W9-AJD-283

NETWORK KNOW-HOW

We are in great haste to construct a magnetic telegraph from Maine to Texas; but Maine and Texas, it may be, have nothing important to communicate.

—Henry David Thoreau, *Walden*

NETWORK KNOW-HOW

An Essential Guide for the Accidental Admin

by John Ross

no starch press

San Francisco

13 12 11   2 3 4 5 6 7 8 9

ISBN-10: 1-59327-191-3
ISBN-13: 978-1-59327-191-6

Publisher: William Pollock
Production Editor: Kathleen Mish
Cover and Interior Design: Octopod Studios
Developmental Editor: Tyler Ortman
Technical Reviewer: Mike Kershaw
Copyeditors: Eric Newman and LeeAnn Pickrell
Compositor: Riley Hoffman
Proofreader: Rachel Kai
Indexer: Sarah Schott

For information on book distributors or translations, please contact No Starch Press, Inc. directly:

No Starch Press, Inc.
38 Ringold Street, San Francisco, CA 94103
phone: 415.863.9900; fax: 415.863.9950; info@nostarch.com; www.nostarch.com

Library of Congress Cataloging-in-Publication Data:

```
Ross, John, 1947-
  Network know-how : an essential guide for the accidental admin / John Ross.
     p. cm.
  Includes index.
  ISBN-13: 978-1-59327-191-6
  ISBN-10: 1-59327-191-3
 1. Home computer networks. 2. Computer networks--Management.  I. Title.
  TK5105.75.R667 2009
  004.6--dc22
                               2008052768
```

BRIEF CONTENTS

CONTENTS IN DETAIL

4
HOW COMPUTER NETWORKS ARE ORGANIZED   35

5
DESIGNING YOUR NETWORK   47

6
INSTALLING THE NETWORK CONTROL CENTER AND
ETHERNET CABLES   55

7
ETHERNET NETWORK INTERFACES   69

12
SHARING FILES THROUGH YOUR NETWORK 131

13
NETWORK SECURITY 151

ACKNOWLEDGMENTS

A book like this is always a collaboration, even if only one author's name is on the cover. The book in your hands is a huge improvement over the original manuscript, thanks to the efforts of editors Tyler Ortman and Kathleen Mish and copyeditors Eric Newman and LeeAnn Pickrell. Technical editor Michael Kershaw protected me from embarrassing technical errors. And compositor Riley Hoffman made this the attractive book you hold in your hands. Thanks to all of you. Of course, any surviving errors or unclear descriptions are my own responsibility.

Thanks also to Jim Cavin for allowing me to connect his MacBook to my network and Tommy Tse for his assistance in obtaining evaluation software from Microsoft.

And thanks as usual to my agent, Carole McClendon, who started the wheels turning on this project.

INTRODUCTION

This book is for people who never expected to build or run a computer network. You were happily using a computer, sending and receiving email, writing reports, and maybe downloading music through the Internet when one day you looked around to discover that one computer had somehow multiplied—now you have two, or three, or more computers. Maybe each of your children needs his or her own computer to do homework or all of your employees have computers on their desks. Or maybe you brought a portable laptop computer home from work and you want to use it along with the family's desktop machine.

Whatever the reason, you now have several computers, and you need a way to connect all of them to the Internet at the same time and to share files, printers, and other resources among them. You need a network.

A network? Yikes! Isn't a network some kind of invisible monster that requires expensive equipment and people to keep it running who speak a mysterious language and go off to seminars with titles like "The Power of Virtualization" or "Removing Internet Anonymity Barriers with IP Intelligence"?

Not necessarily. Networks are not just for geeks any more. Today's small networks are relatively easy to install, and you don't need an advanced course in computer technology to operate them. Even the smallest of small businesses will probably benefit from having a network. And home networks are becoming common household utilities, just like water, electricity, and cable TV. Like those other utilities, you don't need a technical background to use a network. This book will tell you what you need to know to build and use a small, simple network in your home or business without becoming mired in obscure technical details.

We thought about calling this book *Networks for Nitwits*, but that's not quite what the book is about—you're not a nitwit; you're an intelligent computer user who has been dragged into the world of networks. I suggested *The Bridges and Routers of Madison County*, but that would be an entirely different book: the bittersweet tale of an Iowa housewife who finds romance with an itinerant network installer. Somebody should probably write that book, but this isn't it.

This *is* a guide to navigating the jungle of servers, routers, modems, and Ethernet cables and to getting the most out of your small network. I'll explain how networks operate (without getting into too much tedious technical detail), describe each part of a network, and tell you how to use the network with computers running Windows XP and Vista, Macintosh OS X, and several versions of Linux and Unix. I'll also tell you about some other ways you can use your network, including automating household appliances and distributing digital audio and video to computers, home entertainment systems, and "Internet radios" throughout your house.

The ideal network is the one that you—and the other people using your network—never have to think about. You would plug a cable from each computer into an outlet, and every other computer on the network would immediately recognize it. And the network would simply *be* there, ready to use. Or it would be completely invisible, like the wires that provide electricity to the lamp next to the chair where you're reading this. If you think about it, you don't really want a network; you want to see and hear files and other resources that are located beyond your own computer. A network is the means to that end.

As I wrote this book, I kept several goals in mind: First, I wanted to provide enough information that readers with some basic computer knowledge and skills could understand how networks work and how to plan and install their own small network; second, I wanted readers to think about additional uses for their networks; and third, I wanted to offer advice and tools for fixing a network that isn't working correctly. If I have succeeded, your network will be up and running shortly after you follow the book's instructions and recommendations.

Network Know-How begins with a general overview of networks and the things you can do with them. In later chapters, you will learn how networks handle digital data, how different kinds of networks move that data from one place to another, and how the equipment at the core of most networks— hubs, routers, modems, and other devices—works. Next, I'll introduce the important concepts of clients and servers and tell you how to design and install simple wired and wireless networks, how to connect the local network to the Internet, how to build security into your network, and how to use your network for music and video along with computer data. And finally, the last chapter of the book offers advice about troubleshooting and describes some useful tools that might make life a bit easier when it becomes necessary to find and fix a problem.

When you have a network in your home or small business, all the computers connected to the network will become more flexible and more useful. Your new network will change the way you use your computer; within a few weeks or less, you will definitely wonder how you got along without it. When you and the other people connected to your network find yourself using it without thinking about "the network," you and I will both have met our objectives.

1

HOW A NETWORK WILL IMPROVE YOUR LIFE

At the beginning, it's easy. You (or your employer or your spouse) bring a computer into your office or your home, and everything is right there: word processing files, financial records, email, music and video, maybe some games, and a connection to the Internet. It's all in one place. Love it or hate it, that computer has become an important part of the way you work and play. In fact, it's so important and so convenient that you eventually decide to add another computer; it might be a laptop that you can carry from one place to another, or maybe a second desktop machine that allows more than one person to use a computer at the same time. And that's when the trouble starts.

Shortly after you get that additional computer, you will discover that something—a text file or a picture you need for a report, or a music file you want to play, or the modem that connects you to the Internet—is located on the other computer. You have to copy files to a portable disk or a flash drive when you have something to print and carry it to the computer connected to your printer; when you want to scan something you must go to the computer with the scanner; and when you want to connect to the Internet, you must either use the computer with the high-speed connection or wait until another family member has finished using the telephone so you can dial in. Using the computer has risen to a whole new level of inconvenience.

Any time you (or your family or business) use more than one computer, something you want—a file, a printer, or some other resource—is likely to be located on or connected to the computer you're not currently using; it's inevitable that something you need on *this* computer is stored on or connected to *that* computer. The solution to this problem is easy: Simply connect the computers and allow them to share.

Congratulations. You have just created a computer network.

Two or more computers connected through wires, radio signals, flashing lights, or any combination of those and other methods form a *network* that you can use to send and receive instructions and files from one computer to another. Whether you're using your computers at home, at school, in a small business, or even at a temporary gathering such as a business conference or a camping trip (if you're the sort of person who takes computers along on a camping trip), connecting them through a network makes every one of them more useful and more powerful. And when you connect your network to the Internet, every device on your local network also becomes connected to the Internet.

NOTE *When you connect two or more computers in a network, each computer becomes more useful. There's a rule that describes this, called* Metcalfe's Law. *Robert Metcalfe was the original designer of the Ethernet structure used in most modern computer networks; his law states that the value (or power) of a network increases in proportion to the square of the number of devices connected to that network. The math is pretty subjective, but Metcalfe's Law says that two computers connected together are about 4 times as useful as a single computer; if you connect 10 computers, the network is 100 times more powerful, and so forth.*

It's not an exaggeration to say that connecting your computers to a network will change your life. Within just a few days or weeks, you will begin to think about everything connected to the network—other computers, printers, game consoles, the Internet, and anything else—as an extension of your own keyboard and monitor. And shortly after that, you will discover new opportunities and services that a network makes possible.

In this chapter, you will learn about the general nature of computer networks and the things you can do with them. You can find more details about using a network later in this book.

What's a Network?

Before we begin to consider the things you can do with a computer network, it might be helpful to understand a few basic concepts.

First, the idea of networks is not limited to computers. A network can be any kind of structure that connects individual objects. The highway system is a network, and so is the worldwide telephone system. You can use either of these networks to interact or communicate with other people connected to the same system. Broadcasting networks such as CBS and the BBC use wires, microwave radio links, and other methods to distribute programs from one or more studios to a large number of local stations.

Every network has the following elements in common:

- Two or more objects, or *nodes*, that use the network to connect them
- A set of communication *channels* that carry something—speech, TV shows, computer data—between or among nodes
- A set of rules that controls network traffic—on a highway, the rules might specify that vehicles drive on the right and pass on the left, and every car and truck must display a license plate to identify it; in a telephone network, the rules define the form and use of unique numbers (called "telephone numbers") to identify each node and establish connections between them. To assure that a network operates properly, every node and every channel must follow the rules for that particular network.

Next, every network has a maximum carrying capacity. For example, a four-lane Interstate highway can safely carry more cars and trucks at higher speed than a two-lane country road. In a communications network, the capacity of a network connection is the amount of information it can carry, also known as its *bandwidth*. Both a telephone call and an FM radio station use audio channels, but the same voice sounds better on the FM station because the FM channel has a greater bandwidth that allows more of the original information (in this case, higher audio frequencies) to reach your ear. In a data network, the *speed* of a network is usually shown in millions of bits (or megabits) per second (Mbps).

And finally, every node on a network has a name. This name might be the same as the name of the person who uses that node, or a description of the location or the type of device at that node. On some networks, the name is a number, or a combination of letters, numbers, and other characters that have no obvious meaning outside of the network (a telephone number is a good example of this type of name). In order to allow the network to accurately find each node, it's essential that every name be unique.

Sneakernet

The simplest kind of computer network is no network at all. If you have been working with multiple computers without a network, you know the routine: Every time you need something from a different computer, you have to store a file on a floppy disk, a portable drive, or a flash drive, physically carry it from one computer to another, and load the file onto the second computer. Sometimes you'll take the file from the computer you were originally using to the one that is connected to the right printer. If you've been writing a paper on a laptop computer, you might want to add an image that's stored on the desktop system's hard drive. Or maybe you want to give a copy to a colleague for review or approval. Whatever the reason, you have to carry a copy of one or more computer files from one machine to another.

This usually involves some walking, so the process is often known as *sneakernet*. The name reflects the informal dress common in most computer centers, but if you and your family dress for dinner every evening, or if you're a slave to fashionable footwear, you can think of it as "Oxfordnet" or "Slingbacknet" or "Espadrillenet" instead. Whatever you choose to call it, physically carrying files from one place to another is often a distracting, time-consuming nuisance.

However, sneakernet does have its uses. When you travel, it can often be easier and more convenient to carry a few files with you rather than retrieve them from a distant computer through the Internet. If you plan to use computers in two or more locations, such as one at school and another at home, you might be better off storing the file on a small portable drive instead of hauling your laptop around.

When security is an important issue, you might not want to connect your computer to any network. The very best way to protect your confidential data from theft through a network is to make sure the computer where the data is stored has no network access.

Sneakernet is not always the slowest way to move data from one computer to another. If you want to move a lot of data over a relatively short distance when you don't have a high-speed data connection, it can often be faster to drive a handful of DVDs or a box of tapes across town than to send the same files through a dial-up connection or any other slow network link. It's one of the oldest maxims in the world of computers and networks, but it's still true: Never underestimate the bandwidth of a station wagon full of floppy disks.

Data Networks and What You Can Do with Them

The alternative to sneakernet is a network consisting of physical links that connect two or more computers and related equipment. These links can use wires, radio signals, or a combination of both to move computer data (and any other information that can be converted to and from computer data) between any pair of network nodes.

Every computer connected to a network sends and receives data through a connector or radio antenna. Depending on the data transfer speed and the network's specific requirements, the computer might use a parallel port, a serial port, an Ethernet port, a USB or FireWire port, or a Wi-Fi antenna. Because these connectors and antennas move data in both directions, they are *input/output ports* or *I/O ports*, but that term is more often used to describe the computer's serial and parallel data connectors.

After you connect your computers together, you will discover that you can do many things through the network that you may not have expected. By the time you have lived with the network for a few weeks, you won't think much about it, but you'll use it all the time.

File Sharing

When you connect your computer to a network, you can allow other people to read and write files that are located on your computer's hard drives and other storage media, and you can open and store files from other computers. File sharing is one of the most common and the most convenient uses of a network.

File sharing has many uses: You can use it to collaborate with other people on a single document or other file, to play music or watch videos stored on another computer, and for just about everything else that you can do with your own files. In effect, every unprotected file stored on any network computer is as easy to use as a file on your own computer.

For example, Figure 1-1 shows a Windows display of disk drives and individual directories on a home network (other file-sharing methods also exist). You can open a file or folder on a remote computer by double-clicking an icon or a filename, just as you would on your own machine.

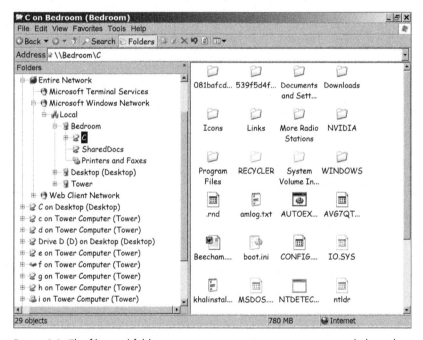

Figure 1-1: The files and folders on a remote computer are easy to reach through a network.

Of course, you probably have some files on your own computer that you don't want to share: personal letters, confidential financial records, medical information, and so forth. A well-designed file-sharing system allows each user to set every file or folder as either "public" or "private."

For more about sharing files with other computers on your home or office network, see Chapter 12.

Sharing an Internet Connection

When you order a connection to the Internet, the telephone company or the cable TV company installs just one connection point. It doesn't matter if the Internet service uses a dial-up telephone line, a high-speed DSL line, a cable TV service, a fiber optic link, or some kind of radio link; your Internet service terminates in just one place, most often in a piece of electronic equipment called a *modem* (that's geek-speak for **modulator/demodulator**, a device that converts between computer data and some other type of communications signal). If you have just one computer, you can connect it directly to the modem; but when you want to connect two or more computers to the Internet at the same time, you'll need a network.

For many families, a high-speed Internet connection provides the reason to start thinking about installing a home network. When you spend that extra money for a DSL or cable Internet link (or fiber optic link), you want easy access to the Internet from every computer in the house. When you connect your network to the modem through a *gateway router* (shown in Figure 1-2), you can reach the Internet through any computer on that network. Some modems require a separate router to distribute the Internet connection to multiple computers, while others have built-in routers.

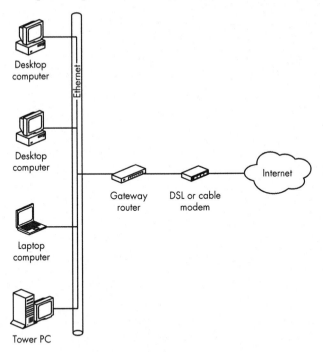

Figure 1-2: A gateway router provides a connection between a local area network and the Internet.

Connecting your network to the Internet is not difficult, but it's easier with detailed instructions. You can find those instructions in Chapter 10.

Instant Messages

Instant message programs display text on a distant computer's screen almost as fast as you can type them. They're useful for exchanging notes, asking questions, and nonspecific chatter within a business or between friends and family members. When a new message arrives, the messaging program pops up in a new window on the recipient's screen. If you attach a microphone and speaker to each computer, you can use a similar program to speak to the person at the distant computer rather than using the keyboard and screen. And if you add a camera at each end, you can use a video messaging system that allows each of you to see the other party during the conversation.

Within a home or small office network, you can use instant messaging, with or without sound and pictures, to communicate from one room to another. It might be a simple message, such as "Dinner's ready," or a more complicated request for information from someone else in the building. And of course, if there are young people in the house, the instant message program will quickly become a channel for gossip and idle conversation.

For more about instant messaging programs, see Chapter 16.

Sharing Printers and Other Hardware

In most homes and small businesses, there's no need for every computer to have a printer available for its exclusive use, because nobody uses a printer all the time. It's often more practical to attach a single printer to a network (or maybe one for black-and-white pages and another for color) rather than buying a separate printer for each computer.

When you only need a single printer, you can often buy one that provides better images and faster performance for considerably less than the price of two or three cheaper models. The same kind of economy can also apply to a flatbed scanner and other specialized input or output devices.

A network printer can either connect directly to the network as a separate node (a *printer server*) or through one of the network's computers. Look for information about both types of printer connections in Chapter 14.

Home Entertainment

The same home network that carries data to computers can also distribute music, movies, and other audio and video to stereo systems, TVs, and home entertainment centers throughout the house. Special-purpose computers called *music servers* can copy music from CDs or older recordings (such as cassettes or vinyl records) or download music files, store the music as digital files, and play them in any room in the house on demand, either through the speakers attached to a computer, through a traditional stereo system, or through a dedicated tabletop device similar to a radio. The same players can also receive and play streaming radio stations from around the world through the Internet. *Video servers* can store movies and other videos and make them available through the network to computers, televisions, and home theater systems. Some network music servers also include docking stations for iPods and other portable music players that can transfer files between the server and the portable unit and play music and videos directly from the portable device.

Audio and video programs can move through the network at the same time as email, web surfing, and instant messages.

For detailed information about setting up and using a home entertainment network, see Chapter 15.

Video Cameras and Home Security Devices

A stand-alone video camera (often with a built-in microphone) connected to your home network can have several uses. You can place a camera at the front door to identify visitors, or use one in a nursery or playroom to keep an eye on your children from computers in other parts of the house. Other devices can use special sensors to detect smoke and fires, unlocked or open doors and windows, broken glass, or flooding and other problems and send alerts to the homeowner on a local computer or to a home protection service through the Internet.

Combined with a wireless network link, the same kind of security monitoring can extend to a detached garage, shed, or other separate buildings, even if the house's wired network does not reach those locations. Chapter 15 explains how to connect and use cameras and other security devices to your network.

Home Automation

Home automation systems usually use separate wiring from a household data network, but sometimes they're closely integrated. Home automation can be as simple as turning on outside lights after the sun goes down, or as complex as opening and closing drapes, monitoring and adjusting heating and air conditioning, operating a lawn sprinkler, or filling the dog's water dish. You can also expect the next generation of "smart" kitchen and laundry appliances to include network connections that will allow them to let you know when the roast is cooked or the clothes dryer has completed its fluff cycle.

Chapter 15 provides basic information about home automation systems and devices and explains how to connect them to a computer network.

2

TYPES OF NETWORK CONNECTIONS

Every computer connected to a network must follow a set of rules and specifications that define the characteristics of both the physical connection and the form and structure of the data that moves from one computer to another. Without these rules, the people using the network cannot be sure that their computers will communicate successfully.

For example, the plugs at the ends of data cables must match the sockets on each computer and other network hardware. If a cable uses a square plug with two pins, but the computer has a round socket with four holes, they won't fit together. The same thing applies to the electrical voltages, timing, error checking, and other issues. There are many different kinds of networks, each with its own rules. This chapter explains a few general principles about networks and describes the network types that you're most likely to see in a home or small office network.

You can use a network without understanding all the internal details of network communications, but if you're designing and building a new network, you should know how to choose the best options for your particular requirements. You can treat individual network components as a series of black boxes, but you still have to know *which* black boxes to use. And when something goes wrong, knowing what's inside those boxes will make troubleshooting a lot easier.

Before we talk about specific network types, let's look at the common elements of every computer network.

As you probably know, computers reduce all information to only two information states: Either a signal is present, or there is no signal. These two conditions are usually described as 1 and 0, or on and off, or mark and space. Each instance of a 1 or a 0 is a "bit." Anything described as "digital" can be reduced to those ones and zeroes.

The form that each 1 or 0 takes is different in different types of communication channels. It could be a light, sound, or electrical charge that is either on or off; a series of long and short sounds or light flashes; or two different audio tones, electrical voltages, or radio frequencies. In a very simple system, the 1 might correspond to "yes" and the 0 to "no," or any other pair of options.

Individual bits only offer two options, so they're not particularly useful, but when you string eight of them together (into a *byte*), you can have 256 different combinations ($2 \times 2 \times 2 \times 2 \times 2 \times 2 \times 2 \times 2$). That's enough to assign a different sequence to every letter of the alphabet (both upper- and lowercase), the ten digits from 0 to 9, spaces between words, and other symbols such as punctuation marks and many letters used in foreign alphabets. A byte is the basic building block of computer communication. The most widely used coding system for converting bytes to characters is called *ASCII* (American Standard Code for Information Interchange). Figure 2-1 shows a typical sequence of two bytes.

Figure 2-1: These bits form the ASCII sequence of A (01000001) and n (01101110).

ASCII is fine for text, but a computer can also convert many other forms of information to digital data. For example, it can divide every second of sound from a microphone or an analog recording into thousands of very short segments and use 16 or 24 bits to specify the content of each segment, or divide a picture into millions of individual points (called *pixels*, short for *picture elements*) and use a series of bits to specify the color of each bit.

A wire or other data link can carry only one bit at a time. Either there's a signal on the line or there isn't. Over short distances, it's possible to send the data through a cable that carries eight (or some multiple of eight) signals in *parallel* through eight separate wires. Obviously, a parallel connection can be eight times faster than sending one bit at a time through a single wire, but those eight wires cost eight times as much as a single wire. That added cost is insignificant when the wires extend only a foot or two, but the additional cost of parallel wires can add up quickly when you're trying to send the data over a long distance. And when you're using existing circuits such as telephone lines, you don't have any choice; you must find a way to send one bit at a time, with some additional bits and pauses that identify the beginning of each new byte. This is a *serial* data communications channel, because you're sending the bits one after another. At this stage, it doesn't matter what medium you use to transmit those bits—it could be electrical impulses on a wire, or two different audio tones, or a series of flashing lights, or even a lot of notes attached to the legs of carrier pigeons—but you must have a way to convert the text or other output of the computer to the signals used by the transmission medium, and to convert the same signals back again at the other end.

Packets and Headers

Communication over a direct physical connection (such as a wire) between a single origin and destination doesn't need any kind of address or routing information to tell a message where to go. You might have to set up the connection first (by placing a telephone call or plugging cables into a switchboard), but after you're connected, the link remains in place until you instruct the system to disconnect. This kind of connection is great for voice and for simple data links, but it's not particularly efficient for digital data on a complex network that serves many origins and destinations, because a single connection ties up the circuit all the time, even when no data is moving through the channel.

The alternative is to send your message to a switching center that will hold it until a link to the destination becomes available. This is known as a *store and forward* system. If the network has been properly designed for the type of data and the amount of traffic in the system, the waiting time will be insignificant. If the communications network covers a lot of territory, you can forward the message to one or more intermediate switching centers before it reaches the ultimate destination.

To make the network even more efficient, you can divide messages that are longer than some arbitrary limit into separate pieces, called *packets* or *frames*. Packets from more than one message can alternate with packets containing other messages as they travel between switching centers, and reassemble themselves into the original messages at the destination.

The great advantage of this approach is that many messages can share the same circuits on an as-available basis. The packets from a single message might alternate with packets from one or more other messages as they move through parts of the network. For example, if you send a message to a recipient in another city, the packets usually move through an inter-city channel along with many other messages.

Each data packet must also contain yet another set of information: the address of the packet's destination, the sequence order of this packet relative to other packets in the original transmission, and so forth. Some of this information provides additional error checking and instructs the switching centers where to forward each packet, while other information tells the destination device how to reassemble the data in the packet back into the original message.

The *headers* (at the beginning of a packet) and *trailers* (at the end of a packet) attached to each packet include the address of the packet's destination, information that allows the recipient to confirm that the packet's content is accurate, and information that the recipient uses to reassemble the packets in the original order. Between the origin and the destination, network routing equipment sometimes adds more headers or trailers that contain routing instructions and other administrative information.

Figure 2-2 shows how a network adds and removes headers and trailers at different stages of a communication session. The specific names of the headers and trailer don't matter right now; the point is that they surround the original data packet.

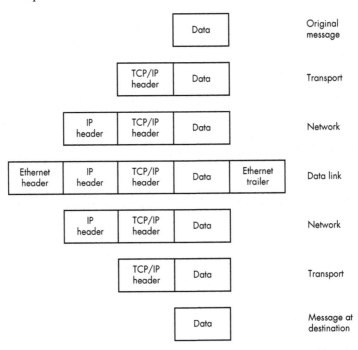

Figure 2-2: A data packet may be surrounded by several kinds of headers and footers.

That same pattern repeats every time you add another layer of activity to a communications system. Each layer may attach additional information to the original message and strip off that information after it has done whatever the added information instructed it to do. By the time a message travels from a laptop computer on a wireless network through an office network and a gateway to the Internet, and onward to a distant computer connected to another local network, a dozen or more information attachments might be added and removed before the recipient reads the original text. A package of data that includes address and control information ahead of the bits that contain the content of the message, followed by an error-checking sequence, is called a *frame*. Both wired and wireless networks divide the data stream into frames that contain various forms of handshaking information along with the original data.

NOTE   *The network deals with packets and frames at different places during the process of transmitting data. Fortunately, this all happens automatically, so you (as a network user) don't have to worry about adding or removing them by hand.*

Error Checking

In a perfect transmission channel, the signal that goes in at one end would be absolutely identical to the one that comes out at the other end. But in the real world, there's almost always some kind of noise along the line that can interfere with the original signal. *Noise* is defined as anything that interrupts or is added to the original signal; it could be caused by a lightning strike, interference from another communications channel, devices not working correctly, or dirt on an electrical contact someplace in the circuit (or in the case of carrier pigeons, an attack by a marauding hawk). Whatever the source, noise in the channel can interrupt the flow of data. In a modern communications system, those bits are pouring through the circuit extremely quickly—millions of them every second—so a noise hit for even a fraction of a second can obliterate enough bits to turn your data into digital gibberish.

Therefore, your data stream must include a process called *error checking*. Error checking is accomplished by adding some kind of standard information to each byte. In a simple computer data network, the handshaking information is called the *parity bit*, which tells the device receiving each byte whether the sum of the ones and zeroes inside the byte is odd or even. This value is called a *checksum*. If the receiving device discovers that the parity bit is not correct, it instructs the transmitter to send the same byte again. More complex networks, including wireless systems, include additional error-checking handshaking data with each string of data.

Handshaking and Overhead

The computer that originates a message or a stream of data can't just jump online and start sending bytes. First it has to warn the device at the other end that it is ready to send and make sure the intended recipient is ready to accept data. To accomplish this, a series of "handshaking" requests and answers must surround the actual data.

The sequence of requests goes something like this:

Origin: "Hey destination! I have some data for you."

Destination: "Okay, origin, go ahead. I'm ready."

Origin: "Here comes the data."

Origin: Data data data data . . . checksum

Origin: "That's the message. Did you get it?"

Destination: "I got something, but it appears to be damaged."

Origin: "Here it is again."

Origin: Data data data data . . . checksum

Origin: "Did you get it that time?"

Destination: "Yup, I got it. I'm ready for more data."

We can leave the specific form of handshaking information to the network designers and engineers, but it's important to understand that not every bit that moves through a computer data network is part of the original block of information that arrived at the input computer. In a complex network such as a wireless data channel, as much as 40 percent or more of the transmitted data is handshaking and other overhead. It's all essential, but every one of those bits increases the amount of time that the message needs to move through the network.

Ethernet

Ethernet was introduced in the 1970s as a method for connecting multiple computers and related equipment in the same building. Ethernet offers several advantages: It's fast, it's extremely flexible, it's relatively easy to install and use, and it's inexpensive. It has become an industry standard supported by dozens of manufacturers, so you can use different brands of equipment in the same network. Today, more than 85 percent of all local area networks (LANs), including just about every modern home and office network, use some form of Ethernet to provide the physical connection between computers through twisted-pair cables, coaxial cables, or fiber optic cables.

One of Ethernet's most important features is the method it uses to prevent conflicts among nodes, called *Carrier Sense Multiple Access with Collision Detection (CSMA/CD)*. Every time a network node is ready to transmit a frame, it checks if another frame is already using the network; if the network is clear, the node sends the frame. But if the node detects that another frame is using the network (a condition called a *collision*), it waits a random period of time before it tries again. CSMA/CD is important because it allows a relatively large number of computers and other devices to operate through the same network without interference.

There are many Ethernet specifications that cover different data transfer speeds and different kinds of cables and connectors. The ones you're most likely to see in a small LAN include the following:

- 10Base-T: 10 Mbps through twisted-pair cables
- 100Base-T or Fast Ethernet: 100 Mbps through twisted-pair cables
- 1000Base-T or Gigabit Ethernet: 1000 Mbps through twisted-pair or fiber optic cables
- Wireless or Wi-Fi: any of several systems that use radio signals instead of wires—the latest 802.11n Wi-Fi networks can operate at speeds up to 70 Mbps.

A 10Base-T network is adequate for a small home network. It's faster than most broadband Internet services, so it's sufficient for handling the inbound and outbound data (including audio and video) that you exchange with the Internet. However, most new network ports, hubs, and switches can handle both 10Base-T and 100Base-T, so there's very little point to limiting the network to the slower speed. 100Base-T will also allow you to move pictures, music, and videos and play multiplayer games within your own network much faster than a 10Base-T network, and it will not limit the speed of an 802.11n link. Considering the insignificant difference in cost, today's 100Base-T networks are always a better choice than the older 10Base-T versions.

If a 100Base-T network can't handle 100 Mbps because of interference or some other problem, it will automatically drop down to 10Base-T. A 10Base-T device can work on a 100Base-T network, but it will force the whole network to drop down to 10 Mbps.

A Gigabit Ethernet network is lightning fast (by today's standards), but it's also more expensive than a network that uses slower equipment. It might be appropriate for a business that moves very high volumes of data through its LAN. As the cost of Gigabit Ethernet drops, it will become the preferred choice for home and small business networks.

You might also see the word *Ethernet* used to identify the connector on a computer, printer, or other network device that mates with an Ethernet cable to connect the device to a network. The instruction manual or the label on every piece of Ethernet-compatible equipment should tell you which type of connection it uses.

Twisted-pair cables are bundles of wires in which each pair of wires is twisted together, as shown in Figure 2-3. Because data normally moves in only one direction through each pair of wires, a 10Base-T or 100Base-T network connection uses two pairs—one for each direction. The most common Ethernet cables include a total of eight wires in four color-coded wire pairs, so you can use the remaining wires as spares.

Figure 2-3: A typical Ethernet cable contains four twisted pairs of color-coded wires.

Most of the remaining chapters of this book are dedicated to features and functions of Ethernet networks.

Wi-Fi

Wi-Fi (short for *wireless fidelity*) is a category of networks that use radio signals instead of wires to connect computers and other devices. Another name for Wi-Fi is *wireless Ethernet*, because Wi-Fi uses many of the same data-handling rules and specifications as a wired Ethernet network. However, every Wi-Fi packet must include additional handshaking data, so the overall data transfer speed is often slower than a conventional Ethernet link.

Wi-Fi offers several advantages: It doesn't need cables to connect every network node, so it's often easier to install and use than a wired network connection. Rather than string cables through walls and provide a network outlet at every desk, you can distribute access to the network through antennas in between each computer and a base station (an *access point*) in a central location. When you travel with a laptop computer, a handheld PDA (personal digital assistant), or a mobile Internet device, such as a BlackBerry or an iPhone, you can often connect it to the Internet via Wi-Fi by simply turning it on.

Many home and small business networks use a combination of Ethernet and Wi-Fi; the Wi-Fi base station doubles as a connection point for Ethernet cables, so the same LAN includes both wired and wireless nodes. Chapter 8 contains information about installing and using Wi-Fi network links.

Powerline Networks

In a powerline network, computer data moves through a building's existing electric wiring. Each computer connects through a parallel port, a USB port, or an Ethernet port to a data adapter that plugs directly into an AC wall outlet. The same power transformer that feeds your house wiring also isolates your data network from your neighbors.

The most widely used standard for powerline networks is called *HomePlug*. The greatest advantage of HomePlug and other powerline networks is that the wires are already in place. Every AC wall socket in the house can double as a network connection point. It's also more secure than Wi-Fi, and it can reach greater distances than a Wi-Fi network with just one base station. Wi-Fi signals are often blocked by thick walls and other obstacles that make no difference to a powerline system.

NOTE   *You must plug all your powerline adapters directly into wall outlets. Surge protectors and powerline conditioners often absorb powerline network data, because they see the data as "noise" on the AC power voltage. Conversely, if you're using a powerline network, you will want to connect your stereo or home theater system to power conditioners to filter out the noise produced by the network.*

All equipment that follows the HomePlug specifications should work together in the same network. Some older types of powerline networking might also be available, but they're less reliable than HomePlug because they can suffer from interference caused by certain electrical appliances (such as vacuum cleaners and other appliances that use big motors or power transformers), and they don't always work well with very old house wiring. Today, it's better to stay away from anything that doesn't carry the HomePlug certification mark shown in Figure 2-4.

Figure 2-4: The HomePlug certification mark indicates that a powerline networking product has been approved by the HomePlug Powerline Alliance.

If installing Ethernet wiring is not practical in your building, a HomePlug network might be your best choice. When it works, which it does in most houses, it provides an easy, reliable network. But some would-be users report slow performance and other problems, so it's best to buy your HomePlug adapters from a retailer who will allow you to return them if they don't work in your house.

Other Alternative Wiring Methods

Two more home networking methods are possible, but they're almost always provided as supplements to other services. These systems use the internal telephone wiring that connects extension telephones in several rooms or the coaxial cable (*coax*) that provides cable TV signals. The industry group that promotes home networks through telephone wires is called HomePNA (the Home Phoneline Networking Alliance); MoCA (Multimedia over Coax Alliance) is the comparable group for coax.

Don't confuse internal telephone or coax wiring with the DSL and cable services that connect high-speed Internet service to your home or business LAN; HomePNA and MoCA are strictly for distributing network service within a building.

HomePNA and MoCA are less flexible than HomePlug network wiring because most homes already have a lot more built-in AC power sockets than telephone or TV outlets. However, if the phone boxes or cable outlets are already in convenient locations, it might be practical to consider HomePNA or MoCA as an alternative to Wi-Fi or separate Ethernet wiring.

DTE and DCE Equipment

There's one more concept that every network planner should understand: the difference between *data terminal equipment (DTE)* and *data communications equipment* or *data circuit-terminating equipment (DCE)*. If you're clear on these two types of network devices, you will avoid a lot of headaches caused by communication failures.

Data can move through a wire in only one direction. When a data link sends and receives signals at the same time, it must use separate wires to send data from the DTE to the DCE, and from the DCE to the DTE. Therefore, a network device uses separate inputs and outputs on the same multipin connector. The specific pin assignment is different in different connection types, but the inputs and outputs are always different pins or sockets.

The problem arises because every output must connect to an input. As Figure 2-5 shows, if you connect an output to another output, the two signals will collide; if you connect an input to an input, there's never any signal.

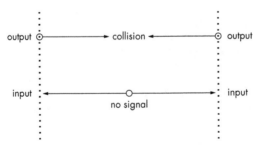

Figure 2-5: Connect an output to an output or an input to an input and nothing useful happens.

Therefore, when you connect two pieces of equipment, the outputs at each end must go to inputs at the other end. If Pin 2 on one device is an output, Pin 2 on the other device must be an input. Most standard data cables connect each connector pin to the same numbered pin at the other end, so connecting two devices through a cable is exactly the same as plugging one device directly into another.

That's why there are two categories of data devices. Data terminal equipment includes remote terminals, computers, some printers, and other network endpoints. Data communications equipment includes modems, hubs, switches, and other control devices. When you connect a terminal to a control device, the output pins on the DTE device connect to the input pins on the DCE device.

The problem arises when you want to connect two computers without a control device in between. Direct computer-to-computer communication requires a special cable because you can't connect a DTE device directly to another DTE device. When you connect two DTE devices with serial data ports, you connect the output on one computer to the output on the other computer, and the input to the input, so neither computer will actually receive any data. Therefore, you must flip the connections, so each output connects to an input. A cable or adapter that connects output pins to input pins is called a *null modem*. Figure 2-6 shows a typical null modem adapter.

Figure 2-6: A null modem adapter or cable
connects inputs directly to outputs.

NOTE   *The "data moves in only one direction" rule does not apply to data moving through coaxial cable, which can handle inbound and outbound signals modulated at different frequencies through the same cable.*

Point-to-Point Networks

Most of the time, we think of a computer network as a structure that can link one computer to any other computer connected to the same network. But sometimes all you need is a direct connection between two computers. This kind of connection is called a *point-to-point* network. Figure 2-7 shows both network types.

A point-to-point connection is handy when you want to transfer data from one computer to another when one or both of them are not already connected to a network. For example, if you're in a meeting where somebody asks for a copy of a report or drawing, you could use the built-in infrared network tools built into many laptop computers to shoot the file across the table from your computer to your colleague's. Or if you want to copy a file from a friend's computer, you could plug a transfer cable into both machines or set up a point-to-point Wi-Fi link.

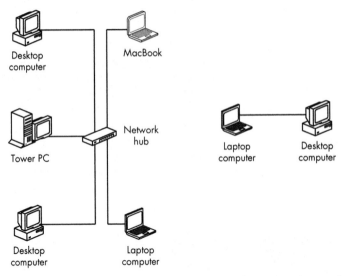

Figure 2-7: A LAN (left) can provide connections between any pair of nodes; a point-to-point network (right) connects two nodes.

Point-to-point networks can use wires, radio signals, or infrared light to exchange data between the two endpoints. If you're using a cable connection, you must use a special point-to-point Ethernet adapter or cable. For a point-to-point Wi-Fi link, you must configure it as an *ad hoc* connection.

Ad Hoc Wi-Fi

Most Wi-Fi networks connect wireless nodes to a LAN through a wireless access point, but Wi-Fi network adapters can also support wireless links directly from one computer to another. This kind of connection is called an *ad hoc* network, because it's usually set up as a temporary link rather than as part of a permanent network infrastructure (wireless networks with one or more central access points are called *infrastructure* networks).

Infrared

Infrared connections use invisible flashing light (it's invisible because it uses frequencies outside the range of human sight) to exchange data between computers, mobile telephones, digital cameras, and other devices. Most of the wireless remote control units that you use with your television, DVD player, and home stereo system also use infrared light signals. Infrared channels are often called *IrDA* connections, because the Infrared Data Association (IrDA) has set the standards for infrared communication.

Many laptop computers have built-in IrDA ports, usually in an inconspicuous location along the edge of the case. The IrDA port is usually an infrared lens under a transparent plastic cover, like the one shown in Figure 2-8. The camera captured the flashing infrared light, even though it's not normally visible to the human eye.

Figure 2-8: The IrDA port on a laptop computer often looks like a blank panel on the edge of the case.

As you have probably noticed with your TV's remote control, infrared signals can bounce off walls and other objects, so it's not absolutely necessary to point a pair of IrDA ports directly at each other, especially when they're both indoors. When two computers with active IrDA ports are in the same room, they will usually detect each other automatically.

NOTE *The infrared port on a laptop computer can detect an IrDA signal from another computer in the same room and automatically set up a network link between the two devices. It's best, then, to disable the infrared port anytime you're not planning to use it. To disable or enable infrared communications in Windows, open the Device Manager (**Control Panel ▸ System ▸ Hardware ▸ Device Manager**), expand the list of infrared devices, right-click the name of the infrared port, and choose **Disable** or **Enable** from the pop-up menu.*

FireWire (IEEE 1394)

FireWire was developed by Apple as a high-speed serial data transfer method for connecting computers to external accessories. It was later adopted by the Institute of Electrical and Electronics Engineers (IEEE) as their Standard No. 1394. IEEE 1394 is used most often for high-speed data transfer from audio and video equipment to computers, but it can also exchange data between two computers through a special cable.

NOTE *Unlike FireWire, it's not possible to use a simple cable between two computers' USB ports as a communications link for direct data transfer. However, special "USB Data Transfer Devices" are available for this purpose.*

Connections Through a Telephone Line

When a high-speed wide area network service such as DSL is not available, you can connect your computer or LAN to the Internet, or directly to a remote computer, through the dial telephone system (the *Public Telephone Switched Network* or *PTSN*, also known as *POTS,* short for *Plain Old Telephone Service*). Dial-up network links are considerably slower than DSL, cable, or other high-speed services, but they're convenient because there's a POTS telephone line in just about every home and business, and because the PTSN often continues to work during power failures.

A network connection through a telephone line uses a modem to convert digital computer data to sounds that can pass through the PTSN. A second modem at the other end converts those sounds back to digital data. The communications programs in Windows and other operating systems send control codes that instruct the modem to transmit telephone numbers and adjust the data transfer speed and other configuration settings.

Most new laptops have built-in PTSN modems. Separate modems for desktop computers are available as internal expansion cards or external devices that connect to the computer through a serial data port or a USB cable.

Figure 2-9 shows the dial-up modem control panel used in Windows XP to connect a computer to a distant network or an Internet service provider (ISP). Figure 2-10 shows the setup screen for the HyperTerminal program. Other programs have different layouts, but they all do essentially the same thing: They dial a telephone number and log in to the computer that answers the call. Advanced properties specify the type of network connection, the data speed, and other configuration settings.

Figure 2-9: The Connect dialog in Windows specifies the telephone number that a modem will call and the login and password that the computer will send after the connection goes through.

Figure 2-10: The Connect To dialog in HyperTerminal includes space for an area code and telephone number.

Remote Terminals

Today, most networks connect two or more computers, but it's also possible to use your computer as a *remote terminal* (a keyboard and screen) to operate another computer that might be located in the next room or halfway around the world. Computers using terminal emulator programs send commands from your computer's keyboard to a distant system, and they display data from the distant computer on your computer's screen. You can connect to another computer as a remote terminal through a LAN, through a dial-up telephone line, or through the Internet.

For example, Figure 2-11 shows the login sequence from a remote terminal program connected to The Well, a text-based online community that runs on a Unix host computer in Sacramento, California. The Well's computer treated my desktop computer in Seattle exactly the same as it would treat a local terminal connected directly to the host. You might see similar text-based host computer displays from library catalogs or mainframe computers.

```
#===================== Connected 9:32 PM 2/10/2008 ===================#

This is The WELL

Find membership information at http://www.well.com/
Forgot your password?  Go to http://www.well.com/newpass

If you already have a WELL account, type your username.

login: 
Password:
Last login: Sun Feb 10 17:17:11 from 
```

Figure 2-11: A remote terminal allows a user to operate a remote computer through a network.

You can connect to a computer as a remote terminal through the Internet, using a category of programs called *telnet* that form the core of most terminal emulators, or you can connect directly to the host computer through a modem and a conventional dial-out telephone line.

Clients and Servers

As your network grows, you might choose to add some computers and other devices (such as printers) to the network. Those additional computers will provide useful resources to all of the network's users.

In a network, a *client* is a computer or program that uses resources supplied by another device; a *server* is the device that provides those resources. Organizing a network into clients and servers is one way to make that network much more flexible and powerful than the individual computers connected to it. As you plan a new network or expand the one you already have, you should think about each network activity as either a client program that runs on local computers or a server that supplies the program from a central source.

NOTE   *It's important to understand that a server is not always a dedicated computer; in many small networks, one or more server programs run on the same computer that is also used by one of the network's users for day-to-day activity.*

For example, if you store your entire collection of music files on one computer and play those files from other computers connected to it through your network, the computer that contains all the files is a "storage server," and each of the players is a client. Or if you print documents by sending them to another computer or a stand-alone printer through the network, the computer or the special network node device that controls the printer is a "printer server."

A server almost always communicates with users (that's you and me) through a client. It's rare for anybody except the system manager or maintenance people to work directly with a server program. The software that sends instructions to a server and receives data or other services is a *client program*. Each server communicates with a client program that sends it the correct set of requests and receives information in a particular format. For example, web browsers such as Firefox, Opera, and Internet Explorer are all clients that use the HTTP (HyperText Transfer Protocol) commands specified by the World Wide Web Consortium; every web server in the world recognizes those commands.

A client and server are not always connected to the same LAN; sometimes they connect through the Internet or through a large corporate WAN (Wide Area Network). For example, when you download a page from a website or a music file from a service such as iTunes or Zune, you're using your own computer as a client to obtain something from a web server.

A network can take advantage of many kinds of clients and servers. Here are just a few:

Mail server   A computer that handles inbound and outbound mail for all network users

File server   A computer that stores data files and makes them available through any computer connected to the network

Music server   A specialized file server that stores music files and makes them available to computers and home entertainment systems

Firewall server   A computer that acts as a security firewall between the other computers on the network and the rest of the world

Game server   A computer that acts as host for a multiplayer game

A server can be a separate computer that runs only specialized server software, a general-purpose computer that runs server programs along with other programs, or an even more specialized device that contains a special-purpose internal computer processor. For example, as Figure 2-12 shows, a printer server could be a computer with a printer attached to it, or a printer with an internal or external network adapter connected directly to the network.

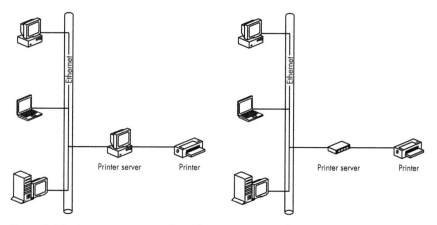

Figure 2-12: A printer server can be either a computer with a printer connected to it or a dedicated printer server.

In a small network, it's not unusual for the same computer to double as a client and a server. For example, in a home network, the family's printer might be located in the kitchen, where Mom has a computer on which she keeps the family's financial records and looks up recipes on the Internet. The kitchen computer is the network's printer server. When others in the house want to print something, they instruct their own computer to send it to the printer through the network to the computer in the kitchen. The computers' operating systems know how to handle such print requests without interrupting other programs running on the printer server.

Clients and servers are important because they are essential network building blocks. A client-and-server structure is often the very best way to add services to a network because it's an efficient way to share expensive hardware and software, and it makes those services equally accessible to everybody.

For more details about adding and using servers, see Chapter 9.

3

HUBS, SWITCHES, AND ROUTERS

Any time a network includes more than two nodes, it must have some way to connect any pair of nodes. Large networks can have very complicated structures with many branches and extensions, but the core of every network can be reduced to just a few patterns. The simplified layout of a network is known as its *topology*.

The most common network topologies are a big loop known as a *ring*; a hub system with everything connected to a central core called a *star*, a common path (not a loop) that connects nodes using a time-sharing method; and a *mesh*, in which there's a direct connection from every node to every other node. Figure 3-1 shows simplified diagrams of each network topology.

In a loop network, such as IBM's old token ring design, data moves around the loop until it reaches its destination. In the much more common hub system, each data packet travels to a central location, where a control device reads the address and sends it back out to the right destination. Ethernet networks, which include most small LANs, are hub systems.

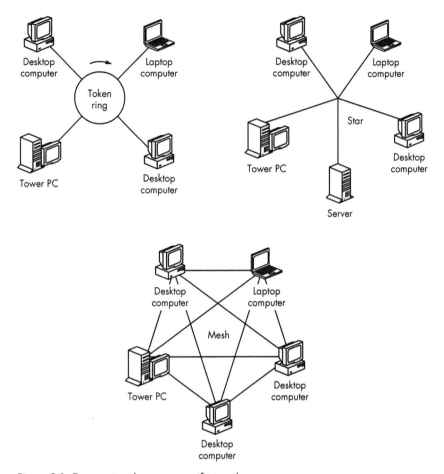

Figure 3-1: Every network uses a specific topology.

Mesh topology is not common in small home or office networks, but the wide area networks that connect your small network to the Internet often use mesh designs.

This chapter describes the equipment at the center of a star network that connects the computers and other nodes to one another, and the related devices that provide connections between networks. Unless you're connecting just two nodes, these hubs, switches, and routers are essential network building blocks.

Hubs and Switches

Both hubs and switches are exchange points at the logical center of an Ethernet network, as shown in Figure 3-2. Each computer or other network node connects to a hub or switch through a cable plugged into a socket called a *port*. In a small network, a hub or switch is almost always a tabletop box with indicator lights on the front and Ethernet ports on the back. In a larger network, the hub or switch might be a panel that mounts in an equipment rack.

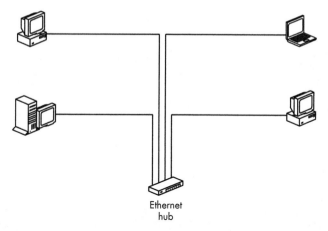

Figure 3-2: A hub or switch is the central connection point in an Ethernet network.

The maximum data transfer speed of a network is the data-handling speed of the hub or switch. You might find a 10 Mbps Ethernet hub, but as faster devices have become less expensive, there's not much reason to use one. Today, the most common hubs and switches are designed for both 10 Mbps and 100 Mbps operation. The latest generation of switches and hubs supports even faster Gigabit Ethernet (1000 Mbps) switches, often at prices only slightly higher than those of older 100 Mbps versions.

Hubs

When a data packet enters a hub, the hub relays that packet to all of the hub's ports (and onward to the nodes connected to those ports). Each node compares the address on the packet with its own address and either accepts it if the address is the same or ignores it if the packet is addressed to some other node. Because the hub sends each packet to every port, only one packet can travel through the network at a time (we're talking about many packets per second, but they still move through the network one at a time). If two or more computers try to send packets at exactly the same time, Ethernet's collision detection feature forces them to stop, wait, and try again a fraction of a second later.

In order to prevent collisions, each node must examine the network to be certain that no other node is already using the hub before it transmits a packet. Therefore, a network with a 10/100 hub is no faster than the slowest node. If all the computers in your network use 100 Mbps network adapters but the printer connects through a 10 Mbps port, the whole network will run at only 10 Mbps or less.

As more nodes try to use a hub at the same time, the data transfer speed through the entire network drops. This could have a significant effect on a busy network that uses a hub: The actual data transfer could be only a fraction of the nominal 10 Mbps or 100 Mbps.

In general, hubs are slow, simple, and cheap. But the difference in cost between a hub and a switch is often insignificant, so a switch is almost always the better choice.

Switches

A data switch performs the same function as a hub—it connects the nodes of a network to one another—but it does the job quite differently. Rather than sending every packet to every port, a switch reads the address section of each incoming packet and sets up a direct connection from the source of each packet to its destination. In the meantime, if some other node tries to send a data packet to another unused port, the switch can set up the link without breaking the other connection. As Figure 3-3 shows, a switch can handle more than one connection at the same time. Because a network node connected to a switch doesn't have to monitor the entire network for possible collisions, it can send and receive data at the same time (this is called *full duplex* mode). Both of these features—multiple segments and full duplex operation—mean that data can move through a switch more quickly than through a hub.

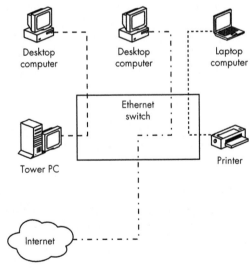

Figure 3-3: An Ethernet switch can support two or more simultaneous connections.

Data switches (and hubs) come in several sizes and shapes. The smallest switches often have four, five, or eight ports, inside a box that can sit on a table or shelf, like the one shown in Figure 3-4. When your network expands to need more ports than your original switch can provide, you can connect one or more additional switches to one of the ports on the original unit.

Photo courtesy of Linksys, a division of Cisco Systems, Inc.

Figure 3-4: This switch connects five network nodes.

Networks in larger business offices usually run cables from each computer back to a central space where all the switching equipment is mounted on a wall plate or an equipment rack. This is often the same room where in-house telephone equipment connects to the telephone company's outside lines. This space is often called a *wiring closet.*

LANs and WANs

The network in your home or office is known as a *local area network (LAN)*. All of the computers connected to a LAN can share peripheral devices (such as a printer or a scanner), they can run programs and read data from other computers on the same LAN, and they all share a common connection to the Internet. In a home network, the LAN might also include home entertainment systems and game controllers.

A LAN also uses the same set of rules and settings to control communication among all the networked computers. These include the name of the network itself and names (or address numbers, or both) for each computer, and sometimes firewalls that protect the privacy of the people using the LAN.

When you want to connect several LANs, you can create a "network of networks" called a *wide area network (WAN)* that can use communications channels such as telephone lines or a cable TV service to provide the links. Figure 3-5 shows a simple LAN connected to a WAN. Your Internet service provider (*ISP*) uses a WAN to connect you to the Internet. The Internet itself is a set of connection points that link a lot of WANs.

It's also possible to connect a single computer directly to a WAN without going through a LAN. If you have just one computer, and it's connected directly to a modem, your computer is on your ISP's WAN.

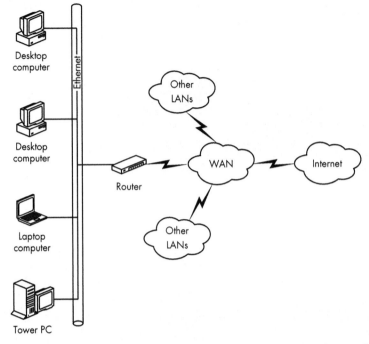

Figure 3-5: A LAN is usually limited to a single building or some other small space; a WAN can connect several LANs.

Bridges and Routers

Any time you connect two networks, you must use a tool that translates the address and control data used by each network into values that the other network can understand. When the device simply examines the address on each packet and decides which packets to forward to the other network, it's a *bridge*. When the device examines the address (or routing) information in each packet and sends the packet along to its ultimate destination (which might be in yet another LAN far from the original), it's a *router*.

NOTE   *Bridges and routers operate between two different networks. Don't confuse them with switches and hubs that distribute data* within *a network. However, many routers combine functions with a switch in a single device.*

When you connect your LAN to the Internet, you add a router as a node on the LAN. This kind of router is sometimes called a *gateway router* because packets from your LAN must pass through it on their way to the Internet (and, of course, packets from the Internet also pass through the router on their way to your LAN). The most common gateway routers are specifically designed to supply the right kind of signaling and address conversion required by DSL or cable TV connections.

Combination Boxes

In relatively small networks, the functions of two or more network control devices are often combined into a single box. For example, a router that connects the network to the Internet could also include a built-in switch that connects several nodes, or a DSL modem might be matched with a gateway router. Many other combinations are also widely available.

If you can find one that meets your network's requirements, a combined package is almost always a better choice than two or more separate pieces. A single unit is almost always less costly than separate components because the case and the power supply account for a major portion of the total price, and it's often easier to configure the network when one device handles several activities.

Using a single device that combines two or more activities offers another advantage that might not be obvious until you have been using your network for a while, and you either need to troubleshoot a problem or you want to add more devices to the network: The connections inside a combined device don't require external cables. As Figure 3-6 shows, the area where your network cables plug into your switches, routers, modems, and so forth is almost always a rat's nest of confusing wiring; anything you can do to reduce the number of cables will make things a lot easier.

Figure 3-6: The cables connected to your network controls can often form a confusing mess.

4

HOW COMPUTER NETWORKS ARE ORGANIZED

In order to exchange files and messages through a network, all the computers connected to that network must use the same set of rules (known to network designers as a *protocol*). The rules that control the Internet are called *transmission control protocol/Internet protocol (TCP/IP)*.

Even if you don't plan to connect your network to the Internet right now, you should use TCP/IP for at least two reasons: First, TCP/IP is built into the Windows, Macintosh, and Linux operating systems and most inexpensive networking equipment; and second, you would waste a lot of time and money finding equipment that works with one of the other, older network protocols.

This chapter offers a relatively simple explanation of the TCP/IP protocols and how your network uses them.

TCP/IP Networks

TCP/IP is really a suite of protocols. The most important are TCP (transmission control protocol), which controls the way commands, messages, and files are broken into packets and reassembled at the other end, and IP (Internet protocol), which provides the rules that guide each data packet through different kinds of networks to the correct destination.

Your computer handles transmission control automatically, so you don't have to devote a lot of attention to individual data packets and their contents. The information in Chapter 2 of this book provides as much detail as most users ever need. But the Internet protocol is another matter; you should understand how your network (and just about every other network connected to the Internet) uses names and addresses for individual computers and other network nodes and how to use some of the standard software tools that are included in every network computer.

Fortunately, internal routing through the Internet is automatic; if you enter a valid address in your web browser, email client, or other program, the Internet will almost always find a path to the computer with that address. If it doesn't, the ping and traceroute commands described in "Network Tools" on page 41 will help you find the source of the problem.

Names and Addresses

An "addressing convention" sounds like an event where people attend speeches and workshops about house numbers and receive awards for sending out five million pieces of junk mail without an error. The formal sessions are often boring, but the after-hours parties are great. In networks, *addressing conventions* are actually the rules that everybody uses to identify the computers and other devices connected to a network and the people who use them. Every computer connected to a network has a unique name and address within that network, and every network connected to the Internet has its own unique numeric Internet address known as an *IP address.*

Numeric Addresses

The technical committees, international standards organizations, and government agencies that manage the Internet have all agreed on a 32-bit numeric address format shown as four numbers between 0 and 255, separated by periods, like this:

192.168.3.200

When you read an IP address out loud, you pronounce each digit separately and each period as "dot." So you would read this sample address as "one-nine-two dot one-six-eight dot three dot two-zero-zero."

You can think of an IP address as similar to your telephone number. Every computer connected to your LAN and every device or network connected to the Internet has a different address.

The agency responsible for assigning numeric IP addresses on the Internet is the *Internet Assigned Names Authority (IANA)*. Some formal contracts with the US government are involved, but the real reason IANA can provide this service to the worldwide Internet community is that everybody agrees to respect their assignments.

As the owner of a small LAN, you will never deal directly with IANA. Your Internet service provider controls a block of numeric addresses, and it will assign you one address (or more) when you set up your new connections.

Reserved Addresses

As Chapter 3 explained, your LAN communicates with other networks through a router. As far as the networks connected to that router are concerned, the router is just one more network connection with an IP address. Therefore, as Figure 4-1 shows, a router has two different IP addresses: one for its connection to the LAN and the other for the WAN or the Internet. The router presents a single address to the Internet that represents all the computers and other devices on your LAN; it performs a function called *network address translation (NAT)* that converts your public address to the addresses of individual network devices. One of the benefits of this system is that you can use the same IP addresses within your LAN as your neighbor across the street (or a LAN on the other side of the world), and the addresses won't interfere with one another.

In order to make this system work properly, IANA has reserved several blocks of IP address numbers for LANs; when a router receives a packet with an address in one of these ranges, it does not relay the packet to the Internet. If you use these addresses for the devices in your LAN, you can be certain that your packets (and the commands, messages, and files that make up those packets) won't end up at the reading room of the National Library of Ecuador when you wanted to send them to your assistant across the corridor.

The reserved IP addresses are:

10.0.0.0 to 10.255.255.255

169.254.0.0 to 169.254.255.255

172.16.0.0 to 172.31.255.255

192.168.0.0 to 192.168.255.255

Fixed and Dynamic Address Assignments (DHCP)

The computers and other nodes in your LAN can obtain their numeric IP addresses in one of two ways: The person who sets up the network connection can assign a permanent address, or a router or other network control device can automatically assign an address every time the device connects to the network. A permanent assignment is called a *fixed* or *static* IP address; an automatic assignment is a *dynamic* address.

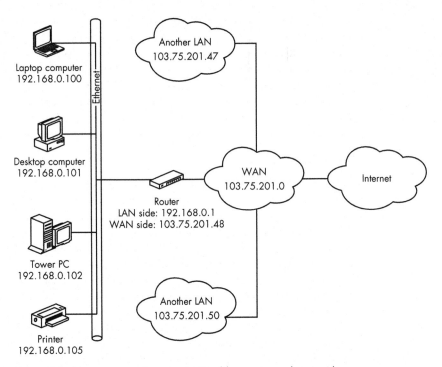

Figure 4-1: A router presents separate IP addresses to each network.

The method for assigning dynamic IP addresses is called *Dynamic Host Configuration Protocol (DHCP)*, so the device that makes the assignments is a *DHCP server*. In a LAN, the DHCP server uses numbers from the reserved range; on the Internet, the servers use numbers from a range provided to your ISP by IANA.

Both fixed and dynamic IP address assignments can work equally well, but all the devices on the network must use the same system; otherwise, more than one device might use the same number at the same time.

NOTE   *If your LAN includes laptops and other portables that connect and disconnect from the network, DHCP is the better choice because it allows the network to assign an address automatically when a user connects and to re-use the same address after the first user has disconnected.*

Some Internet service providers and corporate network managers assign static IP addresses to each user, whereas others use DHCP to generate addresses. Chapters 10 and 11 explain how to set up your own computer and LAN to use either method.

The Domain Name System

Computers have no trouble handling long strings of numbers, but people often do. Addresses in the form of words rather than numbers are generally easier to remember and use. That's why the Internet and just about every LAN use names for each computer connected to a network. In a LAN, each computer reads the name of every other device on the same network automatically; on the Internet, a computer called a *Domain Name System server (DNS server)* converts names to numeric addresses; when you type the name of a website into a browser, a DNS server finds the number that corresponds to that name and returns it to your browser, which connects to that numeric address.

You (or your network manager) will assign a name to each computer when you set up your network; your Internet service provider should set up a domain name for your connection to the Internet. Within a LAN, you can use simple descriptive names for each computer, such as "Sam" or "Kate."

On the other hand, the system for naming computers and networks connected to the Internet (rather than to your own LAN) follows some very specific rules called the *Domain Name System (DNS)*. In the Domain Name System, every name starts with a top-level domain name at the extreme right that can be either a generic description (such as *com, net,* or *edu*) or a two-letter country code (such as *uk* for the United Kingdom or *ca* for Canada). As you move to the left, the next word (or group of letters and numbers) is a name (called a *subdomain*) that has been reserved by a specific owner—an individual, a business, a government agency, or some other formal or informal organization. Large organizations might have one or more additional subdomain names to the left of the first one. Each part of the name is divided from the next one by a period (read as *dot*).

For example, the University of Washington's domain name is *washington.edu.* Within the university, the Department of Genome Science's address is *gs.washington.edu.* And within that department, the addresses of the research group studying evolutionary genetics is *evolution.gs.washington.edu.*

At the extreme left of a domain name, you will sometimes see a subdomain that identifies the type of server. This address might be the familiar *www* or some other Internet service such as *ftp (file transfer protocol).*

Many addresses also include the *type* of Internet service (the *protocol*) that the web resource at that address uses as a leading part of the address, followed by a colon and two forward slashes (//), such as *http://host.sample.com/.* The *http* part stands for *HyperText Transfer Protocol*—the protocol that defines most websites. If you want to reach a different service at the same destination such as a file transfer server, a telnet host, or an Internet Relay Chat server, you might instead use *ftp://host.sample.com/, telnet://host.sample.com/,* or *irc://host .sample.com/,* respectively. When an address does not include the protocol type and the two forward slashes, your web browser will assume it's an http address. Some top-level domains that use country codes have other structures that differ from one country to another. Domain names that have a *us* (for United States) top-level domain sometimes use subdomains (also called *second-level domains*) that identify the state and city where the owner is located, such as *example.sf.ca.us,* which would be in San Francisco, California. In Canada and other countries, the domain name comes right before the country code (such as the Canadian Broadcasting Corporation's *cbc.ca*), whereas other countries use generic identifiers along with the geographic domain, such as *bbc.co.uk* for the British Broadcasting Corporation; the *co* stands for *commercial* and the *uk* for the *United Kingdom.*

Just because a domain name address has a country code, the owner of that address is not necessarily located in that country. For example, many American FM radio stations have obtained addresses in the .fm domain, which belongs to the Federated States of Micronesia, and some television stations use the .tv domain assigned to the Pacific island nation of Tuvalu.

Table 4-1 lists the most common generic top-level domains.

Table 4-1: Generic Top-Level Domains

Top-Level Domain	Used By
.com	Originally commercial, but now a generic domain
.net	Originally reserved for domains related to networks, but now a generic domain
.edu	Reserved for US colleges and universities
.org	Originally reserved for nonprofit organizations, but now a generic domain
.gov	Originally reserved for the US government, but now also used by state and local governments
.mil	Reserved for branches of the US military
.info	A generic domain with no restrictions
.biz	A generic domain restricted to businesses
.name	A generic domain reserved for individuals

Some other top-level domains such as *.asia, .coop, .museum,* and *.travel* are restricted to certain categories of users. Still others, such as

.测试

.испытание

.δοκιμή

.آزمایشی

are for addresses that don't use the Roman alphabet.

Name Servers

DNS name servers are an essential part of the Internet's internal plumbing, but most people don't know that they exist. If your computer can't find a DNS server, your email program, web browser, and other Internet programs won't work unless you use a numeric IP address to identify a destination.

DNS servers perform what seems like a simple task, but this task is more complicated than it first appears because millions of domain names are out there, and new ones are added all the time. Every DNS server in the world has to keep up with all the adds, moves, changes, and deletions. It accomplishes this through a system of *root servers* that are continuously updated. If a local DNS server doesn't recognize a name, it consults the root server that keeps up with that name's top-level domain.

NOTE *There's actually a hierarchy of DNS servers, so a root server might end up consulting yet another server (and so on up the line) if it can't handle a name request itself.*

When you set up your computer for access to the Internet, you must specify the DNS servers that the computer will use to convert domain names to numeric IP addresses. In most cases, your Internet service provider or network manager will give you the numeric address of one or more nearby DNS servers. If your primary DNS server is not accessible, your computer will look for an alternate server if you have provided an alternate address.

It's generally best to use the DNS server address supplied by your ISP because the server with this address is probably closer to your own computer than any other server, and the system works best when total demand for DNS service is spread among as many servers as possible. But if you can't obtain reliable DNS service from your local service provider, a public DNS is often a useful alternative. You can find addresses for several public DNS servers though a Google or other web search for *Public DNS server.*

Some public DNS services can also provide some added features that your ISP might not offer. For example, OpenDNS (*http://www.opendns.com/*) can provide another layer of filtering against spyware, identity theft, adult sites, and other possible problems. It will also allow you to set up two three-letter shortcuts to frequently used addresses and will automatically correct common keystroke errors (such as typing *example.cmo* instead of *.com*). There's some controversy about some of these features, because they could lend themselves to returning names that are links to advertisements rather than the sites the original user requested.

Network Tools

You won't use them often if your LAN and your Internet connection are working properly, but you should know about a handful of troubleshooting tools that allow you to examine the innards of your network and its Internet connection.

All of these tools are simple text commands that you can use with just about any operating system. When you type a command, the system will display the results in the same window or screen. In Microsoft Windows, you can open a Command Prompt window after selecting Start ▸ Programs or by selecting Start ▸ Run and then typing **cmd**. In Mac OS X, select Applications ▸ Utilities and the Terminal program. If you're using Linux or Unix, use a command prompt or an XTerminal.

IPConfig

The IPConfig tool displays detailed information about your computer's current LAN and Internet connection, as shown in Listing 4-1.

```
C:\>IPConfig
Windows IP Configuration
Ethernet adapter Local Area Connection:
        Connection-specific DNS Suffix  . : domain.actdsltmp
        IP Address. . . . . . . . . . . . : 192.168.1.100
        Subnet Mask . . . . . . . . . . . : 255.255.255.0
        Default Gateway . . . . . . . . . : 192.168.1.1
```

Listing 4-1: The IPConfig tool displays the status of a computer's network configuration.

In this example, `Connection-specific DNS Suffix` is an address assigned by a DHCP host. This address is often an arbitrary name used internally within the network, but if your computer is connected directly to the Internet, it might be your computer's DNS address. If you try to connect to a domain name without a suffix (such as "example" rather than "example.net"), the network will assign this suffix to the address when it sends it to a DNS server.

The `IP Address` is the numeric address of this computer within the LAN or WAN. The `Subnet Mask` tells the network which parts of the numeric address identify individual computers, and the `Default Gateway` is the numeric address within the LAN of the gateway router that connects your LAN to the Internet.

For more details about your network connection, add /all to the command, as shown in Listing 4-2.

```
C:\>IPConfig /all

Windows IP Configuration

        Host Name . . . . . . . . . . . . : desktop
        Primary Dns Suffix  . . . . . . . :
        Node Type . . . . . . . . . . . . : Unknown
        IP Routing Enabled. . . . . . . . : No
        WINS Proxy Enabled. . . . . . . . : No
        DNS Suffix Search List. . . . . . : domain.actdsltmp

Ethernet adapter Local Area Connection:

        Connection-specific DNS Suffix  . : domain.actdsltmp
        Description . . . . . . . . . . . : Intel(R) PRO/100 VE Network
Connection
        Physical Address. . . . . . . . . : 00-0C-F1-AA-BF-BF
        Dhcp Enabled. . . . . . . . . . . : Yes
        Autoconfiguration Enabled . . . . : Yes
        IP Address. . . . . . . . . . . . : 192.168.1.100
        Subnet Mask . . . . . . . . . . . : 255.255.255.0
        Default Gateway . . . . . . . . . : 192.168.1.1
        DHCP Server . . . . . . . . . . . : 192.168.1.1
        DNS Servers . . . . . . . . . . . : 198.137.231.1
                                            206.63.63.1
        Lease Obtained. . . . . . . . . . : Wednesday, April 08, 2009 3:11:22 PM
        Lease Expires . . . . . . . . . . : Friday, April 10, 2009 3:11:22 PM
```

Listing 4-2: The IPConfig /all command displays additional information about your connection.

Obviously, this command produces a lot more information. The Host Name is the name that this computer uses on the LAN. The Description identifies the type of network interface adapter that connects this computer to the network. The Physical Address is the *MAC address*—the unique hardware identifier—of the network adapter. The DHCP Server is the address of the device that assigns IP addresses to other devices on the LAN (in this case, this device is the same as the Default Gateway), and the DNS Servers are the computers that this network consults to convert DNS addresses into numeric IP addresses. The Lease Obtained and Lease Expires lines show the date and time that this computer obtained its IP address from the DHCP server and the time the computer will give up that address; the host automatically renews the lease long before it expires, so you don't have to worry about the expiry time.

ifconfig

The ifconfig command is available in Macinstosh OS X and in Unix and Linux. This command displays information about the current network interface, including the connection type and the connection's current status. The format of the information display, however, varies in different operating systems. Therefore, the best place to find a detailed explanation of the ifconfig display produced by your own system is the man page for the ifconfig command.

ping

The ping command is an echo request. When you type ping *target address*, your computer sends a series of "please answer" messages to the target address, and that computer sends you a reply, as shown in Listing 4-3. Your computer measures the amount of time for each roundtrip and displays the duration in milliseconds.

```
C:\>ping nostarch.com

Pinging nostarch.com [72.32.92.4] with 32 bytes of data:

Reply from 72.32.92.4: bytes=32 time=140ms TTL=48
Reply from 72.32.92.4: bytes=32 time=99ms TTL=48
Reply from 72.32.92.4: bytes=32 time=99ms TTL=48
Reply from 72.32.92.4: bytes=32 time=97ms TTL=48

Ping statistics for 72.32.92.4:
    Packets: Sent = 4, Received = 4, Lost = 0 (0% loss),
Approximate round trip times in milli-seconds:
    Minimum = 97ms, Maximum = 140ms, Average = 108ms
```

Listing 4-3: The ping command sends a series of echo requests to a designated address.

Many books and people will tell you that ping is an acronym for *Packet InterNet Groper*, but Mike Muuss, who wrote the original program, always insisted that he chose the name to imitate the sound of a sonar system aboard a submarine; the sonar system makes an audible "ping" when an echo pulse returns from a target.

ping has several uses. It can confirm that the distant computer is alive, and that your computer's connection is working properly. It can also provide a rough idea of the network's performance (less time means higher speed). ping is also useful for finding a DNS problem; if you get a successful ping echo when you enter the target's numeric IP address, but not when you enter the domain name, the glitch is almost certainly someplace in the DNS system.

In Listing 4-3, it took about one-tenth of a second (100 ms) for each test to go from Seattle to San Francisco and back. That's a perfectly reasonable amount of time. But if one or more of the attempts had taken around 500 milliseconds or more, that would indicate some kind of problem.

Ping has also become a verb in computer jargon. You'll hear a technician at a help desk ask you to "ping me" at a specific address, meaning that you should send a ping request to that address. Some people have extended that usage beyond computer networks: They'll talk about "pinging" somebody when they intend to get that person's attention, either by email, telephone, or even poking their head into the recipient's office.

Many large commercial Internet sites, such as *yahoo.com* and *microsoft.com*, have chosen to block ping requests from outside their own network. If you get a no reply response to a ping request, try another address before you assume the problem is with your own Internet connection.

TraceRoute

The TraceRoute tool measures and displays the amount of time it takes for your computer to receive an echo from each network device between your computer and the target. As a result, a TraceRoute display can show you the route between your computer and any other computer on the Internet and pinpoint the segment of that route where a problem is occurring. In Windows, the command is tracert; in OS X, Linux and Unix, it's traceroute. TraceRoute sends three requests to each intermediate node, and shows the timing for each request.

Listing 4-4 shows a TraceRoute from my office in Seattle to No Starch Press in San Francisco.

```
C:\>tracert nostarch.com

Tracing route to nostarch.com [72.32.92.4]
over a maximum of 30 hops:

❶  1     4 ms     3 ms     3 ms  192.168.0.1
❶  2     3 ms     3 ms     3 ms  192.168.0.1
❷  3    71 ms    63 ms    64 ms  --..blv.nwnexus.net [206.63..]
❸  4    57 ms    53 ms    48 ms  fe000.cr1.sea.nwnexus.net [206.63.74.1]
   5     *        44 ms    42 ms  fe000.br4.sea.nwnexus.net [206.63.74.20]
   6    45 ms    43 ms    41 ms  204.181.35.197
   7    42 ms    42 ms    43 ms  sl-bb20-sea-4-0-0.sprintlink.net [144.232.6.121]
```

❹	8	86 ms	85 ms	87 ms	sl-bb25-chi-5-0.sprintlink.net [144.232.20.84]
	9	96 ms	97 ms	97 ms	sl-bb20-kc-2-0.sprintlink.net [144.232.20.108]
	10	108 ms	109 ms	107 ms	sl-crs1-fw-0-4-0-1.sprintlink.net [144.232.20.56]
❺	11	110 ms	110 ms	108 ms	sl-st20-dal-1-0.sprintlink.net [144.232.9.136]
	12	99 ms	98 ms	97 ms	sl-racks-5-0.sprintlink.net [144.223.244.138]
	13	101 ms	98 ms	97 ms	vlan903.core3.dfw1.rackspace.com [72.3.128.53]
	14	101 ms	100 ms	98 ms	aggr115a.dfw1.rackspace.net [72.3.129.109]
	15	97 ms	100 ms	99 ms	squid14.laughingsquid.net [72.32.92.4]

Trace complete.

Listing 4-4: TraceRoute shows the path to a distant computer through the Internet.

In this case, it took 15 hops to complete the connection:

❶ The first two lines show the very fast response from the router sitting on the same table as the computer through a 6-foot cable. Line 2 repeats line 1 because of a software problem in the router.

❷ Line 3, whose domain name and IP address I have hidden, is my Internet service provider's WAN, a couple of miles away in downtown Seattle. Completing that echo takes longer, but it's still pretty fast.

❸ Lines 4 to 7 show the packets moving through various routers in the same switching center in Seattle.

❹ Starting at line 8, the route apparently jumps through routers in Chicago, Kansas City, Fort Worth, and Dallas, which increases the response times.

❺ The path moves around a routing center in Dallas at lines 11 through 15 until it ends up at the Laughing Squid web host that houses the No Starch web server.

This connection goes from origin to destination with several thousand miles of detours. However, the whole thing takes only about a tenth of a second, so those detours don't really matter.

TraceRoute can help identify several possible problems:

- If a TraceRoute report ends with one or more lines of asterisks (***), that usually isolates the problem to either the router named in the preceding line or the connection from that router to the next one.

- If the report shows a very long path that includes router addresses that don't seem to be a on a reasonable route (such as a path from New York to Philadelphia by way of Singapore), one of the network routers is not configured correctly.

- If the route shows that a pair of routers are passing the signal back and forth until TraceRoute times out, that usually indicates that one of those routers has lost a connection and is returning the signal back to the previous router. *That* router still thinks the best path is through the other one, so it tries again.

- If the report shows a long delay that always begins at the same router, it could indicate a problem with that router or very high demand for service through that part of the Internet.

Unless you're a network manager, you probably won't have to analyze TraceRoute reports very often. But if you're having a connection problem, they can sometimes help you to understand why you're not getting through to a website or instant message recipient.

5

DESIGNING YOUR NETWORK

It's quite possible to construct a computer network "on the fly," stringing Ethernet cables from a central hub or switch to individual computers and other devices as you need them. But it's almost always better to spend some time planning your network before you start to install it. It's a lot easier to make changes to your design on paper rather than making adds, moves, and changes in physical space. This chapter offers advice and instructions for preparing a network plan.

I'm assuming in this chapter that you have chosen not to use either power line or video cable as your primary network distribution medium. Both of those methods can be practical in some situations, but a traditional Ethernet system, possibly with a supplementary Wi-Fi base station, is usually a better choice for a small business or household network, because the equipment is widely available, it's often inexpensive, and it's easy to install and maintain.

To begin your network plan, start with a floor plan of the house, apartment, or workspace where you want to install your network. The plan doesn't have to be exactly to scale, but it should be big enough to add notes within each room or cubicle, and it should show the relative positions of each room. Figure 5-1 shows a typical floor plan for a small one-story house. If it's convenient, use a copier or scanner to make several copies of the floor plan.

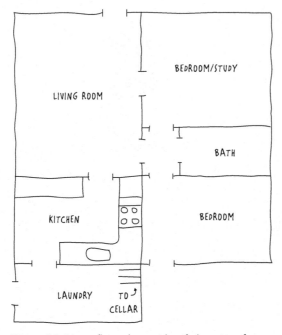

Figure 5-1: Use a floor plan to identify locations for network connection points.

Identifying Current and Future Nodes

The next step is to decide where you will want network connections. Use different colors to note the locations of each of the following items:

Electrical outlets   Network wiring and outlets should be at least 12 inches away from AC wiring, so it will be helpful to identify all of the AC outlets in each room. In addition, you will want access to AC power for your computer, router, modem, and other network hardware.

Your home entertainment systems   Home theater equipment, stereo systems, televisions, and game consoles can all exchange data through your home network, so network outlets should be within close range.

Telephone wall outlets and connection boxes   If you plan to use a DSL or dial-up connection to the Internet, your network will use telephone outlets to connect.

Cable TV or other video outlets   If you get your Internet service from your cable TV provider, you will connect a modem to a cable outlet. Even if you don't use cable Internet service, you might want to use combined wall plates for video and data outlets.

Furniture placed next to a wall   You won't want to plan a network outlet socket in a place that forces you to move a bookcase or a sofa to get to it. On the other hand, if there's a table against the wall, you could probably crawl underneath easily to plug in a cable in a place where it won't call attention to itself.

Closets, stairways, and other hiding places   If your home or workplace includes spaces on more than one floor of the building, be sure to note the locations of closets, stairways, and other places where it will be relatively easy to run hidden cables through ceilings or floors. As with the other wiring in your home or workplace, your goal will be to hide all your network cables inside walls, under floors, and in other invisible locations.

If you're adding the network in an existing home or office, all of these elements are probably in place already. Before you start to add new network wiring and connection points, you must understand how they will relate to the other things in each room. If you're planning a network as part of a major remodeling or new construction, plan to coordinate your efforts with the contractors or outside installers who will provide electrical wiring, telephones, cable or satellite TV, and wiring for a home theater or home entertainment system.

With all this information in one place, it's easy to decide where you will want to install network connection points. Use yet another color of pencil to mark an unobstructed place for the network outlet on the wall nearest to each computer and every other device you plan to connect to the network.

Each outlet should be at least a foot from the closest electrical outlet, both because AC wiring can generate interference that affects data signals, and because it's often required by the local electric code to prevent shorting between AC and data cables.

If your telephone or cable TV outlets are mounted on wall plates (rather than in small boxes attached to the baseboard), consider replacing the existing wall plate with a new one that combines two or three outlets of different types on a single wall plate, as shown in Figure 5-2.

When you design your network, you should also plan for the future. You probably don't need them today, but within a few years, it's quite possible that you will want to connect your household appliances, a bedside radio, and other devices to your LAN and the Internet. And if you plan to eventually add one or more online cameras or home automation devices (such as lighting or climate controls) to the network, it's a good idea to mark their tentative locations.

Figure 5-2: This wall plate combines TV and data network outlets.

Remember, it doesn't cost anything to mark a location for an outlet on your floor plan. You don't have to install every outlet right away, but it's helpful to know where they're likely to be when you plan your cable runs. You can always change the exact locations before you actually pull cable through the walls.

NOTE *Planning for a lot of extra network connection points might seem unnecessary right now, but that will almost certainly change. If you plan for more network connection points than you think you need today, you might have enough for the next ten years. Consider this: If you live in an old house with the original electrical wiring, you probably know that one or two AC outlets in each room was considered more than enough back in 1925; more would have been extravagant. Today, you should have several electrical outlet plates on every wall. In the future, household data networks will be as common as electricity and telephones.*

In your home, consider placing at least one network outlet in each major room—don't worry about hallways and other odd spaces. In the kitchen, place one outlet close to a counter, and plan to place another on the wall next to the refrigerator and range. You might also want an outlet in the laundry room, not far from the washer and dryer—you probably won't want to connect your appliances to the network right now, but remote control and monitoring through your home network is a real possibility in the future. In each bedroom, plan for an outlet near a desk or table where the room's occupant uses a computer or video game console, and (if it's not close to the first outlet) another outlet for a bedside Internet radio or a laptop computer.

In an office, plan for at least one network connection point next to every desk and every other location where you expect to place a computer or other network device, such as a printer.

If you expect to use both Ethernet and Wi-Fi connections to your network, note the locations for one or more Wi-Fi access point on your floor plan.

All of your network wiring should use CAT5e or CAT6 data cable; less expensive CAT5 (no "e") cable can't handle the higher-speed network data that you're likely to need in the future.

The Control Center

The network control center is the location of the switch, router, modem, and other equipment at the core of the network. All of the wiring that connects each outlet to the network converges at the control center. Common locations for a network control center (sometimes known as a *wiring closet*) include closets, utility rooms, and garages or basements. For a very small network (no more than five nodes), you could also consider placing the modem and router on a table next to one of your computers, but that might limit your opportunities for easy expansion of the network in the future.

If you plan to distribute audio, video, telephone, or home automation wiring around the house along with computer network data, your control center should have enough space for all of the necessary equipment required by all those services. It will be easier to pull two or more types of cables at the same time than to install each type separately.

A network control center can have several possible forms: It could be a simple plywood panel attached to the wall, or it might be a pre-wired modular cabinet mounted on a wall or between the wall studs. Or if you have the floor space, it might be in one or more freestanding equipment racks.

The control center's location should have the following characteristics:

- It should be easily accessible. Don't choose a location that forces you to climb over bicycles and storage boxes or push clothes on hangers aside to reach it.
- It should have enough light to allow you to see what you're doing at any time of day or night.
- It should be in a place that remains dry and has a stable temperature.
- It should be close to at least one electrical outlet.
- It should be relatively central, in order to reduce the length of connecting cables.
- It should be at or slightly below eye level, so you can work comfortably.
- It should have enough space to allow for additional wiring and equipment in the future.
- It should *not* be adjacent to the fuse box, circuit breaker box, or other electrical panel. AC power wiring must be kept separate from network, telephone, and video cables to prevent interference and to comply with the National Electric Code.

After you choose a place for the control center, note its location on your floor plan.

Home Run Wiring

When you have identified the locations of your network connection points and found a place for the control center, you can plan the routes for your network cables. The preferred method for network wiring is called *home run wiring* because each cable runs "home" to a central hub or switch. The alternative, which is more practical for telephone and video wiring than for data networks, is *point-to-point* wiring that uses long cable runs that connect to each outlet through a splitter, as shown in Figure 5-3.

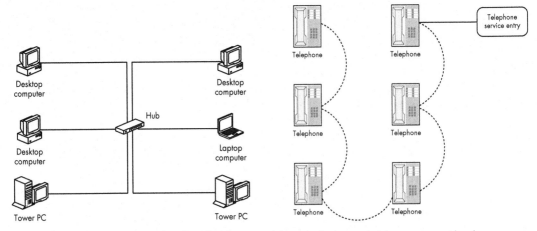

Figure 5-3: Home run wiring (left) is best for data networks; telephones and video can use either home run wiring or point-to-point networks (right).

If you haven't already done so, this is a good time to look around the rooms where you plan to install network outlets, and the spaces directly above and below each room. If you have access to an unfinished basement or attic, you can run cables through the rafters and joists; but if you have to run cables through finished walls and ceilings, you will probably have to hide cables inside walls and behind baseboards and patch some holes after the wires are in place. Either way, look for the best routes for cables from each network outlet to the control center. Use a pencil to mark the routes on your floor plan.

There are two ways to attach a network outlet to a wall. For a finished appearance, use a wall plate similar to the ones used for electrical outlets, like the one shown in Figure 5-2. If the outlet will be hidden behind furniture or in some other place where it won't be visible, you can use a small terminal block mounted on a baseboard like the one in Figure 5-4.

Figure 5-4: A data terminal block can mount directly to a baseboard.

Trunks and Branches: Using Secondary Switches

There's an alternative to a pure home run wiring design for small networks that can make it possible to expand the network without having to run new cables all the way back to the control center. This approach, which vaguely resembles the trunks and branches of a tree or the tributaries of a river, uses data switches to connect additional computers and other devices to the network through a single outlet, as shown in Figure 5-5. Connecting through a switch can be particularly handy when you want to use two or more devices (such as a computer and a game console or a printer server, or two or more computers) in the same room.

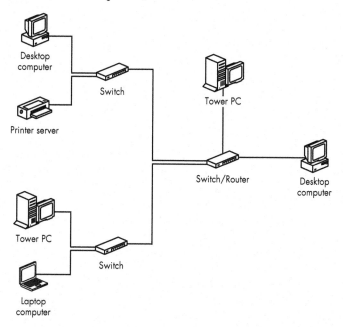

Figure 5-5: An Ethernet switch can extend a network to connect two or more devices to the network hub through a single cable.

A secondary switch can also be useful when you want to place network connection points in adjacent rooms that are difficult to reach from the control center. For example, if you have two second-floor bedrooms that share a wall, you could run a single cable to a switch and connect the switch to computers in both rooms.

Many Wi-Fi access points are combined with switches that allow you to connect one or more devices to the network through wired Ethernet outlets. If you locate your access point in a room where you also use a desktop computer or other network device, a combination unit is often an excellent choice: Place the access point next to the computer and use an Ethernet cable to connect it to the switch.

What About Wi-Fi?

Connecting computers and other network devices through a Wi-Fi network is often an easy alternative to a wired Ethernet system. A single access point is often enough for sending and receiving data to and from computers in many rooms.

A Wi-Fi network can provide Internet access and LAN services, but it has several disadvantages when compared with a wired network:

- Wi-Fi networks are usually slower than wired Ethernet unless all the nodes in the network are compatible with the latest 802.11n standards.

- Wi-Fi networks are less secure than wired networks. Unless you protect your network with a secure encryption method such as WPA, a dedicated intruder can connect to the Internet through your network without your permission and can also steal information from the other computers on the same network.

- Interference between your Wi-Fi network and your neighbors' networks and other wireless devices can reduce your network's data transfer speed.

In spite of those limitations, a Wi-Fi network is often an acceptable choice if you don't want to cut holes through your walls or spend time crawling through your attic or basement. And even if you install a wired network through part of your building, Wi-Fi could be the best way to reach one or two isolated locations such as a top-floor bedroom or a detached garage.

For many families and small businesses, the best approach is to install both wired and wireless in the same network. This will allow you and your users to connect your desktop computers, printer, music server, and other devices that never physically move through wired Ethernet, and use Wi-Fi for laptop computers, Voice over Internet Protocol (VoIP) telephones, smartphones, and other portable devices.

If you decide to include one or more Wi-Fi access points in your network, mark their tentative locations on your floor plan. In most cases, a single access point can exchange data with computers and other devices within about 300 feet (100 meters), so the exact location is not critical. The best location is often either in the network control center, or on the floor or a table next to a computer in a fixed location. For detailed information about installing Wi-Fi access points and connecting Wi-Fi devices to your home or office network, see Chapter 8.

With your network floor plan more or less complete, you're ready to install the control center and string Ethernet cables to each room. The next chapter will tell you how to do that job.

6

INSTALLING THE NETWORK CONTROL CENTER AND ETHERNET CABLES

Whether you connect your computers and other devices to the network through cables or wireless links, your network must have some kind of control center that includes one or more hubs or switches for your wired Ethernet connections, an access point for Wi-Fi, or both. If you plan to connect your LAN to the Internet, the control center must also include a gateway router and a modem. This chapter explains how to assemble a control center and run cables between the control center and the computers, game consoles, printers, and other devices that make up your network.

Connectors, Wall Plates, and Surface Boxes

As part of your floor plan, you chose a location in each room for a network outlet. In places where you decide to use surface boxes, you can attach the outlet block to the baseboard with double-sided adhesive or wood screws. For wall plates, you must cut a hole in the wall and use a mounting bracket like the one shown in Figure 6-1 to attach the plate to the wall. If there's an electrical outlet on the same wall, measure the distance from the bottom of the plate to the floor and mount the data plate at exactly the same height. Remember to keep data outlets at least a foot away from the nearest electrical outlet. When you tighten the screws on the front of the mounting bracket, the wings inside the wall will turn and hold the bracket in place.

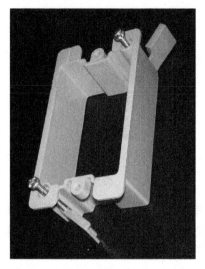

Figure 6-1: Use a mounting bracket to attach data outlet wall plates to a wall.

If you want to install a single combined wall outlet plate for data, telephone wiring, and video, use a modular plate with snap-in connectors. For a single-purpose outlet, use either a snap-in connector or a plate with the data outlet permanently attached.

Ethernet Cable

All Ethernet cables have four color-coded pairs of wires twisted together: green with green and white, brown with brown and white, and so forth. Ethernet cables and connectors are identified as Category 5 (CAT5), enhanced Category 5 (CAT5e), or Category 6 (CAT6), depending on the amount of data that can pass through a cable and the cable's sensitivity to interference. Unless you plan to install a super-fast Gigabit Ethernet network, CAT5e is usually the best compromise between cost and performance in a home or small office network.

NOTE   *Don't use CAT5 cable for new installations. It might be okay for today's networks, but it won't reliably support the next generation of high-speed data services.*

Ethernet cables come in two forms: bulk cable on spools or in boxes, and pre-assembled cables with connectors already attached. Pre-assembled data cables are often called *patch cords*, *patch cables*, or *jumper cables*. They're available in many colors and in lengths ranging from 1 foot to 100 feet. Use different-colored patch cords with a switch or any other device that has lots of connections; multiple colors will allow you to find the right one quickly.

Bulk cable is the right choice for runs inside walls between your control center and the data outlets in other rooms. On the other hand, pre-built cables are better for shorter distances, such as between terminal blocks or wall outlets and computers, control devices, and other equipment, because they're often made with more durable jackets and plugs that have permanent collars. It's possible to build your own patch cords out of bulk cable and loose plugs, but attaching plugs to cables is tedious work that's generally more trouble than it's worth. As a rule of thumb, use bulk cable for permanent installations with a terminal block to each end, and pre-built cables for patch cords and for connections between wall outlets and network devices.

Patch cords are widely available in office supply and electronics stores, but they're often four or five times more expensive than the identical cables sold through industrial electronics suppliers and online sources such as Jameco (*http://www.jameco.com/*), Cyberguys (*http://www.cyberguys.com/*), and Newegg.com (*http://www.newegg.com/*). A 3-foot cable should *not* cost $8 or $10. There's no reason to pay more for "premium" patch cables; any cable that meets the CAT5e specification will do the job. (This piece of advice will probably save you more money than you paid for this book.)

NOTE *In buildings with raised floors or dropped ceilings, it's often convenient to run your data cables through the plenum space above the ceiling or under the floor. However, fire regulations often require special* plenum cable *that won't burn easily and won't produce toxic fumes. Plenum cable is more expensive than regular bulk Ethernet cable, and it's more difficult to use because the jacket is heavier and less flexible, but there's no difference in its data-handling performance. When you're shopping for cable, you might find boxes or spools of plenum cable next to regular CAT5e cable. Sometimes the only difference is a single line on a label. Unless you have a specific need for plenum cable, don't waste your money on the more expensive stuff.*

Pushing Cable Through Walls

This is a book about computer networks rather than home improvement or new home construction, so it's not the place to describe all the special tools and techniques that electricians and telephone installers have been using for more than a hundred years to push wires through walls, under moldings, and inside closets. If you plan to install your own internal wiring, consult some of the do-it-yourself websites or look for a book about home wiring at your local home center before you start.

NOTE *I can specifically recommend* Wiring Home Networks *(Sunset Books, 2004) as a guide to installing network wiring, because I wrote it. However, several other illustrated books about home wiring also include the information you need.*

In order to feed wires from wall plates or surface boxes through your walls to the control center, you will have to drill some holes through base plates, studs, and other structural elements of your house or workplace. If you're working in rooms on the ground floor, you might be able to reach the spaces between the walls from below, drilling upward from an unfinished ceiling in the basement or crawl space. On the top floor, you can work downward from the attic. But if you can't get to the inside of the walls from above or below, your best option will be to cut holes in the wall and drill through the vertical studs, or to hide cables and holes behind mop boards and other moldings. After the wires are in place, you'll have to patch the holes and repaint the walls.

Use an electrician's snake to pull or push cables through places that you can't reach with your hands. When the end of the snake reaches the target location, attach the end of the bulk cable to the snake with electrical tape and pull the snake and cable back from the other end. It's a lot easier to route wires with a rigid snake (a long, thin piece of metal) than to deal with loose cable flopping around inside a wall.

Remember to add a length of heavy twine as a pull line along with each cable or cable bundle that you pull through the walls. In the future, when you want to add another cable along the same route, you can attach the cable to the pull line and pull it through without the need to create new holes in your walls.

You're going to connect a *lot* of cables to and through the control center, so you will want to keep them out of sight in order to maintain a neat and clean appearance. A 2-inch PVC pipe at the back of a closet or in some other hidden location can provide an inconspicuous route for cables between an upper floor or the attic and the basement or crawl space. If the pipe runs through the space where the control center is located, assemble a channel from two shorter pipes and a tee fitting about four or five feet above the floor. Pipes, fittings, and glue are all available at your local hardware store or home center.

NOTE   *Follow the instructions on the package for gluing PVC pipes to fittings, but don't worry about creating watertight seals. Your network data won't leak through a bad pipe joint.*

The Control Center

A network control center always performs these tasks:

- It connects the local network to the Internet through a modem and a telephone line, cable TV service, or some other medium.
- It uses a router to translate addresses between the LAN and the Internet.
- It uses a hub or a switch to exchange data within the network.
- It acts as the central distribution point for data cables.

In addition, it might also include these services:

- A base station for Wi-Fi
- A distribution center for audio, video, and telephone connections

If you're working from the floor plan you created after reading Chapter 5, you have already chosen a location for your control center. If not, find a place that is easy to reach but away from day-to-day traffic: the inside wall of a walk-in closet, a utility room, or a basement wall are all common choices. A garage that's built into the house might be another good spot. The control center should be close to at least one dual AC power outlet.

A network control center can take several forms:

A modular "structured wiring center" Several manufacturers offer structured wiring cabinets and most of the switches, routers, and other control devices necessary to assemble a network control center. The panel mounts on a wall (or between the studs in an unfinished basement or garage) and can include a cover to keep the contents clean and out of sight. These panels and components are considerably more expensive than separate parts from different sources, but they present a finished appearance that might be important if the control center is in a conspicuous location. If you're using one of these systems, follow the installation instructions supplied with each component.

A sheet of plywood attached to the wall A half-sheet (4 feet by 4 feet) of plywood securely bolted to wall studs is entirely adequate to support your network's mounting blocks, control devices, and other equipment. It might not be as attractive as a structured wiring center, but you're not going to see it very often. If you do a neat, workmanlike job, it will work just as well as a fancy sheet-metal cabinet full of matched components.

A freestanding mounting frame or cabinet If you have enough floor space in your utility room, you can assemble the control center from equipment and shelves that mount in a 19-inch-wide *relay rack*. This approach is usually limited to larger networks that include a lot of locations and equipment.

Several wall-mounted outlets and a small number of control devices (modem, router, and/or switch) on a table or shelf If your network is limited to computers in just two or three rooms, it might be easiest to choose one of those rooms as your control center and place the modem, router, and switch near the computer (but remember to allow for additional network nodes in the future). A single wall plate can hold up to six data outlets, so it's possible to run cables to several other rooms without installing an industrial-looking row of mounting blocks.

A data outlet block is the transition between internal data wiring inside a wall and a socket for a cable with Ethernet plugs at each end. Terminating each cable from another room with an outlet will make it easier to make additions and changes to your network wiring.

One side of an outlet block has a set of slotted pins that each holds one of the wires inside a data cable, and the other side has a socket for an Ethernet plug. A data outlet can be located on the side of a small box attached to a baseboard (or to the plywood base of your control center) or on a flush-mounted wall plate. Figure 6-2 shows an outlet block, with cables connected to both sides. The cover has been removed to make the individual wire connections visible.

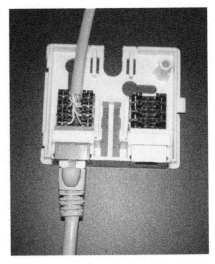

Figure 6-2: An outlet block provides a transition from loose wires to an Ethernet connector.

A completed control center on a plywood panel will look something like Figure 6-3.

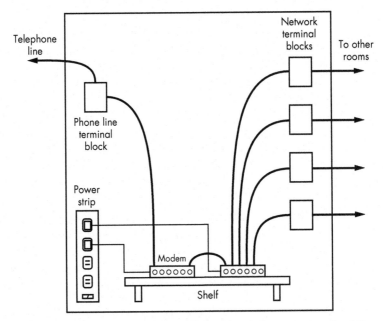

Figure 6-3: A homebrew control panel should include connections for AC power, DSL or video, and several data outlets, along with your modem, router, and switch.

AC Power

Your modem, router, and switches will all need some kind of electric power. If you're using a plywood panel as your control center, attach an AC power strip with enough outlets for all your devices and at least one spare to the side of the panel closest to the nearest AC outlet, near the bottom. The control panel should be close enough to an outlet that the cable attached to the power strip can reach it without an extension cord. In order to protect your equipment from damage caused by lightning strikes or other power surges, use a power strip with a built-in surge protector.

Many network devices use plug-in transformers or power converters (sometimes called "wall warts") that are bigger than a simple AC power plug, so you will want a power strip that provides extra space between outlets, like the one shown in Figure 6-4. This particular model also includes surge protection for a DSL telephone line.

Photo courtesy of APC

Figure 6-4: This power strip is designed for oversize plug-in power supplies.

As an alternative to a power strip, consider using an uninterruptible power supply (UPS) that will provide backup power from a battery when your AC power fails. A UPS is not a replacement for a generator, but it will keep your network alive during short power disruptions. Network control devices don't use as much power as a computer and monitor, so a small UPS should be enough to keep your network alive for up to an hour. Of course, during a power failure you will be able to use the network only with laptops and other battery-powered portables.

The battery in a UPS is relatively heavy, so you will probably want to place the UPS on the floor rather than on a shelf on the control panel. If the UPS does not have enough battery backup outlets for all of the equipment in your control center, plug a power strip directly into an outlet on the UPS.

Modems, Routers, and Switches

If you already have broadband Internet service, take a close look at the modem that connects your computer to the telephone line or TV cable and the instruction sheet that was provided with the modem. Some Internet service providers supply modems (such as the one shown in Figure 6-5) that double as gateway routers, switches, and/or Wi-Fi access points. If you have a combined unit, there's no need to duplicate those functions with one or more separate boxes.

Photo courtesy of 2Wire, Inc.

Figure 6-5: This DSL modem includes a four-port switch and a Wi-Fi base station.

Your floor plan should contain enough information to tell you the number of nodes in your network. You will need one port on a switch or combined switch/router for each node, plus additional ports to connect the control devices. For example, if you have a total of seven nodes in your network, you might use these control devices:

- A DSL or cable modem
- A gateway router combined with a four-port switch
- A four-port Ethernet switch

Figure 6-6 shows how these devices connect to one another.

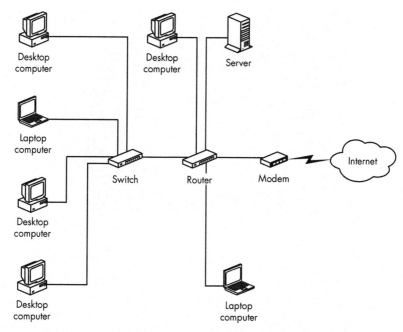

Figure 6-6: A network with seven nodes might use this setup in the control center.

You can find switches and routers at many office supply and electronics stores and through online retailers. It seems as if one brand or another is almost always on sale, so it's worth looking at the advertisements in the Sunday newspaper for this week's hot deals.

If possible, your router or switch should have at least one spare port that you can use with a laptop computer. When you're trying to troubleshoot the network, it's often convenient to send commands from the computer while you watch the responses to those commands on the control devices' status lights.

When you add more nodes to the network in the future, you can expand the network by connecting an additional switch to the control center. If there are no spare ports on the existing switch, disconnect one cable from the active switch, connect the new switch to that port, and plug the original cable into the new switch.

Some switches and routers have keyhole slots on the bottom of their cases that allow you to mount them directly on a wall, like the ones shown in Figure 6-7. When you mount a device on a wall panel, place it below eye level, with the front panel at the top of the box, so the status lights are easy to see.

If there is no allowance for mounting holes on your modem, switch, or router, and you're using a wall-mounted control center, attach a 6-inch shelf to the plywood panel and place the devices on that shelf. If you're using a modular structured wiring center, there's usually space at the bottom of the cabinet that you can use as a shelf. For a rack-mounted control center, use a rack shelf for any devices that don't mount directly into the rack.

Figure 6-7: This D-Link switch has keyhole slots on the bottom of its case.

Use big wire staples from the hardware store to route the power cables neatly along one side of your control panel between each control device and the power strip. Don't mash the staples all the way into the plywood; allow some space to be sure you haven't crushed any of the wires. Be sure to leave enough slack wire at the back of each device to allow yourself to unplug the power connector easily.

Adding a DSL or Cable Connection

Broadband Internet service comes into your building through either a telephone line or a TV cable. Therefore, you will need either a telephone or cable TV outlet in your control center. This is the same kind of outlet that you are already using to connect a telephone or TV set. If you're getting Internet service from your cable TV company, you can sometimes convince the installer to run a cable to your control center. But if you have DSL or some other type of Internet service from the telephone company, you might have to install your own wiring.

Connecting a Telephone Line

If you have DSL or some other kind of Internet service from the telephone company, you will need a telephone outlet with a four-pin socket called an *RJ-11 jack*. This is the same kind of socket that you use to plug in a telephone set.

Mount the outlet block on your panel, about a foot above the power strip. You can use either conventional telephone cable, with two pairs of wires inside, or the same four-pair data cable that you use for your computer network to connect the outlet block on the control panel back to the distribution block that connects your telephones to the service entry. If you use telephone cable, be sure to match the colors of the wires to the letters on the outlet blocks at both ends (R = red, Y = yellow, G = green, and B = black). If you use data cable, use the color codes in Table 6-1.

Table 6-1: Data Cable Color Codes for Telephone Lines

Terminal Color	Data Cable Color
Green	Blue
Red	Blue-White
Black	Orange
Yellow	Orange-White

Use a cable-stripping tool to remove about two inches of the plastic jacket from the end of the telephone cable. If the outlet block has screw terminals, strip about half an inch of insulation off the end of each wire and wrap the bare end around the screw next to the letter that corresponds to the wire's color.

If the terminal uses two vertical pins with a slot between them to hold each wire, don't strip the wires, but use a punch-down tool to force each wire between the pins. If your terminal does not come with a small punch-down tool, look for one at a home center or hardware store; you will need the same tool to connect data cables to their outlet connectors. If excess wire extends from the side of the connector, cut it off. When all four wires are connected, place the dust cover on the plug.

After you have connected the telephone line to the outlet block, plug in a telephone with a modular RJ-11 cable to test for a dial tone. If there's no dial tone, check your connections at both ends; if you have a dial tone, unplug the telephone set and use one of the cables supplied with the modem to connect the modem to the telephone line.

Connecting a TV Cable

Most video wiring inside a building uses coaxial cable called *RG6/U* with a central copper wire surrounded by insulation and a metal shield. The connectors that attach to this cable are called *F connectors.*

Video cables usually require a special tool to attach the F connector to each end of the cable. If you're not installing your own video distribution system along with your data network, and you have to install your own cable from the service entry to the network control center, it might be easier and cheaper to buy a pre-assembled cable with the connectors already attached (look for a cable close to the length you need—don't use a 100-foot cable for a 20-foot run). Use electrical tape or a cable tie to hold excess lengths of cable in a neat loop at one end.

If you have to install the video cable yourself, find the service entry where the cable comes into your house or office. String the cable along the ceiling or through the rafters under the floor to the control center, then attach the cable to the F connector inside the outlet plate. If there's a splitter with a spare connector at the service entry, screw the plug at the end of the cable onto the unused socket. If you can't find a splitter, you'll have to install a new one, or distribute your video from the control panel.

If you're not connecting other outlets through the control center, plug the cable from the service entry directly into your cable modem. If you want to use the control panel to distribute cable TV signals to outlets throughout the house, connect the cable from the service entrance to the input of a splitter and connect the outputs to your cable modem and the cables from each room.

Terminating the Network Cables

If you're using a plywood panel as your control center, mount one or two rows of outlet blocks along the top of the panel, or along the side opposite the power strip. Keep the outlets evenly spaced and allow enough space to add more outlets in the future.

Terminate the wires in each network cable on a terminal block with an eight-pin *RJ-45* socket (be sure to follow the color codes) and attach a tag to the cable that identifies the location of the cable's other end. Use a marking pen or the label supplied with the terminal block to identify each cable on the cover of the block. Your goal is to be able to figure out at a glance which terminal block connects to what destination.

There are two different standard color codes for connecting Ethernet cables to plugs and sockets. Use one of the standard color codes (T568A or T568B) to connect each wire in the cable to the socket inside the terminal block. Table 6-2 shows the correct connections. It doesn't matter which of the two standards you use, as long as both ends of each cable follow the same standard. The best approach is to choose a standard and wire every socket in your network to that standard.

Table 6-2: Wiring for Ethernet Cables and Sockets

Color	T568A Pin Number	T568B Pin Number
Blue	4	4
Blue-White	5	5
Orange	6	2
Orange-White	3	1
Green	2	6
Green-White	1	3
Brown	8	8
Brown-White	7	7

Follow these steps to connect a CAT5, CAT5e, or CAT6 cable to an Ethernet socket:

1. Allow about a foot of slack and cut off the excess cable.

2. Remove about two inches of the cable's outer jacket. Be sure you don't nick any of the internal wires with your stripping tool.

3. Separate the four pairs of wires that extend beyond the jacket, but don't untwist the individual wires.

4. Follow the instructions supplied with the connector to direct each wire to the correct slot. Be sure the jacket extends into the back of the connector.

5. Use a punch-down tool to insert the two wires closest to the back of the connector into their respective slots.

6. Insert the wires from the other three pairs into the correct slots. Don't untwist the pairs any more than is necessary.

7. Double-check to confirm that each wire is in the correct slot according to the color code you are using.

8. If your punch-down tool doesn't automatically cut off excess wire, use a wire cutter to trim each wire.

9. If the RJ-45 socket came with a dust cover, snap it into place over the wires.

10. Insert the socket into the terminal block or the wall plate from the inside of the block or case.

Adding a Telephone

When you're trying to solve a problem with your network connection, it's often helpful to have a telephone next to the control panel, so you can talk to a technical support person while you're looking at the status lights on the modem, router, or switch. You won't need this phone very often, but when something goes wrong, you will be happy to have it. Use a cell phone or a cordless handset if you have one, or install an inexpensive wall phone on or near the control panel. If possible, look for a simple desk or wall phone that does not require an external power supply.

Tabletop Control Centers for Small Networks

You don't need a separate control center for a small network that connects computers in just a few rooms. It's often easier to place the modem and router in one room and run data cables directly to each of the other rooms. You can place the modem and router on your computer table or on a nearby bookshelf.

Leviton and other manufacturers make wall plates that can hold up to six or eight data outlets in the same space as a dual AC outlet. That should be enough for a small network; if you need more, add a second wall plate or replace the first one with a dual-width plate.

When it's time to expand your network, you have two options: You can run new wiring from the original control room to the new location, or you can add a downstream switch in the room closest to the location and run a data cable from there. The second approach can be particularly convenient when the new location shares a wall with a room that already has a data outlet.

NOTE   *It's particularly important to label the wall outlets in a network without a control center. Years from now, when other people try to use your network after you've moved away, they'll need to know where the cable connected to each data outlet goes.*

You can also use a small Ethernet switch to use more than one network device in the same room. For example, if there's a data outlet in a teenager's bedroom, you could connect a four-port switch to the wall outlet and connect a computer, a game controller, and an Internet radio to the household network through that switch.

7

ETHERNET NETWORK INTERFACES

Every computer on a network uses some kind of internal or external connector to send and receive data to and from other computers. This connector, along with the hardware that controls it, is called a *network adapter* or *network interface* because it's the point of contact between the computer and the network. In a small home or business network, the network interface can be either an Ethernet port that communicates with the network through a cable or a wireless transmitter and receiver that exchanges radio signals with a Wi-Fi base station. This chapter describes the most common wired Ethernet network interfaces. Chapter 8 provides similar information about connecting your computer to a network through a wireless interface.

Built into the Motherboard

Every modern wired Ethernet interface has an eight-pin socket (an *Ethernet port* or *jack*) that mates with the plug on an Ethernet cable. Both the plug and the socket follow a standard called *RJ-45* that specifies the size and shape of the connectors and the signals that move through each of the eight pins (*RJ* stands for *Registered Jack*). RJ-45 connectors are similar to the six-pin RJ-11 plugs and sockets used on telephones, but the RJ-45 is slightly larger to allow for the additional pins. Figure 7-1 shows both an RJ-45 Ethernet plug and an RJ-11 telephone plug.

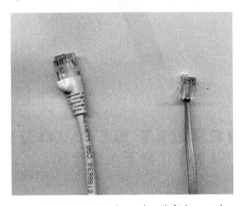

Figure 7-1: An RJ-45 data plug (left) has eight wires; an RJ-11 telephone plug (right) has four or six wires.

In addition to the port itself, an Ethernet interface also includes some internal hardware that converts the data in both directions between the format that the computer's central processor can handle and the format used by the network. This hardware can take several forms. It can be:

- On the computer's main circuit board (the motherboard)
- A printed circuit card that mounts inside the computer
- A PC card that plugs into a laptop computer
- An external unit connected to the computer through a USB cable

Almost all the computers built within the past few years have built-in Ethernet ports. On desktop and tower computers, the RJ-45 jack is on the back of the case, as shown in Figure 7-2. On laptop computers, the Ethernet port is usually on either the back or the side of the case.

If your computer has a built-in Ethernet port, the driver software that instructs the central processor how to handle network data is on the software disc supplied with the computer or the motherboard. If your computer came with the operating system already installed, the driver is already in place. However, if you assemble your own computer from parts, you might have to install the network driver supplied with the motherboard or a third party after you load the Windows, Linux, or Unix operating system.

Figure 7-2: Most new computers come with Ethernet ports as standard features.

Setting the BIOS Utility

If your computer has a built-in Ethernet interface, it's sometimes necessary to turn off that interface and use a network adapter on an expansion card or some other kind of external network interface. This might happen when you want to use a faster network than your built-in adapter can handle (such as a Gigabit Ethernet network) or if the onboard network controller doesn't work correctly.

To turn off the internal network interface, you must open the computer's BIOS settings utility and find the option that enables or disables the onboard LAN controller or some other option with a similar name. In most BIOS utilities, the LAN option is buried under two or three menu levels.

The BIOS settings utility is a set of controls that load configuration settings when you turn on the computer. These settings are an essential part of the computer's startup sequence because they tell the computer where and how to find the operating system. To run the BIOS settings utility, turn off the computer, then turn it on again and immediately press the DEL (delete) or F1 key (depending on the type of BIOS your computer uses).

If you're not comfortable changing the BIOS settings, just leave them alone. When you install another network interface, Windows and other operating systems will recognize both the internal and external adapters. In most cases, it won't matter if both of them are active at the same time.

On the other hand, if your network connection doesn't work when you turn on the computer but the rest of the network is okay and all the network cables are plugged into their appropriate sockets, it's possible that the internal adapter has been disabled by accident. This should never happen unless somebody goes into the BIOS utility and changes the setting, but it's possible, especially if the computer is in a public location where other people can mess with it.

Adding a Network Interface to an Old Computer

If you're using an older computer, it's possible that the computer does not have a built-in network interface. In that case, you must add one before you can connect it to your network. Fortunately, network interface adapters are inexpensive and easy to install.

As a minimum, look for an Ethernet adapter that can handle both 10Base-T and 100Base-T networks. If you plan to connect the computer to a Gigabit Ethernet network, you'll need a faster and more expensive adapter.

Like other computer components, Ethernet adapters are available both as inexpensive no-name products and slightly more costly brand-name versions that come with better documentation and a manufacturer's warranty. As always, you get what you pay for; considering that you can generally find a brand-name adapter for just a few dollars (or euros or pounds) more, it's usually the better choice.

Internal Expansion Cards

Internal network adapters are printed circuit cards that fit into one of the expansion slots on your computer's motherboard, like the one shown in Figure 7-3. Unless you're working with a very old computer, the adapter should be a PCI card; that's probably the only kind you will find at your local computer or office supply store. The PCI sockets on the motherboard are almost always white.

Photo courtesy of D-Link

Figure 7-3: An internal PCI card mounts in an expansion slot inside a desktop or tower computer.

If your computer was made before the mid-1990s, you might need an ISA card instead. ISA sockets on motherboards are usually black. ISA Ethernet adapters are still available, but you'll probably have to go to a specialist source. A Web search for *ISA Ethernet card* will produce pointers to many choices, but be sure to order a "10/100" or "fast Ethernet" card rather than an older design that works at only 10 Mbps.

To install an internal Ethernet adapter, follow these steps:

1. Turn off the computer and unplug the power cable.
2. Remove the cover from the computer's case.
3. Find an empty expansion slot on the motherboard.
4. Remove the metal bracket attached to the computer's frame directly behind the empty slot. Save the screw; you'll need it to secure the adapter card.
5. Line up the bottom of the adapter card with the slots in the expansion socket and push it into place.
6. Use the screw you saved from the old bracket to secure the adapter card.
7. While the computer case is off, clean out the accumulated dust and make sure none of the connectors attached to the motherboard and the drives have come loose.
8. Replace the cover and plug in the power cable.
9. Plug a network cable into the new Ethernet jack in the back of the computer.
10. Turn on the computer. If the operating system does not automatically detect the new network connection, load the driver software.

USB Adapters

A computer that has built-in USB ports but no Ethernet ports can use an external USB network interface as an alternative to an internal expansion card, but the data transfer speed might not be as fast. USB adapters are widely available, but very few computers need them: By the time USB ports became common features on computers, onboard Ethernet ports were also standard equipment.

Network Adapters for Laptops

An old laptop without a built-in Ethernet port must use a network adapter on a plug-in PC card that fits into the PCMCIA socket on the side of the computer. Figure 7-4 shows a network adapter on a PC card.

NOTE   *A new standard for 32-bit PC cards and services called CardBus was adopted in 1995. CardBus PC cards (with a gold grounding strip next to the 68-hole connector) don't fit older 16-bit PC card sockets, but 16-bit cards will fit into 32-bit sockets. If your laptop was made before 1997, look for a 16-bit 10/100 Mbps PC card adapter.*

Very old laptops that don't have PC card sockets can connect to an Ethernet network through a serial-to-Ethernet adapter, but it's probably not worth the effort. Any laptop without a PC card socket is at least a dozen years old, and it won't come close to the performance of today's least expensive models. Considering that a serial-to-Ethernet adapter is likely to cost almost as much as a whole new computer, it's time to replace your "Old Faithful" antique instead.

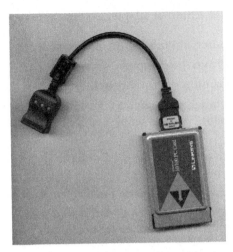

Figure 7-4: This 16-bit PC card network adapter uses a short cable (sometimes called a dongle) to connect the adapter to an Ethernet socket.

Finding the Driver Software for Your Adapter

Windows XP, Windows Vista, Mac OS X, and most current versions of Linux and Unix can automatically detect new network adapters. In some cases, you might have to restart the computer after installing the network adapter, but in general, the operating system will load the device driver software right away.

NOTE   *In some less user-friendly Unix or Linux distributions, it might be necessary to compile the kernel to support a specific network driver and load the module at runtime, but this is not common.*

However, if you're working with an older operating system or a network interface that the operating system can't recognize, you'll have to find and install the correct device driver. A *device driver* is a small program that converts between the generic output signals supplied by the computer's central processor and the specific instructions that control the features and functions of a device connected to the computer. It also converts incoming commands and data from the peripheral device to a format that the central processor can recognize.

New network adapters usually come with a software disc that contains the device driver and other related programs and documentation. If yours is missing, or if the disc doesn't contain the right driver for your operating system, you can probably find a driver program on the adapter manufacturer's website or through an online source of open source device drivers.

Several websites offer direct links to hundreds of sources for device drivers:

http://www.windrivers.com/

http://www.pcdrivers.com/

http://www.driverzone.com/

http://www.driverguide.com/

http://www.helpdrivers.com/

http://www.winguides.com/drivers/

http://www.driversplanet.com/

http://www.totallydrivers.com/

Status Lights on Network Adapters

Most Ethernet adapters have two or three status indicators that light and go dark as data moves through the network connection. On an expansion card, the lights are usually on the metal mounting bracket just above or below the RJ-45 connector; on a PC card, they might be on the card itself, or on the socket that connects to the network cable. Indicator lights on a built-in Ethernet socket are usually right next to the socket itself.

The three indicator lights are:

LINK   Lights in green when the adapter is connected to a live network

10/100   Lights in yellow when the adapter is connected to a 100 Mbps network; goes dark when it's connected to a 10 Mbps network

ACT   Flashes in green as data passes through the network connection in either direction

These lights are useful for troubleshooting and watching network performance, because they can tell you whether your network connection is working properly. For example, when the LINK indicator lights, you know that the computer is connected to a live network; when it's dark, the network connection is offline. When the ACT light flashes, it tells you that the computer is sending or receiving data.

Unfortunately, the lights are often located in a place where it's difficult or impossible to see them while you're using the computer. When you're testing the system, it's often helpful to ask someone else to watch the lights while you operate the computer.

On some computers, the LINK and 10/100 lights might remain on when the computer is turned off. This happens when the computer's BIOS has a "wake on LAN" feature that turns on the computer if the adapter receives an incoming signal. Even if this feature is disabled, the computer keeps the network port alive whenever the power supply is turned on. The only way to disable the network adapter completely is to either unplug the AC power or turn off the power switch on the back of the power supply.

8

WI-FI NETWORKS

Wi-Fi (short for Wireless Fidelity, pronounced "why-fie") networks use radio signals instead of Ethernet cables to connect computers and other devices to a LAN. Wi-Fi is a convenient alternative to conventional wired networks because any wireless-enabled computer within range of the Wi-Fi signal can join the network; there's no need to find a network outlet. This can be particularly useful when it's not practical to pull data cables through walls, ceilings, and floors, and when a user wants to connect a laptop computer or a handheld device such as an iPhone or BlackBerry to an existing network or through a LAN to the Internet. And of course, thousands of Wi-Fi hotspots in public spaces such as airports, coffee shops, libraries, and schools offer easy access to the Internet when you're away from your own home or office.

However, Wi-Fi connections are far less secure than wired networks, because the same data that moves between a computer and a base station by radio can be intercepted by another computer. Even if the data is encrypted, a dedicated intruder with enough time can steal passwords, credit card numbers, and other personal information. However, the latest security tools, including WPA encryption and virtual private networks (VPNs), can go a long way toward making a Wi-Fi network secure.

This chapter describes the types of Wi-Fi networks and explains how to add a Wi-Fi hotspot to your LAN, how to select and use a Wi-Fi network interface with your computer, and how to keep your Wi-Fi network as secure as possible.

Types of Wi-Fi Networks

Wi-Fi networks use the IEEE (Institute of Electrical and Electronics Engineers) 802.11 family of standards to define the radio frequencies, data formats, and other technical details that are necessary to establish a wireless LAN. Today, there are four types of 802.11 networks, as shown in Table 8-1.

Table 8-1: Wireless Network Standards

Type	Maximum Speed	Maximum Range (outdoors)	Radio Frequency Band
802.11b	11 Mbps	300 feet (100 meters)	2.4 GHz
802.11a	54 Mbps	75–100 feet (23–30 meters)	5.2 GHz
802.11g	54 Mbps	300 feet (100 meters)	2.4 GHz
802.11n	248 Mbps	750 feet (250 meters)	2.4 GHz/5.2 GHz

The useful distance that an access point can reach is often considerably less than the promised maximum, especially when the path between the access point and a computer's wireless adapter is indoors. Walls, furniture, and other objects between the two antennas can all reduce the signal strength. 802.11b networks were the first to appear, and they were the most common type until the faster 802.11g version became available. 802.11a uses different radio frequencies, but many network adapters are compatible with both 2.4 GHz and 5.2 GHz access points. Today, the new 802.11n standard is beginning to replace all three older versions.

The three systems that use channels in the 2.4 GHz frequency band are backward compatible. In other words, if your Wi-Fi network interface adapter uses 802.11b only, it will continue to work with an 802.11g or 802.11n base station; both 802.11b and 802.11g adapters will work with an 802.11n base station.

NOTE *The missing letters—802.11c, d, e, and so forth—describe other wireless data characteristics and enhancements that apply to wireless data networks. They're important to hardware designers and manufacturers, but as a network manager or user, you don't have to worry about them.*

You might also see some Wi-Fi access points and network adapters identified as *extreme* or *enhanced*, or with some other word which suggests that they work at faster speeds than a standard network. Most often these systems use a proprietary method that involves two or more parallel channels to increase their data-handling capacity. Enhanced systems usually work as advertised, but only when the adapter and access point were both made by the same company. When you're building a wireless network that will use network adapters made by different manufacturers, or if you plan to allow users of laptops and other portable devices to connect to your network, there's not much benefit to having an enhanced network.

The Wi-Fi Alliance (*http://www.wi-fi.org/*), the industry group that promotes these networks, conducts periodic "bake-offs" where many manufacturers demonstrate that their products will work correctly with equipment made by their competitors. A network adapter or access point that carries the Wi-Fi logo has been tested and certified for compatibility by the Wi-Fi Alliance.

Operating Channels

Wi-Fi uses a segment of the radio spectrum (also called a band) near 2.4 GHz that has been reserved for unlicensed industrial, scientific, and medical (ISM) services, including wireless data networks. 802.11b, 802.11g, and 802.11n all use this band of frequencies. 802.11a uses a different frequency band near 5.2 GHz known as the *Unlicensed National Information Infrastructure (U-NII)*.

Both the ISM and U-NII bands are open to many kinds of unlicensed radio services. This means that the people who make the equipment must demonstrate that their designs meet various regulations related to maximum power, interference, and so forth, but actual users (that's you and me) don't need to obtain licenses before they can operate approved radios. One result of this is that the same radio frequencies used by Wi-Fi networks are also filled with signals from cordless telephones, medical equipment, radio-controlled toys, and microwave ovens, among many other things. Wi-Fi and those other devices use different methods to transmit and receive radio signals, so there's not much danger that the Wi-Fi adapter in your laptop computer will cause a model-train wreck or cause your cordless phone to ring. However, other ISM or U-NII signals, along with Wi-Fi signals from other nearby users, can add noise to your Wi-Fi signal that reduces the network's data transfer speed.

Within the 2.4 GHz band, there are 14 overlapping Wi-Fi radio channels. Japan is the only major country that uses all of them. Only 11 of those channels are used in North America and China, while most of Europe uses 13 channels. In France, only 4 channels are available. Each channel operates on a different frequency, numbered from Channel 1 to Channel 14.

Each channel overlaps the two channels above it and two below it, as shown in Figure 8-1, so the channels with adjacent numbers can interfere with one another. Like the interference from other ISM devices, adjacent-channel interference can create a slower, noisier connection. Therefore, when you're setting up a new network or adding an access point to an existing network, it's best to choose a channel number as far away from the channels used by nearby networks as possible.

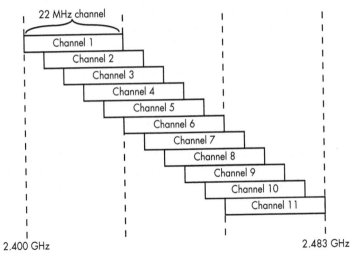

Figure 8-1: Wi-Fi signals use 11 separate overlapping channels. Notice that channels 1, 6, and 11 do not interfere with each other.

Access Points

Every Wi-Fi network must have at least one access point. Wi-Fi access points, or base stations, are radio transmitter/receivers (*transceivers*) that send and receive data by radio and exchange that data with a wired Ethernet network. You can think of an access point as a router between a Wi-Fi network and a wired LAN.

Most access points have one or two short antennas attached to the back panel; some also have a connector that can mate with a cable from a separate antenna. Separate antennas are useful because they can increase the access point's signal strength and sensitivity, but they're usually not necessary in small indoor home or small business networks. There's more about antennas later in this chapter.

Wi-Fi access points are often combined in a single unit with cable or DSL modems, gateway routers, or Ethernet switches. If your network includes both wired and wireless connections, you might want to consider a combined device, which is often less costly than two separate boxes. Figure 8-2 shows a combined access point, Ethernet switch, and router. Indicator lights on the front of this device show power, wireless activity, and data moving to or from each wired network node.

A single 802.11g or 802.11n base station should provide more than enough signal coverage to reach all parts of a house or small office, but if it doesn't (because of obstructions or interference), the best solution is to add a second (or third) access point at a location where its signal will fill in the dead spots. Each access point should be connected to the wired portion of the network through an Ethernet hub or switch or, if that's not practical, through a wireless bridge that retransmits Wi-Fi signals on a different channel. In a Wi-Fi network with more than one access point, they should all use the same network name, but each one should use a different non-overlapping operating channel.

Photo courtesy of D-Link

Figure 8-2: This Wi-Fi access point doubles as a network router.

Network Interface Adapters

Wi-Fi network interface adapters are small radio transceivers that convert from computer data to radio signals that they exchange with a Wi-Fi access point, and back again. A Wi-Fi adapter can be an expansion card inside a laptop or desktop computer, a plug-in PC card, or a separate USB device.

NOTE   *A Wi-Fi adapter can also exchange data by radio directly to and from another computer in an ad hoc network, as described in Chapter 2.*

Most new Wi-Fi adapters are compatible with all four standards (802.11a, b, g, and n), so they can exchange data with any Wi-Fi access point. Older adapters might use only one, two, or three standards, so they'll only connect to compatible base stations. When a network adapter detects a radio signal from a nearby access point, the adapter's control software will automatically match the signal type used by that access point.

Adapters Built into Laptops

Built-in Wi-Fi interfaces are a standard feature of most new laptop computers. The actual interface adapter is on a mini–PCI card that mounts on the computer's motherboard, like the one shown in Figure 8-3. The antennas for internal Wi-Fi adapters are usually flexible wires inside the upper half of a laptop's folding clamshell, in the space surrounding the monitor screen.

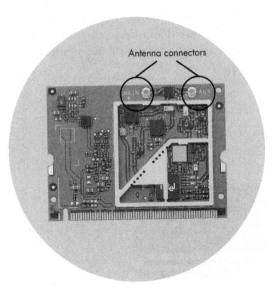

Photo courtesy of Intel

Figure 8-3: Mini–PCI card Wi-Fi adapters mount on the motherboard inside a laptop computer. The "Main" and "Aux" connectors near the top in the photograph are antenna connectors.

One advantage of the mini–PCI card approach (as opposed to making the Wi-Fi adapter a permanent part of the motherboard itself) is that the adapter is what IBM calls a *field-replaceable unit (FRU)*. Other manufacturers use different names, but the meaning is the same: If an adapter goes bad, or if you want to replace an older adapter with a new one that can handle new standards, it's relatively easy to remove the old card and install a new one in its place without changing the motherboard. This feature will be particularly convenient as and when the 802.11n standard becomes more common.

It's important to turn off the Wi-Fi adapter when you're not using a network, in order to reduce battery drain and to avoid transmitting a signal that a hacker could use to link to your computer. There are usually several ways to turn an internal adapter on and off: a physical on/off switch, a set of keyboard commands, and an option in the Wi-Fi control program. The computer's user manual is the best source for instructions on operating a Wi-Fi adapter.

PC Cards

Laptop computers without built-in adapters can use an adapter on a credit card–size PC card or PC ExpressCard. To install the adapter, simply plug it into the PCMCIA socket and wait for your operating system to recognize it and load the appropriate driver software.

Figure 8-4 shows a PC card adapter. The adapters extend about an inch beyond the edge of the PCMCIA socket, in order to place the antenna outside the computer's metal case.

Antenna inside this part

Photo courtesy of D-Link

Figure 8-4: PC card Wi-Fi adapters usually have built-in antennas.

Some PC card adapters also have a connector on the top or on the outside edge of the card for an external antenna. This can allow you to place the antenna in a location where there's a better signal to and from the base station, but the separate antenna is one more thing to carry along with your laptop computer. In general, an adapter with a built-in antenna is usually a better choice for a portable computer.

A few Wi-Fi adapters are also available on the newer PC ExpressCards that are gradually replacing PC cards in the latest generation of laptop computers. However, built-in Wi-Fi adapters were already standard features in most laptops by the time PC ExpressCard sockets were introduced in 2004 and 2005, so there's generally no reason to search for a separate adapter. On the other hand, a PC ExpressCard adapter might be the best way to add Wi-Fi to your desktop if there's a PC ExpressCard socket on the computer's case.

USB Adapters

USB Wi-Fi adapters are available in two different forms: small modules that plug directly into the computer's USB port and stand-alone devices that connect to the USB port through a cable. The separate units often provide better connections because they have more powerful transmitters and more sensitive receivers, but they're considerably less convenient than the small modules, especially with a laptop.

Figure 8-5 shows both a stand-alone USB adapter and a plug-in USB Wi-Fi module.

NOTE *The smaller (and cheaper) plug-in USB Wi-Fi modules are often entirely adequate to connect your computer to a Wi-Fi network unless you're using the computer at the fringe of the access point's coverage. If you can detect a strong signal with a plug-in module, you won't get better performance with a stand-alone device. However, a separate adapter with a more powerful transmitter and a more sensitive receiver might allow you to use a signal that the smaller module won't detect.*

Photos courtesy of Linksys, a division of Cisco Systems, Inc.

Figure 8-5: USB Wi-Fi adapters can be either stand-alone devices (left) or small plug-in modules (right).

PCI Cards

Wi-Fi adapters on PCI expansion cards that mount inside a desktop computer are also available, but they're less convenient than other types of adapters. To install a PCI card, you must open the computer's case and insert the adapter into an unused expansion slot on the computer's motherboard—a considerably more complicated process than plugging in a PC card or a USB device.

The only reason to consider using a Wi-Fi adapter on a PCI expansion card might be to add an old computer that has no USB ports to a wireless network. Even then, you could achieve the same result by installing an expansion card with several USB ports inside the computer and connecting a USB Wi-Fi adapter to one of those ports. That's probably the better approach, because it will also allow you to use other USB devices with the same computer.

Antennas

Every Wi-Fi adapter comes with either a built-in antenna or an antenna that plugs into a socket on the adapter's case. Some adapters include a built-in antenna *and* a socket. As mentioned earlier in this chapter, the antennas for a mini–PCI adapter in a laptop computer are usually built inside the top part of the computer's case, alongside the display panel.

Unless you're trying to send and receive Wi-Fi signals over very long distances, the antenna supplied with your adapter should be all you need. Remember that a more powerful antenna might produce stronger incoming and outgoing signals, but those stronger signals often don't make any difference to network performance—once the signal strength reaches an adequate level, there's no advantage to adding more power or sensitivity.

The antenna used with an access point is a different story. If you install a "high gain" directional antenna or place the antenna as high as possible, the access point's coverage area will increase because radio signals at the frequencies that Wi-Fi uses are *line of sight,* meaning that the signal can reach anywhere that an observer at the same location could see. However, the off-axis signals to or from a directional antenna are a great deal weaker because the antenna focuses most of its output (from a transmitter) or sensitivity (to a receiver) within a limited area. When you install a directional antenna, take the time to make sure the antenna is oriented for the best possible signal strength between the access point and the network interfaces.

On the other hand, *nondirectional* (or *omnidirectional*) antennas have equal signal strength or sensitivity in all directions. The best way to provide Wi-Fi coverage over a wide area is to use an access point with a nondirectional antenna and either increase the height of the access point or antenna or use directional antennas on the network nodes located at the fringes of the access point's coverage area.

Many Wi-Fi adapters and access points use antenna connectors that are not the same as the standard cable connectors on antennas. In order to match the two, you must use a short cable adapter (not to be confused with a network interface adapter) called a *pigtail.* Pigtails are often available directly from the companies that make Wi-Fi adapters and access points, but these *OEM (original equipment manufacturer)* parts are extremely expensive. Cables that do the same job equally well are available for a fraction of the OEM prices from specialty cable suppliers. Run a web search on *Wi-Fi pigtails* to find a place where you can order inexpensive adapter cables.

Wi-Fi Control Programs

Before you can move data through a Wi-Fi network, you must configure the network's base station to specify the operating channel you want to use, the password for data encryption, and other characteristics of the network. In addition, each wireless network adapter must also run a control program.

Access Point Configuration Programs

Your access point should have at least one wired connection to a computer in order to set and change the configuration settings. Depending on the make and model you're using, this connection might be through an Ethernet port, a USB port, or a serial data port. The access point uses this connection to accept configuration and setup commands and to send status information. Some access points can also accept commands through a wireless link, but after you turn off the wireless function, you'll need a wired connection to turn it back on again.

The most common method for configuring an access point is through a web-based configuration utility. In other words, the access point's configuration options all appear on one or more web pages that appear when you point your computer's web browser to the access point's IP address.

Each make and model of access point uses a somewhat different configuration program, so the manual supplied with each device is your best source of specific instructions. However, they all include similar options. The most important settings include:

DHCP   Many networks use *Dynamic Host Configuration Protocol (DHCP)* to automatically assign IP addresses from a *DHCP host* or *DHCP server*. The alternative is to manually assign a numeric IP address to each computer and other device connected to the network. The access point's configuration utility includes an option to use the access point as the network's DHCP server.

IP address   You must either set the access point to accept an IP address from another device (a dynamic IP address) or manually enter an address for the access point.

Wireless network name   Each network should have a distinctive name called a *Service Set Identifier (SSID)*. This is the name that users will select from a list of networks in their computers' control programs.

Channel number   Each access point operates on a single channel. This option sets that channel. For best performance, choose a channel that is different from the ones used by other Wi-Fi networks within your signal range.

Operating mode   Many access points can operate on more than one operating mode (802.11b, 802.11a, 802.11g, or 802.11n), depending on the mode used by the computers with which it exchanges data. This option allows you to set the access mode to detect operating modes automatically and choose the best one available, or to specify a particular mode.

Other wireless settings are often available, sometimes in a separate "advanced" menu or web page. Unless you have a good reason to change something, it's usually best to keep the default settings.

Many Wi-Fi access points are combined with routers or modems, so the configuration process also includes some additional setup options. See Chapter 10 for information about configuring a router or modem. If you're using a separate access point, it's usually best to turn off the DHCP server in the access point and obtain all of the network's addresses from the router or modem.

Wireless Connection Programs

A computer with an installed Wi-Fi adapter uses a wireless control program to select a Wi-Fi network and establish a connection. Windows, Mac OS X, and various versions of Linux and Unix include wireless control programs, and alternative control programs are often provided as part of the driver software supplied with wireless network interface adapters and laptop computers.

For example, Figure 8-6 shows the Wi-Fi control program included in Windows XP, and Figure 8-7 shows the Intel program supplied with its mini–PCI Wi-Fi adapters. Both programs display a list of all nearby Wi-Fi access points and identify those that are using encrypted data. To use either program, select the name of the network you want, and click the **Connect** button at the bottom of the program window. Other programs use different onscreen layouts, but they all operate similarly. In some cases, one of the programs installed on your computer might be more sensitive to weak signals from access points, but that usually doesn't matter—all of them detect the strong nearby access points' signals that you will use most often.

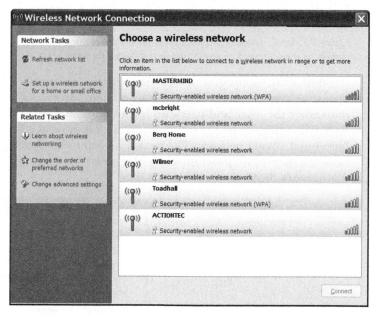

Figure 8-6: The Wireless Network Connection program supplied with Windows detects nearby Wi-Fi signals and sets up a new network connection.

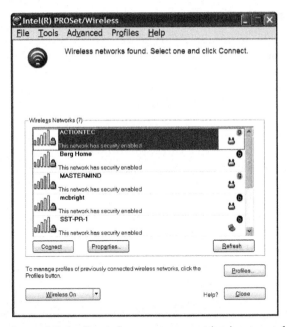

Figure 8-7: Intel's wireless program provides the same information as the Microsoft program, but in a different format.

Both of these programs, and similar programs supplied with other operating systems, network adapters, and computers, can automatically remember the login and password information and other details of each Wi-Fi network you use. For example, Figure 8-8 shows the Properties settings for a hotel's Wi-Fi network. The next time you try to connect to the same network, the control program won't have to ask for a password again because this network profile is set to "Automatic."

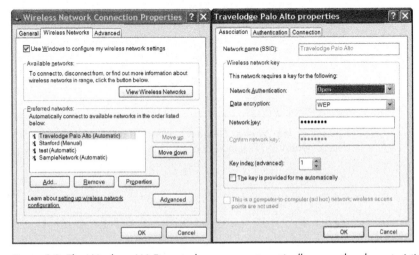

Figure 8-8: The Windows Wi-Fi control program automatically saves the characteristics of past network connections.

If your computer remains connected to the same Wi-Fi network all the time (at home or in your office), or if you frequently connect to the same Wi-Fi hotspot at your favorite coffee shop or lecture hall, the Wi-Fi control program should automatically use the password and other configuration settings for that network every time you turn on the computer within the network's range. The exceptions are public networks that require a new login with every connection.

NOTE *Many Wi-Fi hotspots that require a password display a web-based login screen before they connect you to the first website you try to view. These hotspots won't connect to any other Internet service (such as email or instant messaging) until you log in through a web browser.*

Hybrid (Wired-Wireless) Networks

Most home and business Wi-Fi networks include at least one computer connected to the network's router through an Ethernet cable rather than via a wireless link. The wired connections are often in the same room as the router and modem, where there's little or no advantage to using wireless. In many networks it might be convenient to run a cable to one or more adjacent rooms but use Wi-Fi for computers in more isolated locations.

Other networks limit Wi-Fi connections to laptops, smartphones, and other portable or handheld devices. All the permanent systems use Ethernet cables, because they're faster and more secure.

Wi-Fi Security

Wireless networks are a trade-off between security and convenience. The obvious benefits of a wireless network connection—fast and easy access to the network from a portable computer or an isolated location—come at a cost. For most users, the convenience of wireless operation outweighs the possible security threats. But just as you lock the doors of your car when you park it on the street, you should take similar steps to protect your network and your data.

The simple truth is that someone who wants to devote enough time and effort to monitoring Wi-Fi signals can probably find a way to intercept and read the data they carry. If you send confidential information through a wireless link, an eavesdropper can copy it unless the website or other host is using an end-to-end encryption scheme such as SSL. Credit card numbers, account passwords, and other personal information are all vulnerable.

Encryption and other security methods can make data a little more difficult to steal, but they don't provide complete protection against a really dedicated snoop. An entire catalog of tools for cracking Wi-Fi encryption is easy to find on the Internet. As any police officer will tell you, locks are great for keeping out honest people, but serious thieves know how to get past them.

There are two different kinds of security threats to a wireless network. The first is the danger of an outsider connecting to your network without your knowledge or permission; the second is the possibility that a dedicated eavesdropper can steal or modify data as you send and receive it. Each represents a different potential problem, and each requires a different approach to prevention and protection. Although none of the encryption tools currently available can provide complete protection, they can make life more difficult for most casual intruders. And as long as the tools are out there, you might as well use them.

A few techniques can discourage intruders and crackers. First, you can accept the fact that wireless networks are not completely secure and use the built-in network security features to slow down would-be intruders; second, you can supplement your wireless router's built-in tools with a hardware or software *firewall* (or both) to isolate the wireless network (but remember that a cracker who can grab and decode encrypted network passwords can often grab firewall passwords too); and third, you can use additional encryption such as a *VPN (virtual private network)* to make the network more secure.

The security features of the early Wi-Fi protocols (WEP encryption) were not adequate to protect data. The WEP protocol was flawed in several ways. WEP should be treated more as a "Do Not Disturb" sign than as a real means of protection. The WPA (Wi-Fi Protected Access) and WPA2 standards attempt to fix the shortcomings of WEP, but they work only when all of the users of your network have modern cards and drivers.

Here are some specific security methods:

- Don't use your access point's default SSID. Those defaults are well known to network crackers.

- Change the SSID to something that doesn't identify your business or your location. An intruder who detects something called BigCorpNet and looks around to see BigCorp headquarters across the street will target that network. The same thing goes for a home network: Don't use your family name or the street address or anything else that makes it easy to figure out where the signal is coming from.

- Don't use an SSID that makes your network sound as though it contains some kind of fascinating or valuable content—use a boring name like, say, *network5*, or even a string of gibberish, such as *W24rnQ*. If a would-be cracker sees a list of nearby networks, yours should appear to be the least interesting of the lot.

- Change your access point's password. The factory default passwords for most access point configuration tools are easy to find (and they're often the same from one manufacturer to another—hint: don't use *admin*), so they're not even good enough to keep out your own users, let alone unknown intruders who want to use your network for their own benefit.

An unauthorized person (who could be one of your own children) who gets into the access point's software could lock you out of your own network by changing the password and the encryption key.

- If possible, place your indoor access point in the middle of the building rather than close to a window. This will reduce the distance that your network signals will extend beyond your own walls.

- Use WPA encryption rather than WEP. WPA encryption is a *lot* more difficult to break, especially if it uses a complex encryption key.

- Change your encryption keys often. It takes time to sniff encryption keys out of a data stream; every time the keys change, the miscreants trying to steal your data are forced to start again from scratch. Once or twice every month is not too often to change keys in a home network. An office LAN should change keys at least once a week.

- Don't store your encryption keys in plain text on the network where they are used. This seems self-evident, but in a widespread network, it might be tempting to distribute the keys on a private web page or in a text file. Don't do it.

- Don't use email to distribute encryption keys. Even if you're not sending emails in plain text, an intruder who has stolen account names and passwords will receive the messages with your new codes before your legitimate users get them.

- If it's practical to do so on your network, turn on the access control feature in your access point. Access control restricts network connections to network clients with specified MAC addresses. The access point will refuse to associate with any network device whose address is not on the list. This might not be practical if you want to allow visitors to use your network, but it's a useful tool in a home or small business network where you know all of your potential users. MAC address filtering will not prevent a determined attacker from copying and spoofing the address of an authenticated user, but it could provide an additional layer of protection.

- Turn on the security features, but treat the network as if it's completely open to public access. Make sure everybody using the network understands that they're using a nonsecure system.

- Limit file shares to the files that you really want to share; don't share entire drives. Use password protection on every share.

- Use the same firewall and other security tools that you would use on a wired network. At best, the wireless portion of your LAN is no more secure than the wired part, so you should take all the same precautions.

- Consider using a virtual private network (VPN) for added security.

- Use a firewall program on every computer connected to the network, including both wired and wireless nodes.

It's important to take wireless network security seriously, but don't let the security issues discourage you from using Wi-Fi in your home or office unless you're moving very sensitive information through your network. If you protect your network with encryption and other security tools, you will probably keep all but the most determined hackers and crackers on the outside.

On the other hand, if your small business handles customer billing information, credit card data, sensitive client or patient records, personnel data (such as Social Security numbers), or any similar information that should remain confidential, adding Wi-Fi to your LAN creates an extremely attractive target. If you must add Wi-Fi access to your small business network, use the strongest firewall you can find between the Wi-Fi access point and the other computers on the network.

9

FILE SERVERS

File servers are computers on a network that hold text, data, and other files that all the other computers on the same network can use. A file server can also be used as a workstation, a computer dedicated to file storage, or a single-purpose *network-attached storage (NAS)* device. This chapter describes the advantages of connecting one or more file servers to your network and explains how to set them up and use them.

File servers are much more common in business networks than at home, but they can also be useful as part of a home network. Whether at work or at home, a server can provide these services:

- It can protect files on other computers connected to the network by automatically making and storing backup copies of those files.
- It can store related files in a central location.

- It can help control revisions and updates to documents and other files by assuring that everybody is using the same version.

- It can hold "public" files used by more than one person separate from each user's personal files.

- It can allow coworkers or family members to create and store new files or use existing ones without needing to turn on somebody else's computer.

- It can host web pages and other services for an *intranet,* an Internet-like site that can only be viewed within the local network.

- It can manage email distribution across the network.

- It can provide remote access to files through the Internet.

A server on a home network can also be a central storage location for photographs, music, and video files and allow users to view or play them through any computer in the house, or through a television, stereo, or home entertainment system. Chapter 15 explains how to use a network as part of a home entertainment system.

Choosing a Computer to Use as a File Server

You can use just about any computer as a file server. If you have a spare computer or an older unit that no longer has enough computing power for day-to-day use, that might be a good candidate, especially if you just want to share files and add network storage capacity. You will probably get better performance from an older computer if you add some extra memory and one or more new hard drives—Linux server software only needs about 10GB of hard drive space, but an older hard drive could be more likely to fail due to age and wear. And, of course, you will also need disk space for all the files that you store on the server.

If you want to use the server for more than just storage and file sharing, you can buy or build a new purpose-built server with space for several storage drives and special server software that includes additional features and functions such as web hosting and automatic backups. All of the major office computer manufacturers, including IBM, Dell, Compaq, and Apple, sell server computers with software already installed.

Windows, Mac, Linux, or . . . ?

Every computer needs an operating system, and servers are no exception. If you're resuscitating an old computer to use as a file server, you might be able to salvage the original operating system that ran on that computer, but connecting anything earlier than Windows 2000 or Mac OS X to your network could cause more trouble than it's worth.

If you have some experience with Unix or Linux or if you're willing to learn, one of these operating systems might be a better choice because they have up-to-date features and functions, and they won't demand as much processing power or memory as a newer version of Windows (a good introductory book will help get you started).

If cost is an issue (is cost ever *not* an issue?), many Linux and Unix distributions are available online as free (if time-consuming) downloads or on low-cost CDs and DVDs from distributors such as LinuxCD (*http://www .linuxcd.org/*) and The Linux Store (*http://www.thelinuxstore.ca/*). Several versions, including CentOS and FreeBSD, include server applications along with the core operating system and desktop programs. FreeNAS (available from *http://www.freenas.org/*) is also worth considering if you want a simple file server. On the other hand, if you haven't used Linux or Unix before, you might not want to deal with the distractions involved in installing and learning a new operating system at the same time that you're trying to set up a new network.

Microsoft's Windows Server family and similar products from Apple and Novell include all the features of a simple file server along with many additional business functions such as web and email hosting, calendar coordination, remote access, automated backup, and data management, all with a more-or-less consistent appearance. These server packages are relatively expensive, but their easy installation and available support might be worth the added cost, especially in a large enterprise where additional support staff is an issue. The developers of these commercial server products argue that the *total cost of ownership (TCO)* for their products, including original purchase price and the cost of ongoing maintenance and support, is about the same as the TCO of "free" Linux and Unix servers. Microsoft claims that management and maintenance staffing plus downtime account for roughly 75 percent of a server's TCO, but the experience of many open source software users is quite different. In a very small business, the numbers will probably work out in favor of free or inexpensive server software unless you have to pay for outside support.

If you're already committed to other Microsoft products, including Access, Microsoft SQL, or Windows Media, Windows Server is likely to be the best choice. On the other hand, many Linux and Unix versions include comparable programs (such as the Apache web server) that perform at least as well as or better than the Microsoft products. If you're a Mac household or business, Apple Server is the logical choice.

Unless your family operates like a business, your home network probably needs a different set of features from the ones used by a business: central storage, backup, and maybe web and email hosting. But you probably won't use other common business-server features, such as database services and project management. Microsoft's Windows Home Server is optimized for home rather than business use, so this product might be a better choice for your household network. Windows Home Server is available already installed on server computers from HP and other manufacturers, and Microsoft also offers an "OEM version" that you could install on an existing computer (if that computer exceeds the minimum requirements, which are considerably more than those needed for a Linux server). However, that version doesn't include any kind of Microsoft support, so you're on your own when you have trouble installing or using it. The OEM version can be difficult to find through local retailers, but plenty of web and mail-order suppliers will be happy to sell you a copy.

For mixed networks that include computers using more than one operating system, Samba (*http://www.samba.org/*) is an excellent choice. It's a well-established open source (and therefore free) cross-platform file-sharing program.

Figure 9-1 shows the control console screen for Windows Home Server. The minimum requirements for Windows Home Server are listed in the *WHS Getting Started Guide*, which is available at *http://www.microsoft.com/windows/products/winfamily/windowshomeserver/support.mspx*.

Figure 9-1: The Windows Home Server Console offers many control options on a single screen.

In order to use shared files stored on a Windows Home Server from other computers in your network, you must install the Connector program supplied with WHS onto each client machine. Without this software, the clients won't find the shared files. Connector is only available for Windows XP and Vista, so Home Server is less useful with Macintosh and Linux/Unix clients.

Using a Server for File Storage

The easiest way to set up a file server is simply to connect a computer to the network and designate it as a server. Create one or more folders for shared files, and set the Permissions or Network Sharing characteristics to share files in the directories or folders with network users. If you're storing photos, music, or video files on the server, create one or more separate folders for those files, and set the permissions to *read-only*, allowing network users to open the files but not to change them. Figure 9-2 shows the Sharing tab that controls these settings in Windows XP. For more information about sharing files, see Chapter 12.

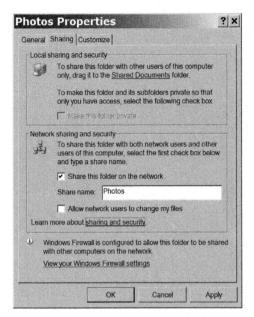

Figure 9-2: Set sharing permissions for the folder
that holds the files you want to store on your server.

When you work on a document or any other type of data file and when you download a file from the Internet, use the Save As command to store the file through the network in one of the shared folders on the server. To read, view, or listen to a file stored on the server, either open the folder that contains the file you want and select the file, or use the Open command in a program associated with that file type (such as a word processor, spreadsheet, or media player) and use the selection window or chooser to find the file. The program should treat the file exactly the same as a file stored on your own computer.

Using Network-Attached Storage

A *network-attached storage (NAS)* device is a dedicated computer—without a keyboard or display screen—used as a network file server. In the small business or home networks that many readers of this book are likely to have, one or more NAS disk drives can be an entirely adequate alternative to a more expensive and complicated network server.

For all practical purposes, a NAS drive is just a disk drive that connects to the network through an Ethernet port. Several disk drive and network equipment manufacturers offer purpose-built NAS devices, including complete hard drive assemblies and network storage enclosures for IDE or SATA hard drives. Some NAS devices have both Ethernet and USB ports, so you can use them with either a direct connection to your network or an external drive connected to a computer with or without a network link. Figure 9-3 shows a network with a stand-alone disk drive operating as a NAS device.

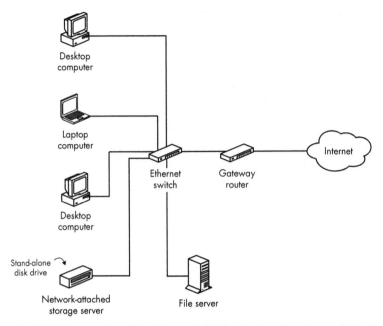

Figure 9-3: A network-attached storage device connects directly to a network.

A NAS server could also be a regular computer, with or without a keyboard and screen. If you already have a spare computer to use as a server, the FreeNAS version of FreeBSD, shown in Figure 9-4, could provide all the services you need for a file server operating system. FreeNAS is designed for remote configuration and operation, and it's relatively easy to set up and use.

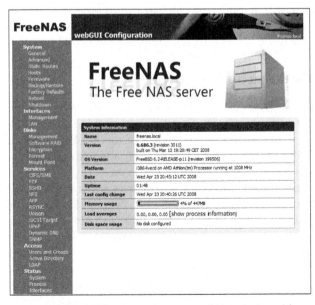

Figure 9-4: FreeNAS is a simple version of Unix designed for use as a file server.

USB Device Servers

To add one or more stand-alone USB disk drives to your network as file servers, consider using a USB device server, such as the Lantronix UBox 4100 shown in Figure 9-5. The server connects directly to the network through an Ethernet cable, and each disk drive or other USB device connected to the server appears as a local device on every computer connected to the network. Similar devices are also made by Silex Technology, including a wireless USB device server that connects to the network through a Wi-Fi access point.

Photo courtesy of Lantronix

Figure 9-5: The Lantronix UBox connects external disk drives and other USB devices directly to your network.

Apple's AirPort Extreme

Whether or not you're using Macintosh computers in your network, Apple's AirPort Extreme product can be an inexpensive alternative to a full-size file server. Along with its functions as a DSL or cable gateway router, an Ethernet switch, and a Wi-Fi base station, the AirPort Extreme also has a USB port that can connect an external hard drive directly to your network. To use more than one external hard drive, connect them to the AirPort Extreme through a USB hub. Figure 9-6 shows the rear panel of an AirPort Extreme.

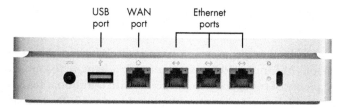

Photo courtesy of Apple

Figure 9-6: AirPort Extreme can connect a USB hard drive directly to your network.

Backing Up Files to a Server

There's more than one way to back up files to a server: You can run a backup program on the client machine and specify a drive and folder on the server as the backup storage location, or you can originate the backup from the server and select files on one or more clients (as explained earlier, *client* computers are the ones that receive services from a server).

Before you create your backups, you must decide exactly what you want to accomplish. Several different kinds of backups are possible, each of them appropriate for certain situations:

- A *complete image* of your hard drive includes copies of all folders, files, and programs. This backup allows you to restore your computer to its previous state after a disk failure. A complete image of a drive is sometimes described as a *clone.*

- An *incremental backup* only includes copies of the files that have been installed or have changed since the last backup. Incremental backups are faster than complete backups because they don't include the unchanged files that are already part of your backup.

- A *selective backup* only includes the important files and programs on your computer. This backup is generally faster and takes up less space on the backup drive than a complete backup because it does not include things like temporary files, old log files, and downloads that you will never use again.

- A *data-file-only backup* can be useful when you expect to restore the backup to another computer that already has the operating system and application programs installed. You can also re-install the operating system and programs from their CDs or other media. If you do choose this option, remember to check each program's website for the latest patches and upgrades before you try to use that program.

- A *limited backup* includes only one or more specific types of files, such as music, photos, or documents. This kind of backup is usually a supplement to a more complete backup that includes all the essential programs and files on a drive.

The backup programs provided with Windows, Mac OS X, and most versions of Linux and Unix are entirely adequate for most people, but there are plenty of other backup programs with additional features and options (often related to automatic scheduled backups). Backup programs are often supplied with network-attached storage (NAS) devices and external USB hard drives. The important thing to remember about using any backup program is that you must store your backed-up files separately from the originals: You can store the backup on a second hard drive on the same computer (*not* a good idea, however, because it doesn't protect against fire or theft); on a set of CDs, DVDs, or data tapes; or on a computer or other storage device connected to the original computer through a network or the Internet. A network is a great way to move your backup data to another computer for storage, but you will still want some kind of backup on removable media stored off-site to protect your data from fire or theft.

NOTE *The backup methods described in this chapter will work equally well on a network without a designated file server; you can use any other computer or network storage device on the same network as the destination for your backup files.*

The Windows Backup Program

Microsoft has supplied a backup program with most versions of Windows, including XP and Vista. This example uses Windows XP, but the general principles are the same for any backup program.

To use the Windows Backup program, follow these steps:

1. From the Windows Start menu, select **All Programs** (or **Programs** if you're using the Classic Start Menu) ▶ **Accessories** ▶ **System Tools** ▶ **Backup**. The Backup or Restore Wizard window shown in Figure 9-7 will open.

Figure 9-7: Use the Windows Backup or Restore Wizard to create backup copies of your files.

2. Click **Next** to advance to the next screen. The wizard will ask if you want to make new backups or restore files that you saved earlier. Select the **Back up file and settings** option and click **Next**.

3. The wizard will ask what you want to back up. To save all the information on the computer, select the All information option; this option will allow you to create a new copy of the original hard disk, but this copy takes up a lot of storage space. To create a more selective backup, select the Let me choose option.

4. Click **Next** to advance to the next screen. The wizard will ask where you want to store the backup.

5. Click the **Browse** button to open the Save As dialog. Use either the Save In field or the finder window to navigate through the network to the folder on the file server where you want to store the backup file. Choose that folder and click the **Save** button and then the **Next** button in the wizard window.

6. The wizard will show you the details about the backup you are about to create. If everything is correct, click **Finish**. The backup program will start.

To restore data from your backup files, run the same Windows Backup program but select the **Restore files and settings** option in the Backup or Restore Wizard.

The reason you're making backups is to protect your data against loss or damage. The most common problems that will destroy your original files are caused by either human error—you really didn't mean to reformat that hard drive, did you?—or damage to a disk drive. When either of those events occur, restoring the files from a network server is easy enough, but if you lose your files because of a fire, a power surge, a lightning strike that damages the server along with the client computers, or some other major disaster, the backup files on the dead server won't do you much good. Therefore, creating at least one set of backup files on a set of DVDs, tapes, or removable hard drives and storing them in another location such as a friend's home or office or a safe deposit box at your bank is always good practice.

Installing Backup in XP Home Edition

In Windows XP Home Edition, the Backup utility doesn't automatically load when you install the operating system. Apparently, somebody at Microsoft thought that Home Edition users didn't need to back up their data. Go figure.

To install Windows Backup from the XP Home Edition CD, follow these steps:

1. Place the XP CD in your computer's drive.

2. When the Welcome message appears, select **Perform additional tasks**.

3. Select the **Browse this CD** option.

4. Open the *ValueAdd* folder and then the *Msft* folder and finally the *Ntbackup* folder.

5. Run the Ntbackup.msi program. This will start a wizard that installs the Backup program.

Installing Backup in Windows Vista

Most versions of Windows Vista (except Vista Starter and Home Basic) include an automatic utility that can store backup files on a network server, but it doesn't run until you turn it on.

To configure the Vista Backup utility, select **Start ▸ All Programs** (or **Programs** in the Classic start menu) ▸ **Accessories** ▸ **System Tools** ▸ **Backup Status and Configuration**. The Backup Status and Configuration tool shown in Figure 9-8 will appear.

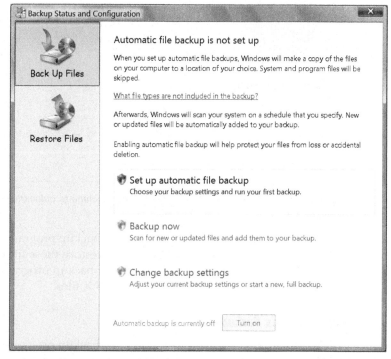

Figure 9-8: Use the Backup Status and Configuration tool to set up an automatic file backup.

The Backup Status and Configuration tool will step through a series of windows that request the specific information needed to run automatic backups.

Macintosh Backup Programs

The same general principles apply to creating and restoring backups on a Mac: Make backups on a regular schedule and store the backup files on a file server, removable media, or both. The Time Machine program included in OS X can automatically create backups to an external drive or a networked drive, as shown in Figure 9-9. Several alternative Mac backup programs can also send backup files to a network, including:

SuperDuper!   *http://www.shirt-pocket.com/SuperDuper/ SuperDuperDescription.html*

Synk Backup   *http://www.decimus.net/comparison.php*

iBackup   *http://www.grapefruit.ch/iBackup/*

.Mac Backup   *http://www.mac.com/1/solutions/backup.html*

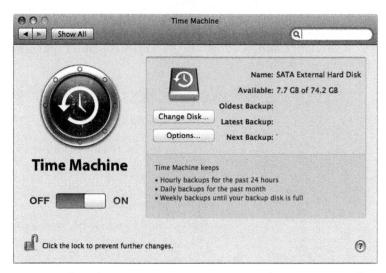

Figure 9-9: If you have a new Mac, turn on Time Machine to automatically create backups.

Before you trust your critical files to any backup program, run some tests to confirm that the program can accurately restore those files, including the metadata embedded inside them. Some Mac backup programs designed for earlier versions have trouble dealing with OS X files.

Linux and Unix Backups

Linux and Unix users have a wide choice of backup programs, including several that can originate the backup process from either the server (pulling backup data from client computers) or from individual client computers (pushing the backup files to a server). The Linux Online! website includes an up-to-date list of backup programs at *http://www.linux.org/apps/all/ Administration/Backup.html*. Distributions with graphic environments such as Gnome and KDE usually include at least one graphic backup program. One possible backup solution on computers running Linux, Unix, or Mac OS X is to use rsync over SSH to an external system, and schedule it via cron. This doesn't have a nice graphical front end, but it gets the job done securely and efficiently, because rsync does not copy bytes across the network that already exist on the other side—it only copies the "changed" bytes.

Server-side programs run on the server and collect backups from each client computer. BackupPC is a good choice as a server-side Linux backup program because it can back up Windows, Linux, and Mac computers through a network. BackupPC is available for download from *http:// backuppc.sourceforge.net*.

Amanda, the Advanced Maryland Automatic Network Disk Archiver (*http://www.amanda.org/*), is another server-side backup program that supports Windows and multiple versions of Linux and Unix.

Using a Server at Home

A server on a home network can do all the same things that a server on a business network can do, but many of those business functions are probably not particularly important at home. A typical home network server is mainly useful for storing and sharing files (such as music and videos), making automatic backups, and maybe hosting web pages and email.

However, a local server is not always the best way to manage email or host web pages. Using the hosting services that are included with your Internet connection is often easier; a good hosting service will handle all of the security issues and other maintenance for you. Many Internet service providers will give you a separate email address for each family member and provide space on an existing web server for your family's web pages. Or if you prefer, you can obtain individual addresses from one or more of the free or low-cost email services such as Hotmail, Gmail, or any of the others described at *http:// www.emailaddresses.com/*. Adding one or more file servers to a network to share resources goes a long way toward increasing the value of your computers. You can certainly operate your small network without any servers, but like the network itself, a central storage location for documents, images, and other files is often a lot more convenient than storing everything on individual users' machines, especially if you can use an old computer as a server that would otherwise continue to collect dust in a storage closet.

10

CONNECTING YOUR NETWORK TO THE INTERNET

All of the other benefits of a home network—file sharing, internal web hosting, and so forth—are handy, but the main reason that most people want to connect all of their household computers together is to share a high-speed Internet connection. In a business, those other services are more important than they are at home, but Internet access for everybody is still important. This chapter explains how to connect a network to the Internet and how to set up each computer to connect to the Internet through the network.

The Internet is often described as a "network of networks." In other words, the Internet provides a way to exchange data between your own LAN and millions of other networks. Before you can exchange data between your local network and the Internet, however, you (or your network manager) must configure your network gateway, and before you can connect a computer to the Internet through that gateway, you must configure that computer's Internet settings.

The Internet: From the Cloud to You

Network diagrams traditionally show the Internet as a big cloud. Inside that cloud are millions of computers, routers, and other equipment located all over the world, but the internal operation of that equipment is Somebody Else's Problem; when you're hooking up your own network, the Internet is simply a huge, shapeless *thing* that performs in a predictable manner.

Figure 10-1 shows the connection from the Internet through your local network to individual computers. Those computers can be any kind of network-attached device, such as a printer, a network-attached storage (NAS) device disk drive, or a pocket-size smartphone, but for the sake of this discussion, let's think of all those things as types of computers. In order to send and receive data between your computer and the Internet, you must supply certain information to the Internet, and the Internet provides other information to you.

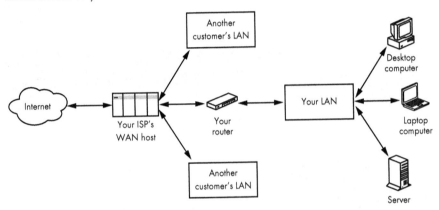

Figure 10-1: The Internet communicates with your computer through a local network.

The Modem

Your LAN probably connects to the Internet through a high-speed telephone line or a cable TV system. The device that converts digital data to and from the LAN to signals that can move through the phone line or cable is a *modem (modulator/demodulator)*. In most cases, the modem is combined with a gateway router, but some cable TV companies and telephone companies provide stand-alone modems that can connect either directly to a single computer or through a router or switch to a LAN.

For the purposes of this chapter, you can think of a modem as a type of router. The differences between a modem and a router are that a modem includes the internal hardware that performs *modulation* and *demodulation* activities along with the software that provides the connection settings. The configuration settings that control the connections between the Internet and your local network are generally the same in both modems and routers.

NOTE   *A dial-up modem that uses the voice telephone network to connect your computer to the Internet operates in a similar manner to a high-speed modem, but it uses a much slower connection.*

The Gateway Router

As Chapter 3 explained, the router that connects the Internet to your local network has a point of presence in two different networks: your Internet service provider's wide area network (WAN) and your own local area network (LAN). The WAN is part of the much larger Internet cloud.

Therefore, the router has two different addresses: one address on the WAN and a different address on the LAN. The router's job is to exchange data in both directions between these two networks. In certain respects, the Internet treats the router the same way that the router treats the other computers on the network, but the Internet uses different addresses to accomplish those goals. One of the important activities that occurs inside the router is network address translation.

Your router's Setup utility shows two groups of settings: one for the WAN and one for the LAN. The WAN side identifies the router to the Internet with a unique numeric address. That address can be either *fixed* or *static*, which means that it is always exactly the same, or *dynamic*, which means that a server at the WAN assigns the next available address from a pool every time the router connects to the WAN. Dynamic address assignment uses a process called Dynamic Host Configuration Protocol (DHCP), which is described in "DHCP Servers On or Off" on page 110.

The gateway router typically specifies the numeric address of one or more *Domain Name System (DNS)* servers that convert Internet addresses that use words (such as *nostarch.com*) into numeric addresses. Without a DNS server to consult, the WAN won't know where to direct email messages, requests for web pages, or any other attempts to communicate with a destination on the Internet. Your Internet service provider will provide the addresses of one or more DNS servers.

The router also needs a *gateway address* and a *subnet mask*. The *gateway* is the next router in line between the WAN and the rest of the Internet; the subnet mask tells the WAN which numbers in the router's IP address identify the router and which generic numbers identify the WAN. For example, the most common subnet mask is 255.255.255.0, which means that the last of the four numbers is different for each node. In other words, if your WAN controls all the addresses in the 123.223.123.*XXX* group, your address might be 123.223.123.103, and another customer's address on the same WAN might be 123.223.123.117.

The specific numbers your router uses are absolutely essential; if you don't have them exactly correct, the router won't connect to the Internet. But understanding what they mean is less important than getting them right. Your Internet service provider will supply the numbers to use when you set up a new account. Write the numbers in the same place where you keep account numbers and other important computer-related information.

NOTE *When a separate DSL or cable modem is between the gateway router and the Internet, the modem often provides the static IP address and other information to the Internet and the local network. In this situation, the gateway router relays the necessary addresses between the modem and the rest of the local network.*

The LAN settings for your router or modem control the way your local network operates. The specific settings in each computer connected to the network must be within the ranges defined by the router or modem. The next section explains how each of these LAN-side settings works.

Individual Computers

Each computer connected to a LAN must have the same configuration settings in relation to the router that the router has with the WAN: a numeric IP address, a network mask, and addresses for a gateway to the Internet and one or more DNS servers. As the person responsible for your network, you must set up a DHCP server and either provide these values to each of your users and make sure they enter them correctly or type them into each computer and network device yourself.

The differences between setting up a router to talk to the Internet and setting up a computer to talk to the local area network are (1) the router has two groups of settings (the WAN and the LAN), but the computer has only one; and (2) the router obtains its WAN settings from your Internet service provider, but the local computer gets many of the same settings from the router. Therefore, you should almost always set up the gateway router in your network first—before you add computers to the network.

NOTE *When you connect a single computer directly to the Internet through a high-speed (DSL or cable) modem, you must use the settings supplied by your ISP or the modem.*

The essential settings for connecting a computer to the Internet through a LAN are similar to the ones that you use to set up the modem and the router. The next sections explain how to deal with each of them.

DHCP Servers On or Off

A DHCP server automatically assigns IP addresses and other configuration information to all of the devices in a network. In a LAN, the DHCP server is most often part of the router or modem that connects that network to the Internet or built into a network hub. In most small networks, using a DHCP server is more convenient than assigning a static IP address to each network device one at a time.

The DHCP setting is a common cause of connection problems. If a computer is configured to obtain its IP address and other settings from a DHCP server, the DHCP server on the router or modem must be active. Other (less common) DHCP problems can occur when more than one server is active at the same time. In some cases, the other network devices will obtain DHCP settings from the "wrong" server, or the settings will not allow you to connect to the Internet. If you can't successfully connect a computer to the Internet through your LAN when testing your network, you should always check the DHCP server settings.

There are several important things to know about using DHCP in a LAN:

- A network can have just one active DHCP server.

- When a network is using a DHCP server, each computer and other device (such as a printer or game console) connected to the network must be configured to accept an address from the DHCP server. In Windows, the Obtain an IP address automatically option, shown in Figure 10-2, must be active.

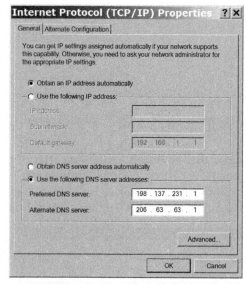

Figure 10-2: When the Obtain an IP address automatically option is active, Windows uses the network's DHCP server to set its IP address.

In Macintosh OS X, the Configure IPv4 option, shown in Figure 10-3, must be set to Using DHCP.

- The IP address number assigned by the DHCP server must be within one of the reserved ranges. In almost all cases, you don't have to change the server's default values.

Most hubs, routers, modems, and Wi-Fi access points use one or more web-based pages (such as the one shown in Figure 10-4) to display and change the DHCP server's settings. However, the pages supplied with just about every make and model of network control device are organized slightly differently. So you must consult the manual supplied with your device or the manufacturer's website for specific instructions.

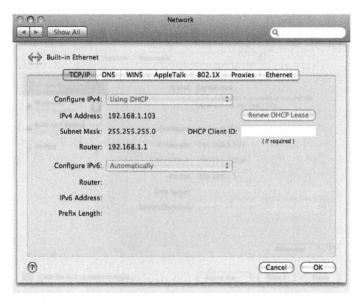

Figure 10-3: In OS X, choose the Using DHCP option to obtain an IP address from a server.

In this example, the important settings are DHCP Server and Starting IP Address. When the DHCP server is enabled, the server provides IP addresses for the entire network. When the server is disabled, each computer and network node uses a static address that you must set on that computer or node.

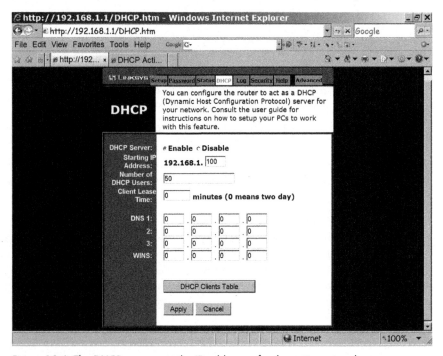

Figure 10-4: The DHCP server sets the IP addresses for the entire network.

The Starting IP Address setting specifies the lowest IP address number that the server will assign to a client device. The Number of DHCP Users setting defines the highest number in the address range (in this case, 192.168.1.149). In some systems, the server asks for a range of numbers instead of the starting number and the number of users. In either case, allow for more DHCP users than the number of machines currently connected to the network, so the server can continue to support your network after you add more devices.

Subnet Masks

The subnet mask setting specifies which part of the IP address changes for each device connected to the network. Unless you have a reason to use a different mask, set the subnet mask to 255.255.255.0. If the network uses DHCP to assign IP addresses, you don't have to enter a subnet mask on each client device.

For most of us, the subnet mask is another of those settings that we have to enter correctly to make the network work properly, but we really don't need to know what it means. In a large or complex network, however, you can use subnet masking to separate the network into smaller subsidiary networks, or *subnets*. Computers and other network nodes within the same subnet can exchange data more quickly because they don't have to go all the way out to the larger WAN or the Internet and back again to locate one another.

As you know, numeric IP addresses are divided into four groups of numbers, each of them within the range from 0 to 255. One part of the address identifies the network, and the other identifies a specific computer. For example, your ISP might use a WAN with the network address 203.23.145.*XXX*; the individual computers and LANs connected to that WAN would have addresses from 203.23.145.000 to 203.23.145.255. In this case, the subnet mask would be 255.255.255.0 because the local address is limited to the last part of the address (the zero). A maximum of 256 devices (numbered 0 through 255) can be connected to this subnet.

Within your own LAN, you can use subnet masking to divide the network into two or more subnets. Dividing the network into subnets is useful when you want to separate your wired connections from the Wi-Fi access point or when you want to use an internal firewall to isolate computers that contain sensitive personnel or financial data from the rest of the network. To divide your LAN into two equal-size subnets, assign the subnet mask *XXX.XXX.XXX*.0 to one subnet and use local addresses from 1 to 126 (use 0 for the router). For the other subnet, use the subnet mask *XXX.XXX.XXX*.128 and assign addresses between 129 and 255. You will need a separate router for each subnet.

NOTE   *Using subnets to split a LAN into separate groups counts as an advanced networking practice; you're not likely to see this setup in a simple home or very small business network.*

IP Addresses

As Chapter 4 explained, several groups of numeric IP addresses have been reserved for computers and other devices connected to LANs. Because these addresses are only visible within each LAN, it's practical to use the same addresses in different networks. Every computer and every other device connected to your network must have a different address within one of these reserved number ranges.

Each network device, including the LAN side of the router itself, must have a different IP address from one of the reserved groups. A DHCP server (usually part of the router or modem) will take care of this automatically and assign new addresses whenever users connect another computer to the network. This can be especially convenient if users connect and disconnect laptops and other portable devices to and from the network.

If you're *not* using a DHCP server, you'll have to set the address for each device, one machine at a time. The LAN side of your router or modem usually has a default address that you use to reach its configuration utility (look in the device's manual to find the address). You do *not* have to change the default address on a router or other control device unless another device (such as a Wi-Fi access point) has the same default address. To make sure that you haven't assigned the same address to more than one device, keep a master list of IP addresses that includes every device connected to the network, including laptops and other portable devices that use part-time connections. You can keep the list in a text file stored on your own computer, but you should also print a copy of the current list (including the date) and keep it separately from the computer. When it's time to add one or more additional devices, consult the list to find and add a new address that isn't already assigned.

DNS Servers

Your LAN needs one or more DNS servers to convert Internet addresses to numeric IP addresses, but the DNS servers don't have to be part of the LAN; you can use a DNS server anywhere on the Internet. Use the same DNS server addresses for each computer that you used for the WAN side of the router.

NOTE   *If you can't get a DNS server address from your ISP, run a web search for* public DNS server *to find addresses for alternative servers. One widely-used public DNS is OpenDNS* (http://www.openDNS.com/).

Gateways

The *gateway* address is the address of the router or other control device that relays data between computers on a LAN and the Internet. This gateway is sometimes called the *default gateway*. The gateway address is the same as the numeric address used for the LAN side of the router. Consult the router manual to find the correct address for your network.

Computers connected to the network don't use the same gateway address as the router or modem. The router/modem is the gateway between your network and the ISP's WAN. Your ISP's gateway address identifies the path between their WAN and the rest of the Internet.

Configuring the Network Gateway

The best place to find specific instructions for configuring the WAN side of a modem, router, or other network control device is in the information provided by your ISP. Specifically, when you set up a new ISP account, you should obtain your connection's static IP address or DHCP setting, the DNS server addresses, the subnet mask, and the gateway address. The ISP will probably give you addresses and a password for your email account at the same time, but you don't need them to configure the network connection (although you will need them to send and receive messages).

If your ISP requires a login and password every time you connect, you will need a router or modem that uses the same set of connection rules (the *protocol*) that your ISP's equipment expects. If your ISP does not provide a modem, ask them for a list of compatible makes and models.

The LAN side of the router uses addresses and other settings that don't extend beyond your own network, so your network can use the same settings as your neighbor's network. Therefore, many manufacturers ship their routers with preset addresses that should work for most networks. The user's manual or setup guide supplied with the device usually contains step-by-step instructions for changing the settings. If you can't find a printed copy of the manual, look for one on the manufacturer's website.

NOTE   *Chapter 11 contains detailed instructions for connecting routers using Windows, Macintosh OS X, and Linux or Unix to a LAN. To connect a NAS device, printer, or other device to the network, follow the instructions supplied with each device.*

Summary

Your network connects to the Internet through a gateway router that appears as a node on both your own LAN and your ISP's WAN. In order to exchange data between a network computer and the Internet, you must configure the WAN side of the router with addresses and options supplied by your ISP.

The LAN side of the router controls the way your own network handles communication with the Internet. Therefore, the router's LAN-side settings must be compatible with the settings on each computer and other device connected to the LAN.

11

CONNECTING YOUR COMPUTER TO A NETWORK

Regardless of the operating system that a computer uses, it requires the same configuration settings to connect to a LAN and to the Internet. Each operating system organizes configuration information differently, but they all require the settings described in Chapter 10. This chapter describes the configuration settings for Windows, Macintosh OS X, and for Linux and Unix, and it offers step-by-step instructions for connecting computers running those operating systems to your network.

Before you try to configure the computers in your network, set up the LAN and WAN settings on the network's modem and router; the configuration of your network's computers must be compatible with those settings.

If your network includes an active DHCP server, your computer should automatically obtain the settings needed to connect to the LAN and to the Internet. When no DHCP server is present or if the DHCP client isn't working perfectly, you should assign an address manually and enter other settings for each computer individually.

NOTE *You can use a computer with a fixed IP address in a DHCP network, but using one is a bad idea because the fixed address can cause collisions with an automatic assignment. Some routers and other devices that contain DHCP servers may also allow you to assign a specific IP address to a network node with a particular MAC address.*

The user's manual for your modem or router and the information supplied by your Internet service provider are the definitive sources for network configuration information. Make a note of the following settings on your modem or router since you will need them to configure the individual computers:

- DHCP status: on or off
- IP address
- Subnet mask
- Default gateway
- DNS servers

Connecting Your Windows Computer to a Network

In Windows XP and Windows Vista, the Network Setup Wizard creates a profile that connects your computer to a LAN. To make changes to an existing profile, use the Properties settings for that profile.

Creating a New Network Profile

Follow these steps to run the Network Setup Wizard:

1. From the Start Menu, select **Connect To ▶ Show all connections**, as shown in Figure 11-1. If you're using the Classic Start Menu, select **Settings ▶ Network Connections**.

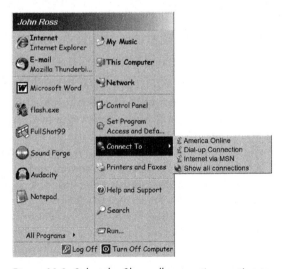

Figure 11-1: Select the Show all connections option to open the Network Connections window.

2. From the Network Connections window, select **Network Setup Wizard**. The wizard's Welcome screen will appear.

3. From the Welcome screen, click **Next**. The Wizard will remind you to install and turn on all the computers and other components in your network.

4. Click **Next** again. The wizard will look for a network connection and ask what kind of connection you're making, as shown in Figure 11-2.

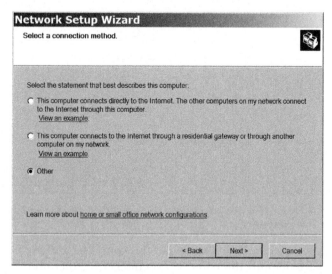

Figure 11-2: Select the Other option to add this computer to your LAN.

5. Select **Other** and click **Next**. The Wizard will ask for more details, as shown in Figure 11-3.

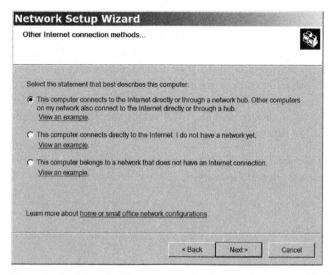

Figure 11-3: Select the This computer connects to the Internet directly or through a network hub option to connect to your LAN.

6. Select the **This computer connects to the Internet directly or through a network hub** option and click **Next**. The Wizard will ask for a brief description and a name for this computer, as shown in Figure 11-4.

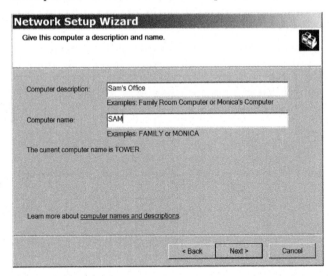

Figure 11-4: Assign a unique name and description to each computer on your LAN.

7. Type a brief description of this computer and the name you want to use to identify this computer on the LAN. Other users will use this name to connect to this computer through the LAN. Click **Next**.

8. The Wizard will ask for a workgroup name. Type the workgroup name and click **Next**. You must use the same workgroup name for every computer on the LAN.

9. The Wizard will ask about file and printer sharing, as shown in Figure 11-5. If you want to allow other network users to use the printer (or printers) connected to this computer or if you want to share files stored on this computer with other network users, select the Turn on file and printer sharing radio button; if you do not have a printer connected to this computer (or you don't want other users to use the printer) and you don't want to share files, select the Turn off file and printer sharing radio button.

NOTE   *If you don't turn on file sharing, you won't be able to view or change files on this computer through the network.*

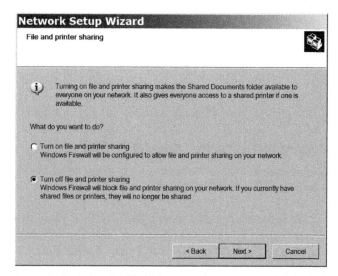

Figure 11-5: Select the file and printer sharing option that applies to your network.

10. The wizard will configure your computer for the settings you have selected. When configuration is complete, the Wizard will display the window shown in Figure 11-6, which offers to create a Network Setup Disk or finish the wizard. Select the option that describes what you want to do. If you select Create a Network Setup Disk, you can use a floppy disk, a USB flash drive, or other removable disk as your setup disk.

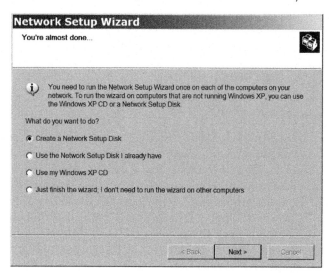

Figure 11-6: The Network Setup Wizard will offer to create a Network Setup Disk.

11. The wizard will follow your instructions and display the Completing the Network Setup Wizard window. Click **Finish**.

Repeat the process for each Windows computer connected to your network. If you created a Network Setup Disk (or flash drive) at the end of the Network Setup Wizard for the first computer, you can use the program on that disk instead of running the Wizard each time.

Changing Your Computer's Network Settings

To change one or more of your computer's network configuration settings manually, follow these steps:

1. From the Start Menu, select **Connect To ▸ Show all connections**, or from the Classic Start Menu, select **Settings ▸ Network Connections**. The Network Connections window, shown in Figure 11-7, will open.

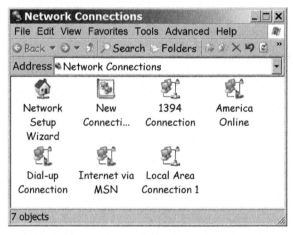

Figure 11-7: The Network Connections window shows all of your computer's network profiles.

2. Your wired connection profile is the one called *Local Area Connection* and sometimes includes a number. The number is usually 1, as shown in Figure 11-7, but if you have added or deleted additional profiles, some other number might be used. If you're using a Wi-Fi or other wireless network connection, the network profile will be called *Wireless Network Connection.* Open the Local Area Connection and click the **Properties** button, or open the Wireless Network Connection profile and click **Change Advanced Settings**. A status window similar to the one shown in Figure 11-8 will open.

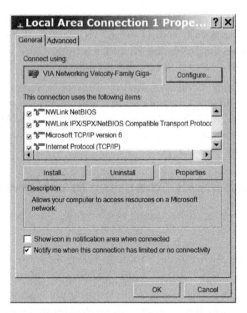

Figure 11-8: The Local Area Connection status window
shows information about your network connection.

3. Scroll down to the end of the list of items, select **Internet Protocol
(TCP/IP)**, and click the **Properties** button. The Properties window
shown in Figure 11-9 will open.

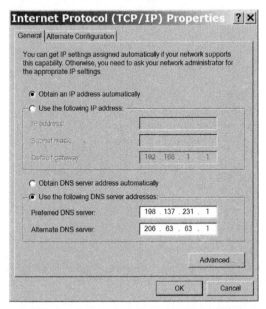

Figure 11-9: The Internet Protocol Properties window
controls your network and Internet settings.

4. To use this computer with a DHCP server, select the **Obtain an IP address automatically** radio button. To assign and use a static IP address, select the **Use the following IP address** option and type the numbers of the IP address, subnet mask, and default gateway.

5. To use the DNS server specified by the DHCP server, select the **Obtain DNS server address automatically** radio button. To specify one or more DNS servers on this computer, select the **Use the following DNS server addresses** radio button and type the addresses for the preferred and alternate DNS server.

Connecting Your Macintosh Computer to a Network

To connect a Macintosh computer running OS X to your network, follow these steps:

1. If it's not already in place, install an Ethernet cable between the computer and the network's hub, switch, or router.

2. From the Macintosh desktop, click the Apple icon at the extreme left side of the Menu Bar to open the Apple Menu. The System Preferences window shown in Figure 11-10 will appear.

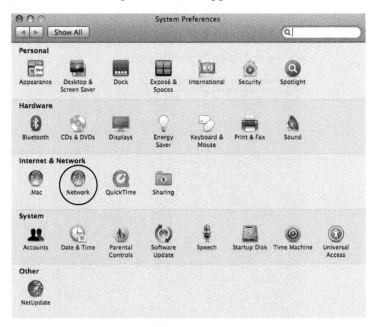

Figure 11-10: Use the System Preferences window to set up your network connection.

3. Click the **Network** icon in the Internet & Network group. The Network window shown in Figure 11-11 will appear, with detailed information about your network connection. If your network has a DHCP server providing IP addresses, the settings will automatically appear in the Network window.

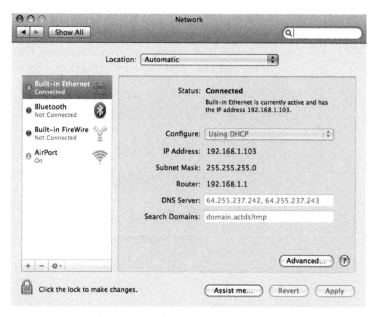

Figure 11-11: The Network window shows the current network connection settings.

4. If the settings that appear in the Network window are not the ones you want to use, click the padlock icon in the lower-left corner of the window to change them. The icon will change to an open padlock.

5. To change the network configuration settings, click the **Advanced** button near the bottom of the window. The Built-in Ethernet window shown in Figure 11-12 will appear.

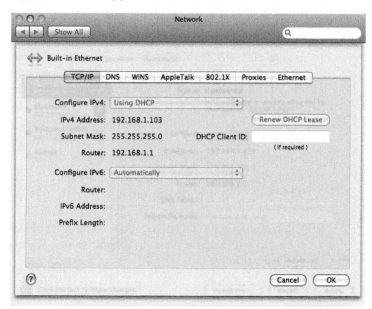

Figure 11-12: The Built-in Ethernet window controls the network configuration settings.

6. The bar along the top of the window contains seven network options. Click **TCP/IP** to enter or change your Internet connection settings.

7. The Configure IPv4 field is a drop-down menu. Click the arrows at the right of the field to open the menu shown in Figure 11-13.

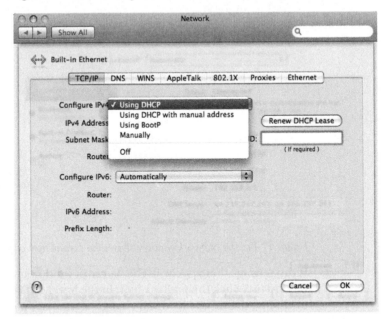

Figure 11-13: Use the Configure IPv4 drop-down menu to enable or disable DHCP on this computer.

8. Select the option you want to use to assign IP addresses on this computer. Select **Using DHCP** to obtain an address from the network's DHCP server, or select **Manually** to assign a fixed address.

9. If you select the Manually option, enter the numeric IP address, the subnet mask, and the gateway router address in the appropriate fields, and click **DNS** in the menu bar along the top of the window. The window shown in Figure 11-14 will appear.

10. Click the plus sign (+) at the bottom of the DNS Servers box, and type the IP addresses of one or more DNS servers. You should obtain these addresses from your Internet service provider.

11. Click **OK** to save your changes and close the Advanced Network window. The main Network window will appear with your current settings in place.

12. Click the open padlock icon at the lower-left corner of the window to lock the settings, and then click **Apply** to save your settings and close the Network window.

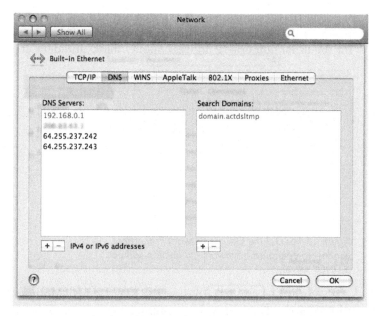

Figure 11-14: Enter the addresses of your ISP's DNS servers in the DNS window.

Connecting Your Linux or Unix Computer to a Network

Different Linux and Unix distributions use different network configuration programs, but they all require the same information that Windows and Macintosh computers use to connect to a LAN and through the LAN to the Internet. Like the network connections for Mac and Windows, most Linux and Unix systems will automatically set up a connection when a DHCP server is active.

Figure 11-15 shows the Gnome Network Administration Tool provided with Ubuntu. To change the settings, select the **Wired connection** box and click **Properties**.

Figure 11-15: Gnome uses a tabbed window to set network configuration options.

The DHCP control and the manual IP address and DNS settings are shown in the Properties window in Figure 11-16. This window includes fields for the usual numeric IP address, subnet mask, and default gateway address.

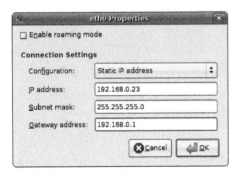

Figure 11-16: Use the Gnome network Properties window to configure a network connection without a DHCP server.

Figures 11-17 and 11-18 show the KDE Control Module utility included with PC-BSD. To change the configuration settings, select the adapter connected to the network and click the **Configure** button.

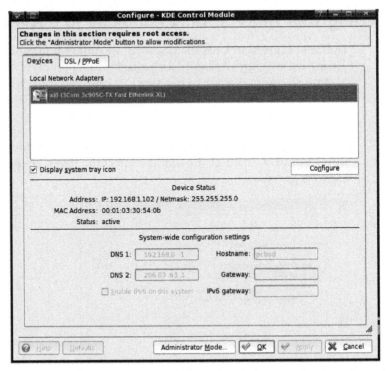

Figure 11-17: The KDE Control Module utility includes network settings for each network adapter.

Figure 11-18: The KDE configuration window for each network adapter includes settings for DHCP, IP address, and the subnet mask (Netmask).

Other desktop environments might use different configuration utility programs, but the settings are similar. You can generally find the controls and settings by searching around each version's desktop.

Remember that some network control settings programs don't make permanent changes (especially when you're loading the operating system from a CD or DVD or you're using versions of the ifconfig/route command to assign IP, netmask, or other addresses). To make a permanent change, you must load the operating system on the computer's hard drive and edit the system configuration. Checking the settings each time you start the computer is always good practice.

Summary

No matter what kind of computer you're using, the basic network configuration settings are the same: Either the computer obtains an IP address and related settings from the network's DHCP server, or it uses settings from the network configuration utility. The procedures in this chapter should give you enough information to set up a working network connection with any commonly used operating system.

12

SHARING FILES THROUGH YOUR NETWORK

File sharing requires a compromise between convenience and security. You want to make some of the files stored on your computer available to other people, but you probably have other files that contain information you would prefer to keep private. Therefore, Windows and other network operating systems allow you to assign different files or directories to different access levels. Some files are available to every network user, while others might be limited to specific users, and still others are only available to the file's owner.

One of the most common network systems for sharing files, printers, and other resources is the Server Message Block (SMB) protocol. This protocol is at the core of Microsoft Windows networking, and it also works with Macintosh OS X and Linux/Unix systems. Therefore, exchanging files among computers that run different operating systems is not a problem, even though the files themselves might not always be compatible (for example, you probably can't run a program written for Windows on a Linux system).

Many operating systems support more than one networking protocol, but when you run a mixed network, or if it's remotely possible that a visitor with a different kind of computer (such as a Mac or Linux laptop) might want to connect to your network, it's best to use the most common protocols.

Control of file sharing rests with the computer that holds each file, so other people can't open and read your files without your permission—even if they have a login account (or they're using a guest account) on the same computer. In order to share files with other users, you must turn on your operating system's file-sharing service and then assign an access level (universal, limited, or none) to each folder or directory. This chapter explains how to set up file sharing in Windows XP and Vista, Macintosh OS X, and in the Gnome and KDE environments used by many Linux and Unix distributions.

File Sharing in Windows XP

Windows XP uses a set of programs called *Simple File Sharing* to exchange files among computers on a network. In XP Home Edition, Simple File Sharing is always on; in XP Professional, file sharing is normally turned on, but you can turn it on or off.

To turn Simple File Sharing on or off in XP Professional, follow these steps:

1. From the Windows Desktop, open My Computer.
2. Select the **Tools** menu and choose **Folder Options**.
3. In the Folder Options window, click the **View** tab to open the window shown in Figure 12-1.

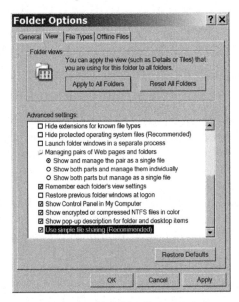

Figure 12-1: Use the Folder Options window to turn Simple File Sharing on or off.

4. In the Advanced Settings box, scroll down to the bottom.

5. To turn Simple File Sharing on or off, click the **Use simple file sharing (Recommended)** checkbox. The file-sharing function is active when you see a checkmark in the checkbox.

6. Click **OK** to save your setting and close the Folder Options window.

In spite of its name, Simple File Sharing offers five access levels, which you might consider more complicated than simple. However, each of the five levels is useful in certain situations.

Level 1	My Documents (private)	Files are only accessible to the file owner.
Level 2	My Documents (default)	Files are accessible to the file owner and administrators.
Level 3	Locally shared documents	Other users on this computer have read-only access; the file owner and administrators have full access.
Level 4	Read-only shared documents	Local and network users have read-only access; the file owner and administrators have full access.
Level 5	Read and write	All users have full read and write access.

WARNING   *If you want to restrict access to any of your files, be sure to protect your Windows user account with a password.*

Level 1

The owner of Level 1 files and folders is the only person who can read them. All the files in a Level 1 folder are also private.

Level 1 files and folders are only possible within your user profile (the My Documents, My Music, My Pictures, and other folders in *<drive letter>: \Documents and Settings\<username>*).

To assign a folder or disk drive to Level 1 access, follow these steps:

1. From the Windows desktop, open My Computer.

2. Select **Documents and Settings** and then select the *username* folder.

3. If the folder you want to assign to Level 1 is not visible in the My Computer window, open the drive or folder that contains that folder.

4. Right-click the drive or folder icon.

5. Select **Sharing and Security** from the pop-up menu. The Properties window shown in Figure 12-2 will appear.

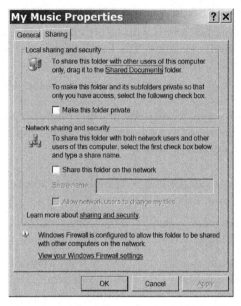

Figure 12-2: Check the Make this folder private checkbox to restrict access to this folder.

6. Check the **Make this folder private** checkbox to limit access to the files in this folder. Click again to remove the checkmark and allow other users to see this folder.

7. Click **OK** to save your choice and close the Properties window.

Level 2

Files stored in Level 2 drives and folders are accessible to the owner of those drives and folders and to anybody with an administrator-level account on the computer where the folders and files are stored. Other users on this computer and all users on other computers connected to this computer through the network can't open these files.

To assign a drive or folder to Level 2, follow these steps:

1. From My Computer, right-click the drive or folder icon you want to assign to Level 2. A pop-up menu will appear next to the icon.

2. Select **Sharing and Security**. A Properties window will appear with the Sharing tab visible.

3. Disable the **Make this folder private** option and the **Share this folder on the network** option. If a checkmark appears in either box, click the box to remove it.

4. Click **OK** to save your choice and close the Properties window.

Level 3

The owner of Level 3 folders and files and any user with an administrator-level account on the same computer can read, change, or delete Level 3 folders and files; all others using the same computer can read or open these files, but they can't change or delete them. In Windows XP, Power Users can also change and delete Level 3 files. These files are not accessible through the network.

All Level 3 files and folders are located in the *<drive letter>:\Documents and Settings\All Users\Shared Documents* folder. To assign a file or folder to Level 3, simply copy or drag it to the Shared Documents folder.

If you expect to create many Level 3 files and folders, consider creating a shortcut to Shared Documents on the Windows Desktop. Dragging an icon to a shortcut has the same effect as dragging a file or folder directly to the original folder.

Level 4

Level 4 drives, files, and folders are accessible through the network as read-only documents. Anybody with a network connection can open and read a Level 4 file, but only the file owner and the administrator of the local computer can change or delete the file.

To assign a drive, folder, or file to Level 4, follow these steps:

1. From My Computer, right-click the icon of the drive or folder you want to assign to Level 4. A pop-up menu will appear.

2. Select **Sharing and Security** from the pop-up menu. A Properties window like the one in Figure 12-3 will appear with the Sharing tab visible.

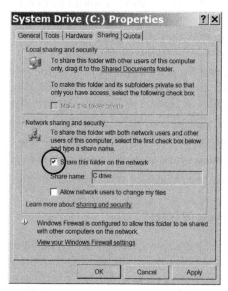

Figure 12-3: Select Share this folder on the network to assign a drive or folder to Level 4.

3. In the Network Sharing and Security section of the Properties window, check the **Share this folder on the network** option.

4. Make sure a checkmark does not appear in the **Allow network users to change my files** checkbox. Click the box to remove an existing checkmark.

5. Click **OK** to save your changes and close the Properties window.

Level 5

Level 5 drives, files, and folders have no protection against changes or deletions by any network user. Anybody with access to a Level 5 file, whether on the same computer or through the network, can add, change, or delete that file. In a Level 5 folder, any user can also create a new file or folder or delete an existing one.

Obviously, Level 5 is the lowest level of security (essentially no security at all), so you should only use Level 5 for files that you want to allow everybody on the network to change or delete. As added protection, make sure your network is protected with a firewall; if the network includes one or more Wi-Fi access points, be sure to use WPA encryption.

On the other hand, don't let these security concerns scare you away from using Level 5 access when it's appropriate. In a business where two or more people work together on the same project, you will want to allow those involved to create or make changes to the relevant documents. On a home network, you may want to provide universal access to music, photos, and video files, and documents such as school term papers that a parent might want to review before they're turned in. And if you share files between your home or office computer and a laptop, you will want to allow Level 5 access between the two.

To assign the contents of a drive or folder to Level 5, follow these steps:

1. From My Computer, right-click the icon of the drive or folder you want to assign to Level 5. A pop-up menu will appear.

2. Select **Sharing and Security** from the pop-up menu. A Properties window will appear with the Sharing tab visible. This window is the same one you used to assign files or folders to Level 4 (Figure 12-3).

3. In the Network Sharing and Security section of the Properties window, check the **Share this folder on the network** option.

4. Check the **Allow network users to change my files** checkbox.

5. Click **OK** to save your changes and close the Properties window.

File Sharing in Windows Vista

Microsoft introduced a completely new file-sharing method in Windows Vista. It's still necessary to turn on file sharing, but the whole process is no longer as complicated as the earlier "Simple File Sharing" method because many of the network file-sharing functions are consolidated into the Network and Sharing Center shown in Figure 12-4. To open the Network and Sharing Center, start at the Control Panel, and select **Network and Internet ▸ Network and Sharing Center**. If you're using the Classic View of the Control Panel, you can go directly to the Network and Sharing Center.

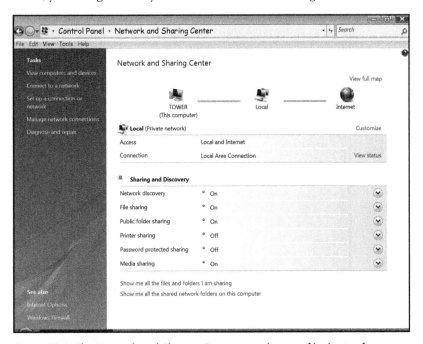

Figure 12-4: The Network and Sharing Center controls many file-sharing functions.

Network Discovery

One important new setting in Vista is called *network discovery*. When network discovery is turned on, your computer is visible to other computers on the same LAN, and your computer can detect other computers; when network discovery is off, the computer can't see other computers and other users can't see yours. In other words, network discovery is one more setting that must be turned on in order to view files among computers. You might also encounter a custom state if a firewall exception has been disabled or one of the services that controls network discovery is not active.

To turn network discovery on or off from the Network and Sharing Center, click the **On** or **Off** button, or click the arrow at the far right of the Network discovery option, then click the **Turn On** or **Turn Off** button, and click **Apply**.

File Sharing

Vista allows two kinds of file sharing through a network: sharing from the Public folder and sharing from any folder. You must turn on either method in the Network and Sharing Center before you can use it.

Public Folder Sharing

When you turn on Public folder sharing from the Network and Sharing Center, any folder or file within the Public folder is accessible to anyone on the network. You can set the Public folder to allow read-only access or you can allow any user to create new files and to read, change, and delete existing ones, as shown in Figure 12-5, but you can't set different access levels to the Public folder for specific users; the Public folder is an all-or-nothing (or, more accurately, an everybody-or-nobody) deal.

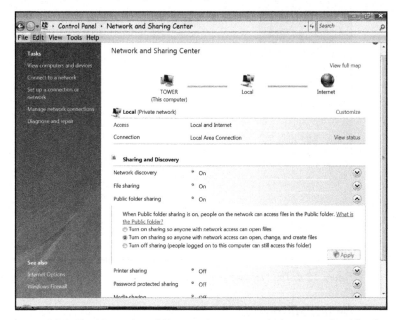

Figure 12-5: The Network and Sharing Center controls the access level for the Public folder.

Regardless of the network access settings, others using the local computer can always open and edit files in the Public folder.

Sharing through the Public folder is a good choice when you want to keep all your shared files in one place, separated from the files and folders that you want to keep private. The Public folder is also an easy way to share files with everybody on the network, without needing to set specific permissions for individual users.

To open the Public folder, select the **Start** menu and choose **Documents ▸ Documents**. Then select **Public** from the Favorite Links list in the left panel of the Documents window. If the left panel is not visible, select **Organize** from the taskbar directly under the menu bar, and then select **Layout ▸ Navigation Pane**. Figure 12-6 shows the Public folder.

Figure 12-6: Windows Vista's Public folder contains subfolders for different categories of shared files.

To add a folder or file to the Public folder, either move or copy the file or folder into the Public folder or into one of its subfolders. The preset subfolders are intended for common file types, such as documents, music, photos, and videos; you can add new categories or remove the existing ones to meet your own needs and preferences.

You can also place shortcuts to local files and web pages in the Public folder. If you place a copy of your Favorites folder (*<drive letter>:\Users\ <username>\Favorites*) in the Public\Favorites folder, you can share your Internet Explorer Favorites list with other network users.

To open or view a file or folder in a Public folder from another computer on the same network, use that computer's network browser and open the *<drive letter>:\Users\Public* folder for the target computer.

Sharing from Any Folder

The alternative to the Public folder is to treat each shared file or folder separately. Outside of the Public folder, you can set sharing permissions for each folder or individual file to allow read-only or read-and-change access for specific users or groups of users. A shared folder is also known as a *network share* or simply a *share*.

To share folders or files outside the Public folder, follow these steps:

1. From My Computer, select one or more folders or drives that you want to share.

2. Click **Share** in the toolbar at the top of the window. The Share icon is only visible when you have selected one or more drives or folders; it's not available for individual files. The File Sharing dialog shown in Figure 12-7 will appear.

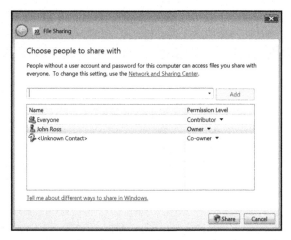

Figure 12-7: The File Sharing dialog specifies the people with whom you can share a folder's contents.

3. To add an individual name to the list of people who have access to this folder, click the arrow next to the empty field near the top of the dialog, and either select that person's name from the list or select **Create a new user** from the drop-down menu.

4. If you select Create a new user, the User Accounts dialog will appear. Select **Manage another account**, and then select **Create a new account** in the Manage Accounts dialog.

5. Step through the rest of the process to create a new account, and then return to the File Sharing dialog. You should now see the name of the new account in the drop-down menu.

6. Select the person you want to share access to this folder with and click the **Add** button. That name will appear in the list of users, as shown in Figure 12-8.

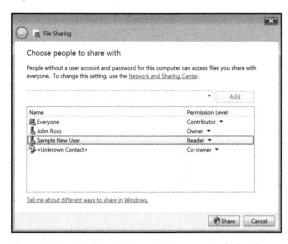

Figure 12-8: The File Sharing dialog now includes the new user's name.

7. Click the Permission Level to the right of each user's name to assign that person one of these permissions for the shared files in this folder:

Reader   A reader can view the contents of files but cannot edit or delete them.

Contributor   A contributor can view files and add new ones to the folder but cannot edit or delete existing files.

Co-owner   The co-owner of a file or folder can open and view files, create new ones, and edit or delete existing files.

8. Click the **Share** button at the bottom of the dialog to save your changes and close the window.

9. The File Sharing utility will display a window confirming that the folder in question is now shared with other computers on the network. The utility offers to email other users to advise them about the new shared folder, but you do not need to send such a message; the new share automatically appears whenever an authorized user opens a link to your computer (as shown in Figure 12-9).

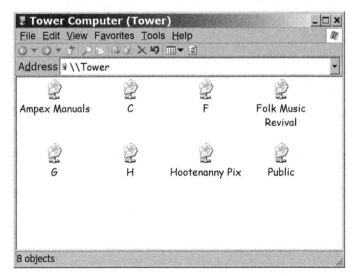

Figure 12-9: This network link shows a computer with four hard drives (C:, F:, G:, and H:), along with three shared folders and a Public folder.

10. Click the **Done** button at the bottom of the dialog to close the window.

To change permissions for an individual file within a shared folder, follow these steps:

1. Open the folder that contains the file.

2. Right-click the name or icon for the file whose permissions you want to change. A Properties window for that file will appear.

3. Click the **Security** tab to view the dialog shown in Figure 12-10.

4. In the Group or User Names list, choose the name of each user to see current permissions. If you can't see the name you want, use the scroll bar at the right side of the list.

5. To change a user's access to this file, click the **Edit** button. The Permissions dialog shown in Figure 12-11 will appear.

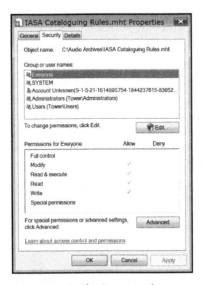

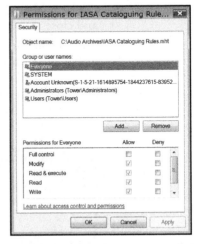

Figure 12-10: The Security tab controls file-sharing permissions for individual files.

Figure 12-11: Use the Permissions dialog to change permission settings for one or more users.

6. The lower part of the dialog includes Allow and Deny checkboxes for each of six different options. To change a setting, click to add or remove a checkmark from the appropriate box. The options are:

Full control   A user with full control can read and write data files, run program files, edit or delete files, and change a file's permissions.

Modify   A user with Modify permissions can run a program file and read, write, or delete a data file.

Read & execute   A user with permissions to Read & execute can view the contents of a file and run a program file but can't make changes or delete the file.

Read   A user with Read permissions can view the contents of a data file but can't make any changes or delete the file.

Write   A user with Write permissions can make changes but can't delete the file.

Special permissions   Special permissions are administrative controls that most users don't need. Click the **Advanced** button to set these options.

7. Obviously, some of these permissions overlap, so if, for example, you allow full control, you will also allow permission to modify, read, and write to the file. To save your choices and close the Properties dialog, click **OK**.

Printer Sharing

The Network and Sharing Center also controls printer sharing. Chapter 14 explains how to use this feature.

Password Protected Sharing

Password protection assigns one more level of security to shared files. When password protected sharing is turned on, you can't open or edit files without a user account and password on that computer.

Media Sharing

Media sharing in Windows Vista transmits music, still pictures, or videos through your network to a *digital media receiver (DMR)* such as a game console or a compatible home theater receiver. Chapter 15 explains how to use media sharing.

File Sharing on a Macintosh

Starting with OS X 10.2, the Macintosh operating system supports Windows file sharing (SMB), so that's the best way to exchange files between an up-to-date Mac and another computer through a network. I'll discuss connecting older Macs to a network later in this section.

If your home or business uses Macintosh computers exclusively, you could use one of the older Apple sharing services, but you're on your own for that; we're concerned here about connecting your Mac to a non-proprietary network.

Connecting a Mac to a Windows (SMB) Network

When a Macintosh is connected to an SMB (Windows) network, it appears the same as any other computer connected to the network: You can find drives, directories, files, and other resources connected to the Mac directly from your Windows or Linux/Unix desktop.

In most cases, connecting a Mac to a Windows network is a plug-and-play process. Simply plug an Ethernet cable into the socket or turn on your Wi-Fi adapter and the computer will automatically detect the network. However, your computer won't accept connections from the network unless the user logged in on the other computer also has an account on your Mac. Unlike Windows, Mac OS X won't accept connections from a guest account.

Adding a New Account

To establish a new account in Mac OS X, follow these steps:

1. From the **Apple** menu, select **System Preferences**.
2. Select **View ▸ Accounts**.
3. In OS X 10.2, select **New User**; in later versions, click the + button. The window shown in Figure 12-12 will appear.

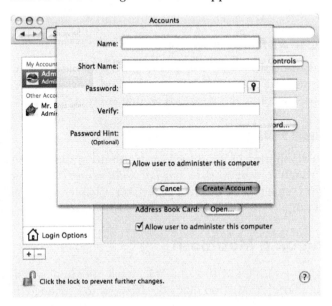

Figure 12-12: Create a new account using this window.

4. Type the name and a short name for the new account. The short name should be identical to the user's Windows or Linux/Unix username.
5. Type the user's password in the appropriate field.
6. In OS X 10.2, check the **Allow user to log in from Windows** checkbox and then click **OK.**
7. Close the System Preferences window.

When an existing user wants to connect to a Mac, the user's computer should automatically set up the link in versions later than OS X 10.3, but sometimes you have to instruct the Mac to accept the link. This is always required in OS X 10.2. Follow these steps to allow a user to log in from a Windows network:

1. From the **Apple** menu, select **System Preferences**.
2. Select **View ▸ Accounts**.
3. Select the account you want to authorize.

4. If the computer requests a password, type it in the appropriate field.

5. Check the **Allow user to log in from Windows** checkbox. The system will instruct you to reset your password.

6. Enter your existing password or a new password and click the **Save** button.

7. Confirm that you can now log in to the Mac from another computer connected to the network. If it works, the process is complete.

8. If you can't log in to the Mac from another computer, try changing the user's password.

Setting the Workgroup Name

Each computer on the network should use the same SMB workgroup name, but the default in Mac OS X is WORKGROUP, which is probably not the name your Windows network uses.

To change the workgroup name on a Mac, follow these steps:

1. Select **Applications ▸ Utilities ▸ Directory Access**.

2. Click the padlock icon to identify yourself as an administrator.

3. Select **SMB/CIFS** from the list of services, as shown in Figure 12-13.

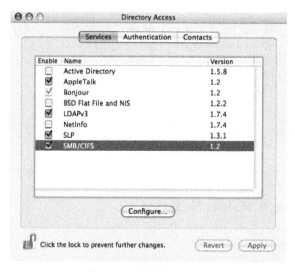

Figure 12-13: Select SMB/CIFS from the list of services.

4. Select **Configure**. The program will scan the network and display a list of workgroups. On most small networks, you will see only one workgroup name.

5. Select the workgroup name you want to use and click **OK**.

6. Click **Apply** and quit Directory Access.

Turning on Windows File Sharing

Before you can share files through a Mac, you must turn on Windows file sharing:

1. From the **Apple** menu, select **System Preferences**.
2. Select **View ▸ Sharing**.
3. Check **Windows Sharing** in the Service column, as shown in Figure 12-14. The list of network preferences will now include Windows Sharing On.

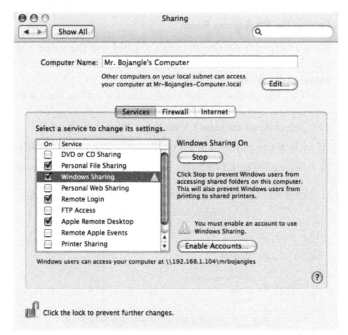

Figure 12-14: Select Windows Sharing in the Service column.

Connecting to Windows File Sharing

To view or open a shared file on another computer through the network, follow these steps:

1. Click the Finder icon in the dock, and select **Connect to server** from the **Go** menu.
2. When the Connect to Server dialog appears, either browse to find the share you want or type the address, using this format: *smb://<ServerName>/ <ShareName>*.
3. Click the **Connect** button to make the connection.

Connecting from Older Mac Versions

Apple did not include SMB file sharing in Mac OS until OS X 10.2. You can use one of the Apple sharing services to share Mac files using older software with another computer through a network, but the process is somewhat different.

To share files from OS X 10.1 or 10.2 with another computer on the same network, select **Go ▸ Connect to Server**. A list of other computers will appear. Select the name of the computer that contains the files you want to use and click the **Connect** button.

To connect to another computer from OS 8 or 9, follow these steps:

1. From the **Apple** menu, select the **Chooser**.
2. Click the AppleShare icon.
3. If a list of AppleTalk Zones appears, choose the zone that includes the computer you want to reach.
4. Select the name of the computer that contains the file or other resource you want to open from the list, and click the **OK** button.

File Sharing in Linux and Unix

The latest Linux and Unix distributions all include support for Windows file-sharing (SMB) protocols, so sharing files with computers using other operating systems (or other Linux/Unix distributions) should be easy. The terminology is not always the same, but if you understand the underlying principles involved in network file sharing, you shouldn't have any trouble working with a mixed network.

NOTE   *In this section, I'm describing tools for sharing files that are part of the most commonly used Linux and Unix desktop environments—Gnome and KDE. If you're a hardcore user who works from the command line rather than a desktop, I'm assuming you already know how to create and use network shares or, if not, that you can find specific instructions from man pages and other documentation.*

Sharing from Linux or Unix Computers

Both of the major Linux/Unix desktop environments—Gnome and KDE—include relatively easy-to-use network file browsers. In Gnome, the program is called Nautilus, as shown in Figure 12-15. To open the network file browser, go to the **Places** menu on the Gnome desktop, and select **Network**.

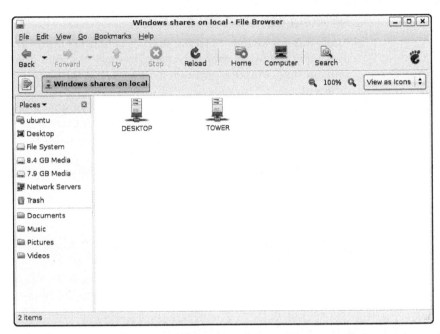

Figure 12-15: Gnome's Nautilus file browser includes access to network shares.

In KDE, the comparable function is part of the Konqueror file manager, as shown in Figure 12-16.

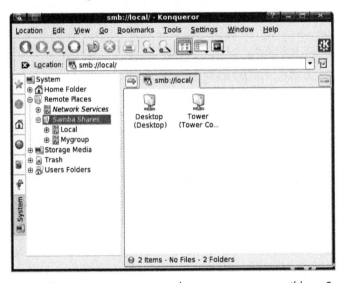

Figure 12-16: In Konqueror, network computers are accessible as Samba Shares under Remote Places. Click an icon to open a drive or folder.

Both Nautilus and Konqueror are basic graphic browsers that support the usual set of file management activities: You can click an icon to open a folder or a file or drag-and-drop to copy a file from one computer to another.

Creating Shares on Linux and Unix Computers

The general procedures for creating a shared directory in Gnome and KDE are similar: Open a browser window that contains the directory you want to share, right-click the directory, and change some settings.

Sharing from Gnome

From a Gnome file browser, follow these steps to create a share:

1. Right-click the folder you want to share. A pop-up menu will appear.
2. Choose **Sharing options** from the menu. The dialog shown in Figure 12-17 will open.
3. Check the **Share this folder** option. The additional options shown in Figure 12-18 will become available.

Figure 12-17: Use the Folder Sharing dialog to configure a directory as a network share.

Figure 12-18: When you turn on the Share this folder option, the Folder Sharing dialog reveals more options.

4. Select the options you want to apply to this share, and click the **Create Share** button to save your choices.

Sharing from Konqueror

If your desktop uses KDE and Konqueror, follow these steps to create a share:

1. Right-click the folder or drive you want to share.
2. Select the Permissions tab in the pop-up Properties window, as shown in Figure 12-19.

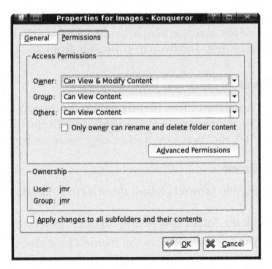

Figure 12-19: Konqueror's Permissions tab controls
network access to a folder's contents.

3. To configure a folder as a share, use the drop-down menus next to
   Group and Others to change access permissions, and check the **Apply
   change to all subfolders and their contents** option.

Samba

Samba is a suite of programs that uses SMB to allow file and print sharing
from non-Windows operating systems (including Linux, Unix, and several
others). If it's not included with your Linux or Unix package, you can
download it from *http://samba.org/*.

Samba itself uses text commands rather than a *graphical user interface
(GUI)*, but several add-on GUI interfaces are available at Samba's website.
Unless the people using Linux or Unix on your network are comfortable
using a command-line shell, you will want to install at least one of these
GUIs along with Samba.

Using Shares

Shared folders and *directories* (which are two names for the same type of
resource) are a basic networking tool. Any time two or more people want
to collaborate on a project, they can share access to the documents and
information files by creating a project share and allowing any member of
the group to work on those files.

Your computer displays shared folders and other network resources just
like files and folders stored on your own computer, so where the file is actually
stored doesn't matter—you can place a shortcut to a share on your desktop
and open a shared document or other file with a couple of mouse clicks, just
as if the file was stored on your own computer.

13

NETWORK SECURITY

Any time you operate a network, you must protect it against intrusions from outsiders and damage caused by intentional or accidental misuse or abuse by internal network users. Computer networks are vulnerable to several forms of attack, including unauthorized access to files, theft of service, and denial of service caused by excessive network-connection requests. Strictly speaking, attacks on individual computers, such as viruses, worms, and Trojan horses, are a separate issue from network vulnerabilities, but a good network security plan will include firewalls and other tools that also protect the computers connected to the network.

This chapter describes the basic steps that every home and small business network manager must take to keep his or her network secure.

Keeping Intruders Out

Intruders break into networks for several reasons:

- They want to open files and read documents, either to steal confidential information or just to overcome the challenge of "cracking" protected files.

- They want to use the network to obtain a high-speed Internet connection.

- They want to use the network to forward unsavory or illegal data (such as spam or pornography) to the Internet or download similar material.

- They want to steal passwords, credit card numbers, bank account information, and other forms of data that they can either sell or use to order items of value.

- They want to interfere with normal network operation by overloading the network's ability to handle data, altering or deleting essential software, or causing hardware to break down.

Two important objectives of network security are to limit access to authorized users and to keep those same users away from configuration settings and confidential data. The most important tools for maintaining a secure network include different access levels for different users, passwords, and firewalls. If they're not adequate, more complex methods are also possible, including kernel-level mandatory access control systems, authentication and authorization mechanisms, and data encryption.

User Accounts and Access Levels

Almost all computer operating systems have at least two levels of user accounts: administrators and users. *Administrators* have access to all of the computer's configuration settings, such as installing or removing printers, joining a network, and so forth. *Users* can read and write programs and data files assigned to their own accounts and to resources whose owners allow other people to use them. On a network, a *guest* account has its own access settings for those who use a computer's resources through the network rather than through the keyboard and other input devices connected directly to each computer.

Each user has exclusive control of his or her files. The owner of every account can set access controls on files that keep them either private and confidential or public and accessible to other users. Even if other users have accounts on the same computer, they can't read somebody else's private files. The exception is a system administrator account that provides access and control to almost all files.

Passwords

Passwords are the first line of defense against unwanted access to a computer or a network. If a would-be intruder can't get the computer to start the operating system, opening data files or using the network is a lot more difficult (but not impossible—a determined intruder with enough time and resources can often get around a password to open and read unencrypted files).

You may be tempted to set up your computer without a startup password, but that completely defeats most of the computer's security features and those of the network connected to it. Unless you're absolutely certain that no strangers will ever get close enough to turn on your computer or gain access through a wired or wireless network, and you trust everybody else in the house or office to respect your privacy, it's worth the extra time needed to enter a password every time you turn on the computer or connect to it through a network.

An effective password should be difficult to guess and long enough to make it hard to find with a brute-force program (a program that applies massive computing resources to trying one password after another until it stumbles upon the right one).

Too many people use one of these items as a password:

- Your own first name or middle name
- The name of your spouse, child, or pet
- Your mother's maiden name or any other family name
- Your favorite entertainer, band, team, or song
- Your own first initial and last name (such as *JSmith*)
- An obvious string of numbers, letters, or both (such as *123456*, *abcxyz*, or *abc123*)
- Your birthday or some other significant date
- Your home town or country
- A string of characters from your keyboard (such as *qwerty* or *!@#$%*)
- The word *password*
- The phrase *letmein* (that is, *let me in*, not the name of a Chinese noodle dish)
- The phrase *trustno1* (Fox Mulder's password on *The X-Files* TV series)
- The word *swordfish* (originally used in the Marx Brothers' *Horse Feathers* and in many subsequent movies, books, and computer games)
- The word *sex* or any common curse or obscenity
- The word *God* or *Jesus* (or any other deity of your choice)
- Any of these words or phrases spelled backward

When a "computer security expert" in a movie or TV show finds the right password to break into the bad guy's computer on the third try, he probably tried some of the passwords on this list.

Many network routers, modems, and other hardware come with default passwords preset at the factory. These passwords are well known by crackers and easy to find in equipment manuals and on the Internet.

The best passwords are random strings of letters, numbers, and other characters, at least seven or eight characters in length. One expert tested a brute-force password-cracking program; Table 13-1 shows the amount of time that one programmer (Jimmy Ruska) needed to discover passwords of different lengths by creating and testing every possible combination. (The specific numbers in this table apply only to his particular program. You should pay attention to how the amount of time increases as you add more characters to a password rather than the exact times.) The time to crack is even greater if your password includes one or more symbols, such as !, @, #, $, &, and +.

Table 13-1: Time to Test All Possible Passwords[*]

Password Length	Letters Only	Letters and Numbers
3 characters	1 second	2 seconds
4 characters	3 seconds	10 seconds
5 characters	1 minute, 17 seconds	6 minutes
6 characters	26 minutes	3 hours, 30 minutes
7 characters	14 hours	6 days
8 characters	15 days	205 days

[*] Source: *http://blog.jimmyr.com/Most_Common_Passwords_20_2008.php*

Other cracking methods can be slower or faster, but the general point—that longer passwords are more difficult to crack—still applies.

Firewalls

A *firewall* is a server that uses a set of rules established by the network manager to inspect incoming data and to block data from a source that isn't on a list or files that match a particular description (such as a virus). Or the firewall might pass all data moving from the LAN *to* the Internet but only allow certain types of data *from* the Internet. The most common use of a firewall in a LAN is at the gateway to the Internet, as shown in Figure 13-1. The firewall monitors all inbound and outbound data between the computers on the local network on one side and the Internet on the other. This kind of firewall is intended to protect the computers on the LAN from unauthorized intrusion from the Internet.

Firewalls in Wireless Networks

In a wireless network, a firewall can also be placed at the gateway between the wireless access points and the wired network. This firewall isolates the wireless portion of the network from the wired LAN, so intruders who have connected their computer to the network without permission can't use the wireless connection to reach the Internet or the wired part of the LAN. Figure 13-2 shows the location of a firewall in a mixed network that includes both wired and wireless connections.

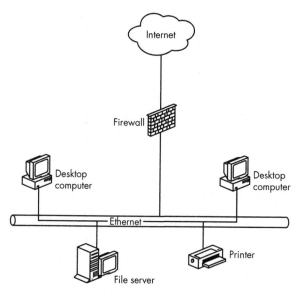

Figure 13-1: A network firewall isolates a LAN from the Internet.

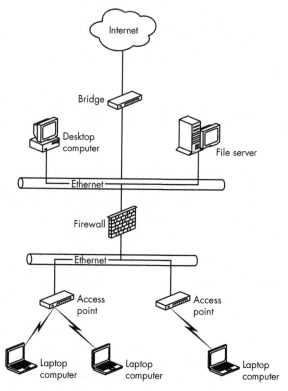

Figure 13-2: A firewall can also protect the wired portion of a LAN from wireless intruders.

A firewall in a wireless network can perform several functions:

- It can act as a gateway router between the wireless network and a wired LAN.
- It can protect a direct connection from a single computer to the Internet.
- It can block all traffic moving from the wireless side to the wired network that doesn't come from an authenticated user.
- It passes commands, messages, and file transfers from trusted users to the Internet.

Therefore, a legitimate user can connect to network nodes on the wired part of a mixed LAN or on the Internet, but an intruder would be cut off at the firewall.

Because authorized wireless users and intruders are both on the unprotected side of the firewall, it does not isolate the wireless nodes from one another. An intruder can still gain access to another computer on the same wireless network and read shared files, so it's a good idea to turn off file sharing on any computer connected to a wireless network and to use firewall software on individual computers.

A firewall for a wireless network should use some kind of authentication to allow legitimate users through the gateway, but it should reject everybody else. If access control based on MAC addresses is built into Wi-Fi networks and the added authentication in 802.1x are not adequate, then an outboard firewall should require all users to enter a login and password before they can connect to the Internet.

If your wireless network includes computers running more than one operating system, your firewall must use a login tool that works on any platform. The easiest way to accomplish this is with a web-based authentication server, such as the one included with the Apache web server (*http://httpd .apache.org/*).

The Apache web server is available as a Linux or Unix application that can run on an old, slow computer with an early Pentium or even an antique 486 CPU, so you can often recycle an old junker and use it as a firewall. Both the Apache application and the operating system are available as open source software, so it ought to be possible to build an extremely low-cost Apache firewall.

If you prefer to use Windows, or if you don't want to assemble your own firewall, you have several options. You can use the Windows version of Apache, or you can use a commercial utility such as the ones listed at *http:// www.thegild.com/firewall/*.

Attacks on a wireless LAN don't all come through the air. A wireless network also requires the same kind of firewall protection against attacks from the Internet as an entirely wired network. Many wireless access points include configurable firewall features, but if yours does not, the network should include a firewall program on each computer, along with a separate router or a dedicated computer acting as a network firewall.

Protecting Individual Computers

Client firewall programs provide another line of defense against attacks coming from the Internet. Some of these attacks come from miscreants who are looking for a way to read your files and other resources that you don't want the entire world to see. Others might want to use your computer as a relay point for spam or attempts to break into some other computer halfway around the world in order to make the real source more difficult to identify. Still others spread viruses or use *really* unpleasant programs called rootkits that take control of a PC or display threatening messages.

An unprotected system with a lot of unused storage space can be an attractive target for hackers who want to distribute pirated software, music, or video files (you didn't think they store that stuff on their own computers, did you?).

The number of such idiots and creeps on the Internet is surprisingly large; if you install a firewall that notifies you when an outside computer tries to connect to your network, your firewall log will probably list several break-in attempts every day.

Wireless Access Points with Firewalls

The easiest firewall to use with a wireless network is one that's built into an access point. Many wireless access points combine the functions of a wireless access point with a broadband router and an Ethernet switch, so they support both wired and wireless network clients.

As you know, a network router translates addresses between the numeric IP address that identifies the LAN to the Internet and the internal IP addresses that identify individual computers within the local network. The firewall normally blocks all incoming requests for data to network hosts, but this creates problems when you want to use one or more of the computers on the local network as file servers. So the firewall redirects certain types of requests to the appropriate computer inside the firewall.

Each request to connect to a server includes a specific port number that identifies the type of server. For example, web servers operate on port 80, and FTP servers use port 21, so those port numbers are part of the request for access. To accept access requests to a server, you must instruct the firewall's *Network Address Translation (NAT)* function to forward those requests to a specific computer within the LAN. Table 13-2 lists the most common service port numbers.

Hundreds of other port numbers have been assigned, but you will never see most of them in actual use. The official list of port assignments is available online at *http://www.iana.org/assignments/port-numbers.*

NAT assumes that each internal server's IP address doesn't change from one request to the next. A web server on 192.168.0.23 today won't migrate to 192.168.0.47 next week. That's generally not a problem on a wired network, but in a wireless setting where network clients join and leave the network all the time, the DHCP server automatically assigns the next available address to each new client. If one of those clients is the home of one of the network's service ports, the NAT probably won't find it. This problem is not common, because most networks don't use portable computers as servers, but it can happen. The solution is to turn off the DHCP server and assign a permanent IP address to each client.

Table 13-2: Common TCP/IP Service Port Numbers

Port Number	Internet Service
20	FTP-Data (FTP default data)
21	FTP (File Transfer Protocol)
23	Telnet
25	SMTP (outgoing mail)
37	Time
53	DNS (Domain Name System)
70	Gopher
79	Finger
80	HTTP (web server)
88	Kerberos
110	POP3 (incoming mail)
119	NNTP (network news)
1863	Microsoft MSN Messenger
5190	AOL Instant Messenger
7070	Real Audio and Video

Firewall Software

A wireless gateway firewall at the interface between the access point and the wired part of your LAN will keep intruders from using your network to reach the Internet, and a firewall at the Internet connection will turn away attempts to connect to your network *from* the Internet, but a wireless network still needs one more form of protection. If somebody gains access to your wireless LAN without permission, you want to keep them away from the other legitimate computers on the same network, so each network node needs a client firewall program.

Client firewalls perform the same functions at a computer's network interface that a LAN or enterprise firewall performs for the entire network; a client firewall detects attempts to connect to TCP service ports and rejects them unless they match one or more of the firewall program's configuration settings. Several good firewall products are available as shareware, and others are free to noncommercial users. It's easy to try them on your own system and choose the one you like best. ZoneAlarm (*http://www.zonealarm.com/*) and LANguard (*http://www.languard.com/*) are both well-regarded Windows firewall software products. There's also a firewall built into Windows XP and Windows Vista that is adequate for most home and small business networks.

Linux and Unix users also have plenty of firewall options. Most of them were written for stand-alone firewall computers that are commonly used as network gateways, but they could be equally appropriate as protection for individual network clients.

In Linux, the iptables firewall is part of the kernel. It's well-documented at *http://www.netfilter.org/projects/iptables/index.html*. Port Scan Attack Detector (psad) is another set of tools that identify port scans and other intrusions on many Linux systems. For more information, see *http://www.cipherdyne.org/psad/*.

IP Filter is a software package that provides firewall services to FreeBSD and NetBSD systems. The official IP Filter website is *http://coombs.anu.edu.au/~avalon*, and you can download an excellent HOWTO document at *http://www.obfuscation.org/ipf/ipf-howto.txt*. The program can deny or permit any packet from passing through the firewall, and it can filter by netmask or host address, establish service port restrictions, and provide NAT services.

OpenBSD, FreeBSD, and NetBSD can all use the Packet Filter, or PF, facility to perform firewalling. More information is available at *http://www.openbsd.org/faq/pf/*.

NetBSD/i386 Firewall is another free Unix firewall. It will operate on any PC with a 486 or later CPU and as little as 8MB of memory. The NetBSD/i386 Firewall Project home page is *http://firewall.dubbele.com/*.

Virtual Private Networks

A virtual private network (VPN) can add another effective form of security to data that moves from a remote client to a host network that can be located anywhere with a connection to the Internet.

A VPN uses a *data tunnel* to connect two points on a network through an encrypted channel. The endpoints can be a single network client and a network server, a pair of client computers or other devices, or the gateway to a pair of LANs. Data that passes through a public network such as the Internet is completely isolated from other network traffic. VPNs use login and password authentication to restrict access to authorized users; they encrypt the data to make it unintelligible to intruders who intercept the data; and they use data authentication to maintain the integrity of each data packet and to assure that all data originates with legitimate network clients.

NOTE *VPN functions occur at the IP or network layer of the ISO model. Therefore, they can operate on top of the Wi-Fi or other wireless protocols, which operate at the physical layer. VPNs can also pass data across a network connection that includes more than one physical medium (for example, a wireless link that passes data onward to a wired Ethernet network). In other words, a VPN is an end-to-end service; the data can use a wireless link, an Ethernet cable, an ordinary telephone line, or some combination of those and other transmission media.*

In a traditional VPN, a remote user can log in to a distant LAN and obtain all the same network services that are available to local clients. VPNs are commonly used to extend corporate networks to branch offices and to connect users to the LAN from home or from off-site locations such as a client or customer's office.

A connection through a VPN server looks to the rest of the network exactly like a client device connected directly to the LAN. The only difference is the data from the VPN passes through a VPN driver and a public network instead of moving directly from the network adapter to the LAN. Figure 13-3 shows a typical VPN connection to a remote network.

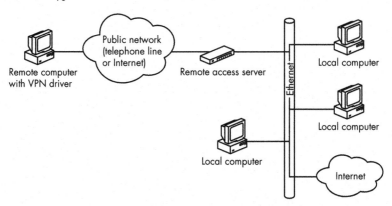

Figure 13-3: A remote network can connect to a LAN through a virtual private network.

All of the same security benefits also apply to short-range VPNs that tunnel through a wireless link and longer-range VPNs that start on a wireless network and relay the data to a remote server. These are two different uses for a VPN: a *local* VPN that only extends across the wireless portion of a network between the client devices and the access point, and an *extended network* that carries VPN-encoded data beyond the access points to a VPN server through a public network, such as the Internet or a dial-up telephone connection. An extended network is a traditional VPN that happens to originate from a wireless network client. The same VPN can also support connections that don't include a wireless segment and logins from public wireless services, such as the ones at airports or coffee shops. This setup is conventional for a VPN.

Local, short-range VPNs are interesting to people who operate wireless networks because they add another layer of security to wireless links. Because the data moving between wireless clients and the network access point is encrypted (using an algorithm that is more secure than WPA encryption), it is unintelligible to any third party who might be monitoring the radio signal. Because the VPN server won't accept data links at the access point from wireless clients that are not using the correct VPN drivers and passwords, an intruder can't break into the network by associating a rogue client with the access point.

The goal of a wireless VPN is to protect the wireless link between the clients and the access point and to lock out unauthorized users. Therefore, the isolated and encrypted data can only move across a single room rather than over hundreds or thousands of miles. Of course, the access point might also relay VPN-encoded data onward through the Internet to a network host in another location.

Figure 13-4 shows a wireless connection to a VPN. The VPN server is located between the wireless access point and the host LAN, so all of the packets that move through the wireless portion of the network are encoded. For clarity, the diagram shows the VPN server as a separate component, but the most practical way to add VPN security to a wireless LAN is to use a router or gateway that incorporates VPN support. VPN-enabled routers are available from several vendors, including Cisco, NETGEAR, and TRENDnet.

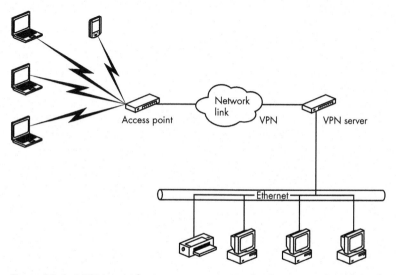

Figure 13-4: A VPN provides a secure connection between a wireless network and an Internet gateway or a local LAN.

VPN Methods

A VPN moves data through one or more intermediate networks to a destination on another network. The VPN's tunneling client encapsulates the existing data packets or frames by adding a new header with the routing information that instructs the packets how to reach the VPN's endpoint. The transmission path through the intermediate networks is called a *tunnel*. At the other end of the tunnel, the VPN server removes the tunneling header and forwards the data to the destination specified by the next layer of headers. The exact form of the tunnel doesn't make any difference to the data because the data treats the tunnel as a point-to-point connection.

The tunneling headers can take several forms. The methods used most widely in VPNs are Point-to-Point Tunneling Protocol (PPTP), Layer Two Tunneling Protocol (L2TP), and IP Security (IPsec) mode. PPTP and L2TP can move data through IP, IPX, and NetBEUI networks; IPsec is limited to IP networks. Both the client and the server must use the same protocol.

In PPTP and L2TP, the client and server must configure the tunnel for each transmission before they begin to exchange data. The configuration parameters include the route through the intermediate network and the encryption and compression specifications. When the transmission is complete, the client and server terminate the connection and close the tunnel.

Unfortunately, several data security analysts have identified significant flaws in PPTP that allow intruders to break into a PPTP-based VPN and sniff passwords and then decode encryption, read data, or inflict damage to a network server. Therefore, PPTP headers are not secure and should not be used.

In an IPsec network link, the client and server must establish the tunnel through the intermediate networks in a separate transaction before they begin to exchange data.

Both L2TP and IPsec offer specific advantages and disadvantages, but they're both good enough to create a secure link between a wireless network client and an access point. The differences among the three are technical rather than practical. You can find an excellent explanation of the internal operation of all three protocols in Microsoft's white paper entitled "Virtual Private Networking in Windows 2000: An Overview," which is available online at *http://technet.microsoft.com/en-us/library/bb742566.aspx* (but remember that the flaws in PPTP networks were identified *after* that whitepaper was written).

VPN Servers

A VPN server (or *host*) can be part of a Linux/Unix or Windows server, or it can be built into a stand-alone network router or gateway. If your network already uses a separate computer as a dedicated server, you can use that computer as the VPN server. A separate piece of hardware might be a better choice if your network does not already have a full-blown network server.

Dozens of VPN equipment makers offer routers, gateways, and other products that support one or more of the VPN protocols. Each of these products has a different feature set, so testing the specific combination of client and server that you intend to use on your own network before you commit to them is essential. The Virtual Private Network Consortium (VPNC) is moving toward a set of interoperability tests and certification standards (much like the Wi-Fi standards for wireless Ethernet equipment). The VPNC website (*http://www.vpnc.org/*) lists the products that have passed the interoperability tests, and the site also provides links to information sources for a long list of VPN products.

Configuring a Windows Server for a VPN

If you're committed to using a Windows server, you can use either L2TP or IPsec with Windows Server 2003 or Windows Server 2008; if your server runs the older Windows NT Server 4.0 or Windows 2000 Server software, you're limited to L2TP (or the seriously flawed PPTP). The server also requires two network interface cards: one connected to the wired LAN or the Internet gateway and the other connected to the wireless network. The interface card that is connected to the wireless port normally connects directly to the wireless access point's Ethernet port. The exact process of installing an L2TP host on a Windows server is slightly different in each version of Windows, but the general steps are the same. For specific information about configuring a particular operating system, consult the online Help screens and Microsoft's Resource Kit and other online documentation for your server's operating system. The following sections describe the configuration steps in general terms.

NOTE   *For more information about deploying and using VPNs with Microsoft servers, see the Microsoft TechNet articles at* http://technet.microsoft.com/en-us/network/bb545442.aspx.

Configure the connection to the LAN.
> The link to the LAN or other network is a dedicated connection through a network adapter. The network connection profile for this connection must include the IP address and subnet mask assigned to this connection and the default gateway address assigned to the network gateway.

Configure the VPN connection.
> The VPN connection is usually an Ethernet link to one or more access points. The connection profile on the server for the VPN connection must include the IP address and subnet mask assigned to this port and the addresses of the DNS and WINS name servers used by this network.

Configure the remote-access server as a router.
> The server must use either static routes or routing protocols that make each VPN client reachable from the wired network.

Enable and configure the server for L2TP clients.
> Windows uses Remote Access Service (RAS) and point-to-point protocol (PPP) to establish VPN connections. The Routing and Remote Access service enables RAS. A VPN connection requires the following RAS configuration options:

>> **Authentication method**   Encrypted PPTP connections use the MS-CHAP or EAP-TLS authentication methods.

>> **Authentication provider**   Either Windows 2000 security or an external RADIUS server can verify network clients.

>> **IP routing**   IP routing and IP-based remote access must be active. If the wired network acts as a DHCP server for the wireless clients, DHCP must be active.

Configure L2TP ports.
Set each L2TP port to accept remote access.

Configure network filters.
Input and output filters keep the remote-access server from sending and receiving data that does not originate at a VPN client. These filters will reject data to or from unauthorized users, so those intruders will not be able to obtain an Internet connection (or a connection to the wired LAN) through the wireless network.

Configure remote-access policies.
Set the remote-access permission for each VPN client to allow access to the RAS server. The port type must be set to the correct VPN protocol (for example, PPTP or L2TP), and the profile for each connection must include the type of encryption in use. Windows offers three encryption strength options:

Basic   Uses a 40-bit encryption key

Strong   Uses a 56-bit encryption key

Strongest   Uses a 128-bit encryption key

VPN Servers for Linux/Unix

All of the BSD variations (including FreeBSD, NetBSD, OpenBSD, and Mac OS X) include an IPsec VPN client and server as part of the release package.

Linux FreeS/WAN is the most popular implementation of IPsec for Linux. Go to *http://www.freeswan.org/* for downloads, documentation, and access to the community of FreeS/WAN users.

OpenVPN is an SSL-based VPN solution for Linux, BSD, OS X, and Windows. OpenVPN is easy to configure and offers both *routed VPN* (traffic to specific destinations is sent through the VPN) and *tunneled virtual interfaces* (emulating a physical layer Ethernet device, which can pass non-IP traffic through the VPN). OpenVPN can be found at *http://openvpn.net/*.

If you're using a Linux firewall, you might want to consider VPN Masquerade. Linux uses the IP Masquerade function in the Linux kernel to share a single connection to the Internet among multiple clients. VPN Masquerade is the section of IP Masquerade that supports IPsec clients. The HOWTO for Linux VPN Masquerade is at *http://tldp.org/HOWTO/VPNMasquerade-HOWTO.html*.

Network Hardware with Built-In VPN Support

A dedicated computer running Linux or one of the BSD versions of Unix can be an inexpensive VPN server. Or if you're using a Windows server for other purposes, a dedicated computer can also provide VPN support at little or no additional cost. But a full-size network server is often a bigger and more complicated solution to a relatively simple problem. They're not always the best choice. Many switches, routers, gateways, and firewall devices also include VPN support. Cisco, 3COM, Intel, and many other manufacturers make VPN products that are often easier to install and maintain than a separate computer.

In a wireless network, the VPN server does not need all the same bells and whistles as a server in a larger corporate network. As Figure 13-5 shows, a router located between the wireless access point and the wired portion of an enterprise network can easily double as a VPN server. In a home network, the VPN server can operate between the access point and a DSL or cable modem.

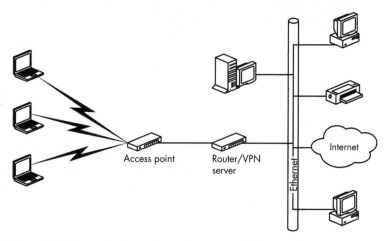

Figure 13-5: A network router can also act as a VPN server for a wireless network.

Stand-alone VPN client hardware that sits between the computer and the network is also available, but this setup isn't as practical in a wireless network because the wireless network adapter is almost always plugged directly into the computer itself.

VPN Client Software

A wireless client connects to a VPN server through its wireless Ethernet link to the network access point, which the operating system sees as a LAN connection. To set up a VPN tunnel through that connection, you must install the tunneling protocol as a network service.

Configuring Windows for VPN

Windows XP and Vista include support for virtual private networks, but this support is not part of the default installation, so the first step in setting up a VPN client is to install the protocol.

In Windows XP and Windows Vista, a wizard makes the whole process easy. In XP, follow these steps to set up a VPN connection:

1. From the Control Panel, open Network Connections.

2. Double-click the **New Connection Wizard** icon.

3. When the Network Connection Type window, shown in Figure 13-6, appears, select the **Connect to the network at my workplace** option and click the **Next** button.

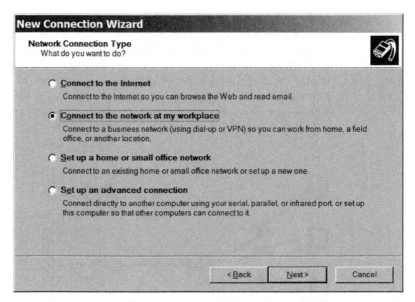

Figure 13-6: The option for creating a VPN link specifies connecting to a workplace network, but this option also applies to a wireless VPN.

4. In the Network Connection window (shown in Figure 13-7), select the **Virtual Private Network connection** option and click the **Next** button.

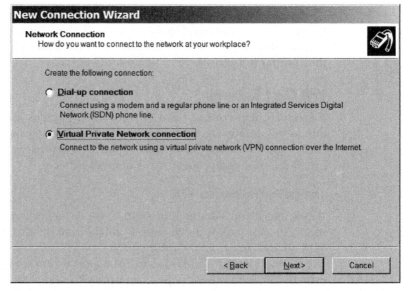

Figure 13-7: Select the Virtual Private Network connection option to create a VPN connection.

5. In the Connection Name window, type a name for the wireless VPN connection. This name will appear on desktop shortcuts to this connection. Click the **Next** button.

6. In the Public Network window (shown in Figure 13-8), select the **Do not dial the initial connection** option because you don't need to connect through a telephone line. Click the **Next** button.

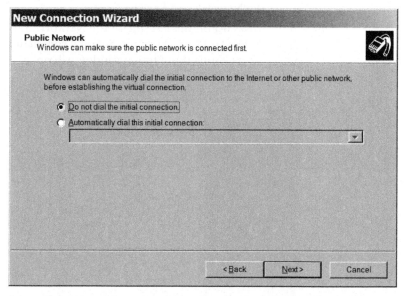

Figure 13-8: In a wireless network, the VPN does not require a dial-up connection.

7. In the VPN Server Selection window, shown in Figure 13-9, type the host name or IP address of the VPN server.

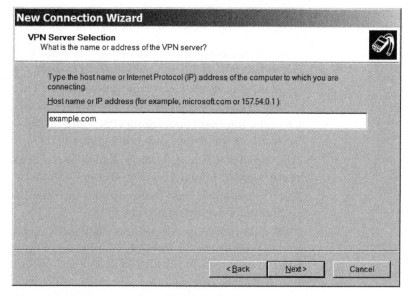

Figure 13-9: The host name or IP address identifies the VPN server at the other end of the wireless link.

8. Click the **Next** button and then the **Finish** button to complete the wizard.

In Vista, follow these steps:

1. Open the Control Panel.
2. Select the **Network and Sharing Center**.
3. In the Tasks list on the left side of the Network and Sharing Center, shown in Figure 13-10, select the **Set up a connection or network** option. A Choose a Connection Option window will open.

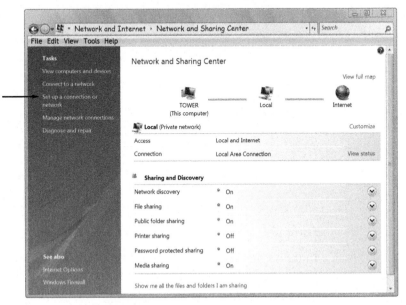

Figure 13-10: Use the Set up a connection or network option to create a VPN link.

4. Select the **Connect to a workplace** option and click the **Next** button. The wizard will ask if you want to use an existing connection.
5. Select the **No, create a new connection** option. The wizard will ask if you want to use a VPN or a dial-up connection.
6. Select the **Internet connection (VPN)** option. The wizard will then ask for details in the screen shown in Figure 13-11.
7. Type the VPN server's address provided by the network manager in the Internet address field. This can be either a numeric address or a name.
8. Type the name you want to use on your own computer for this VPN connection in the Destination name field.
9. If you want to test the connection, click the Next button. If you don't want to connect, select the Don't connect now option and then click Next. The wizard will ask for your name and password.
10. Type the name and password you use for this VPN account. If you want your computer to automatically send your password, turn on the Remember this password option. Click the **Create** button to establish the VPN connection and close the wizard.

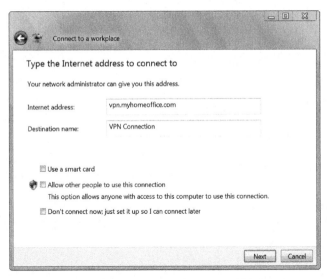

Figure 13-11: Use this screen to configure your VPN.

To create a shortcut to a VPN on your desktop in Windows, follow these steps:

1. In XP, open the Control Panel and select **Network Connections**. In Vista, open the Control Panel, select the **Network and Sharing Center**, and select **Manage Network Connections** from the Tasks list.
2. From the Network Connections window, right-click the icon or listing for the VPN and select **Create Shortcut** from the pop-up menu.
3. A pop-up window will ask if you want to place the shortcut on the desktop. Click the **Yes** button. A shortcut will now appear on the desktop.

The Microsoft L2TP/IPsec VPN Client

Microsoft includes a client for L2TP connections with Internet Protocol security (IPsec) in Windows 2000, Windows XP, and Windows Vista. A similar client program for Windows 98, Windows Me, and Windows NT Workstation 4.0 is available for free download from *http://download.microsoft.com/download/win98/Install/1.0/W9XNT4Me/EN-US/msl2tp.exe*.

Making the Connection in Windows

When the VPN connection profile is in place, it's easy to connect a Windows client to the host LAN or the Internet through the wireless VPN link: Just double-click the icon for the connection profile. Windows will ask for a login and password and then make the connection.

If you mostly use your wireless connection to connect to the Internet, you can make it the default connection, which will open whenever you run a network application such as a web browser or email client program. To make the VPN profile the default, follow these steps:

1. Open the **Internet Properties** window from the Control Panel.
2. Select the **Connections** tab.
3. In the Dial-Up Settings section, select the VPN connection profile from the list, and click the **Set Default** button.
4. Click the **Settings** button. In the Dial-Up Settings section, type your login and password on the VPN server.
5. Select the **Dial whenever a network connection is not present** option.

Selecting Windows XP and Vista Options

Windows XP and Windows Vista offer many VPN options that were not available in earlier versions of Windows. To set these options, follow these steps:

1. Choose the **Network Connections** window from the Control Panel. If you have a shortcut to your VPN connection on the desktop, you can skip this step.
2. Double-click the VPN icon. A Connect VPN to Internet window, like the one in Figure 13-12, will appear.

Figure 13-12: Use the Connect VPN to Internet window to configure a VPN in Windows XP.

3. Click the **Properties** button. The Properties window for your VPN client will appear. Figure 13-13 shows the General tab of the VPN to Internet Properties window.

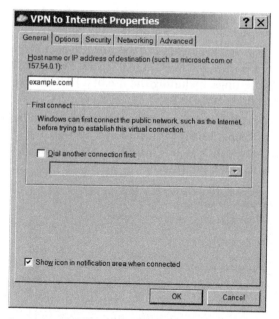

Figure 13-13: The General tab controls the destination of
a VPN connection.

4. The IP address of the VPN server should already be visible in the Host
name or IP address of destination field. The **Dial another connection
first** option should be disabled. Click the **Networking** tab to view the dialog shown in Figure 13-14.

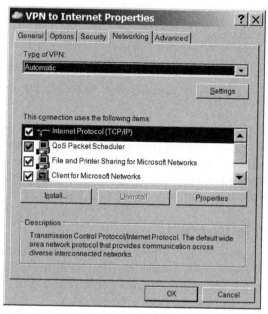

Figure 13-14: The Networking tab controls the VPN's
network configuration options.

5. Select the type of VPN server your network will use from the Type of VPN menu. If you don't know the VPN type, select the Automatic option.

6. Select Internet Protocol (TCP/IP) or Internet Protocol Version 4 from the list of connection items, and click the **Properties** button to change the network settings, including the use of a DHCP server or manual settings for IP address and DNS.

7. Click the **Advanced** tab to open the dialog shown in Figure 13-15. If your network is not already protected by a firewall, select the Internet Connection Firewall option. This will protect the wireless client from attacks coming through the Internet.

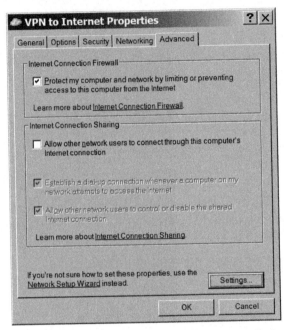

Figure 13-15: The Advanced tab controls the use of a firewall on the VPN.

The Options and Security tabs in the VPN to Internet Properties window control connection options that normally don't change from the default settings. Network managers who want to change the security settings should instruct their users on how to configure these options to comply with the network's specific requirements.

VPN Clients for Linux/Unix

Using a VPN client on a computer running Unix is more complicated than running a VPN from a Windows machine because the client is not integrated into the kernel. Therefore, you must find a client program that works with the version of Unix and the VPN protocol you're trying to use. No single program offers a universal VPN client, and some combinations, such as PPTP on BSD Unix versions, don't seem to exist at all.

Linux users, however, can choose from several IPsec implementations:

FreeS/WAN   *http://www.freeswan.org/*

pipsec   *http://perso.enst.fr/~beyssac/pipsec*

NIST Cerberus   *http://w3.antd.nist.gov/tools/cerberus/*

IPsec is included in the OpenBSD distribution. You can find a tutorial that explains how to use it at *http://tutorials.papamike.ca/pub/obsd_ipsec.html*.

The IPsec implementation for FreeBSD is at *http://www.r4k.net/ipsec/*. For information about NetBSD IPsec, take a look at *http://www.netbsd.org/Documentation/network/ipsec/*.

OpenVPN: A Cross-Platform Alternative

OpenVPN (*http://openvpn.net/*) is an open source VPN that does not use IPSec. It can operate on Windows, Mac OS X, Linux, and Unix. It's designed for ease of use and security, even through noisy or otherwise unreliable networks.

Using a VPN Through a Public Network

When you connect your laptop to your corporate LAN through a public network at an airport or in a conference center, or if you're using a broadband wireless service, you can connect through that network to the Internet and onward to your corporate VPN server. Because you'll have to log in to the public network before you initiate the VPN connection, you should create a separate *VPN via Public Network* connection profile in addition to the one you use from your own office. The profile should point to your corporate VPN server, but it should not be your default connection.

To connect through a public network on a computer running Windows, follow these steps:

1. Turn on the computer with the wireless network adapter in place.
2. Use your wireless configuration utility to select the public network you want to use.
3. Start Internet Explorer, Netscape Navigator, or another web browser. You will see the public network's login screen.
4. If the computer doesn't do it automatically, type your account name and password. The public network will acknowledge your login.
5. Minimize the browser window and open the **Network Connections** window or find the VPN shortcut on your desktop.
6. Double-click the icon for your VPN via Public Network profile. The computer will connect through the Internet to your corporate LAN.
7. Type the login and password for your corporate network.

VPNs are an important part of many networks' security plans for off-site users. With just a few keystrokes or mouse clicks, you can establish access to your network resources from anywhere with an Internet connection. If any Internet technique can eliminate the apparent distance between you and your LAN, your office, and your colleagues without sacrificing security, a virtual private network is that technique.

Wireless Security

Wireless networks are not secure. They are safe enough for many users most of the time, but it's just not possible to make a network that uses radio to exchange data absolutely private.

Wireless networks are a trade-off between security and convenience. The obvious benefits of a wireless network connection—fast and easy access to the network from a portable computer or an isolated location—come at a cost. For most users, the convenience of wireless operation outweighs the possible security threats. But just as you lock the doors of your car when you park it on the street, you should take similar steps to protect your network and your data.

The simple truth is that a wireless network uses radio signals with a well-defined set of characteristics, so somebody who wants to dedicate enough time and effort to monitoring those signals can probably find a way to intercept and read the data contained in them. If you send confidential information through a wireless link, an eavesdropper can copy them. Credit card numbers, account passwords, and other personal information are all vulnerable.

An entire catalog of tools for cracking Wi-Fi encryption methods is easy to find on the Internet. Although 3G broadband and WiMAX networks might be more secure than Wi-Fi (primarily because capturing data from them is more difficult), and WPA encryption is better than WEP encryption, no wireless security is perfect. Encryption and other security methods can make data a little more difficult to steal, but these methods don't provide complete protection against a really dedicated snoop. As any police officer will tell you, locks are great for keeping out honest people, but serious thieves know how to get past them.

To make things even more dangerous, many network managers and home wireless users leave the doors and windows to their networks wide open to intruders by failing to use encryption and the other security features that are built into every Wi-Fi access point and network node. "Drive-by logins" to unprotected private networks are possible in many urban and suburban business districts and in a surprising number of residential neighborhoods.

Most people have gotten the message about using encryption on their home and office networks, but too many of them are still using the older WEP encryption system rather than the much more secure WPA method. The technical support people at one major telephone company, Qwest, were still advising their DSL customers to use WEP encryption as late as mid-2007.

If you're located in a city center or a suburb, you can probably see this for yourself. When you use your Wi-Fi control program to scan the networks in your neighborhood, you will probably see a list of nearby networks in addition to your own access point. The control program will also tell you what kind of encryption (if any) each network is using. In the example shown in Figure 13-16, one network (RedGoldandGreen) is wide open, and four others are encrypted; two of the encrypted networks use WPA, and the two that are listed as "security-enabled" without an encryption type use WEP.

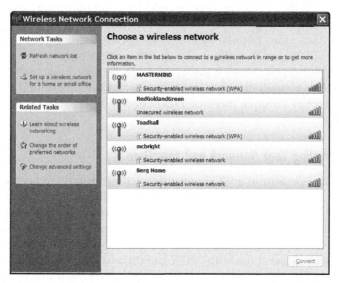

Figure 13-16: Four of the networks in this neighborhood require an encryption key before they will connect.

Do the math: Your access point can reach 150 feet or more in all directions, so the signal probably extends beyond your own property lines (or the walls of your apartment or office). A network device in the building next door or across the street can probably detect your network. If you don't take some precautions to prevent it, your neighbor, or somebody using a laptop or PDA inside a car parked on the street, can log in to your LAN, steal files from your servers, and tie up your Internet connection with streaming videos, multiplayer games, or worse.

It's important to understand that we're talking about two different kinds of security threats. The first is the danger of an outsider connecting to your network without your knowledge or permission; the second is the possibility that a dedicated eavesdropper can steal or modify data as you send and receive it. Each represents a different potential problem, and each requires a different approach to prevention and protection. While it's certainly true that none of the encryption tools currently available can provide complete protection, they can make life more difficult for most casual intruders. And as long as the tools are out there, you might as well use them.

An unsecured wireless network presents many opportunities to an attacker. Not only are the network crackers able to monitor any data that moves through the network, but they might also be able to modify that data. If, for example, your web browser has a vulnerability, an attacker can replace images as you view them with an image that exploits that vulnerability and installs a Trojan horse program on your computer, allowing the attacker to steal data stored on the computer, *even if you never sent that data over the wireless network.* This type of attack might be relatively rare (casual snoopers are unlikely to take the time to snoop around on the chance you have something interesting), but it still presents a real risk.

Also, many popular websites encrypt the login page with SSL encryption via HTTPS, but they don't encrypt subsequent pages to reduce the drain on processing power—your password might be secure, but any email you read via the web mail interface might not be, and attackers might be able to steal the *cookie* (a unique piece of data passed with web data) that identifies your login and open your mailbox directly.

Protecting Your Network and Your Data

As the operator of a Wi-Fi network, what can you do to keep outsiders out? You can employ a few techniques that can discourage them. First, you can accept the fact that wireless networks are not completely secure and use the built-in network security features to slow down would-be intruders; second, you can supplement your wireless router's built-in tools with a hardware or software firewall (or both) to isolate the wireless network; and third, you can use additional encryption such as a VPN to secure traffic to the network.

The security features of the early Wi-Fi protocols (WEP encryption) were not adequate to protect data. The wireless equivalent privacy (WEP) protocol had several serious flaws: The basic encryption method (the RC4 algorithm) was known to have weaknesses in certain applications, all users had to know the key, and no secure mechanisms for distributing new keys existed. Most of these shortcomings were acknowledged and dismissed as being outside the scope of providing the same protection that a user on a standard wired network would receive, but in fact, they meant that wireless equivalent privacy was little better than no protection at all. Recent attacks (such as those performed by the aircrack-ptw tool) have further undermined WEP because these tools have often been able to disclose an encryption key in a matter of minutes by analyzing a limited amount of traffic. With these developments, WEP should be treated more as a "do not disturb" sign than as a real means of protection.

The WPA and WPA2 standards attempt to fix the shortcomings of WEP, but they only work when all of the users of your network have modern cards and drivers. Most, if not all, network interfaces made in the last few years support WPA or WPA2.

For most of us, the more serious danger is not that people will eavesdrop on our messages but that they will create their own connection to your network and either read files stored on computers on the LAN or use your broadband connection to the Internet without your knowledge.

However, business networks must take extra precautions to protect their (and their customers') data. Several high-profile compromises of customer credit card data in major store chains have been traced to inadequate network protection.

Maintaining control of your network and keeping it secure is essential. "Wi-Fi Security" on page 89 includes a list of specific actions you can use to keep intruders out of your wireless network.

The security tools in the Wi-Fi specifications aren't perfect, but they're better than nothing. Even if you choose not to use them, it's essential to understand what they are and how they work, if only to turn them off.

Network Name

Every wireless network has a name. In a network with just one access point, the name is the basic service set ID (BSSID). When the network has more than one access point, the name becomes the extended service set ID (ESSID), but your computer's control program displays both types in the same list. The generic designation for all network names is the *service set ID (SSID)*, which is the term you will see most often in wireless access point and client configuration utility programs.

When you configure the access points for a network, you must specify the SSID for that network. Every access point and network client in a network must use the same SSID. When a network client detects two or more access points with the same SSID, it assumes that they are all part of the same network (even if the access points are operating on different radio channels), and the client associates with the access point that provides the strongest or cleanest signal. If that signal deteriorates due to interference or fading, the client will try to shift to another access point on what it thinks is the same network. This transfer is called a *handoff.*

If two different networks with overlapping signals have the same name, a client will assume that they're both part of a single network, and it might try to perform a handoff from one network to the other. From the user's point of view, this misdirected handoff will look like the network has completely dropped its connection. Therefore, every wireless network that could possibly overlap with another network must have a unique SSID.

The exceptions to the unique SSID rule are public and community networks that only provide access to the Internet but not to other computers or other devices on a LAN. Those networks often have a common SSID, so subscribers can detect and connect to them from more than one location. In other words, if you have an Internet access account at your local coffee shop, you might find and use exactly the same SSID when you visit another shop owned by the same company.

A network's SSID provides a very limited form of access control because it's necessary to specify the SSID when you set up a wireless connection. The SSID option in an access point is always a text field that will accept any name you care to assign, but many network configuration programs (including the wireless network tools in Windows XP and those supplied with several major brands of network adapters) automatically detect and display the SSIDs of every active network within their signal range.

It's not always necessary to know the SSID of a network before you try to connect; the configuration utility (or a network monitor or sniffer program like Network Stumbler) will show you the names of every nearby network in a list or a menu (the exceptions are networks in which the broadcast SSID feature has been turned off). For example, Figure 13-17 shows the result of a Network Stumbler scan at Seattle-Tacoma Airport, where Wayport served the passenger terminal and MobileStar provided coverage in the American Airlines VIP club.

WARNING *Every access point comes with a default SSID setting and password. These defaults are well known and documented within the community of network snoops (run a web search for* default SSID *to find several lists). Obviously, the defaults should never be used in any active network. Make sure you change the access point's administrative login and password while you're at it.*

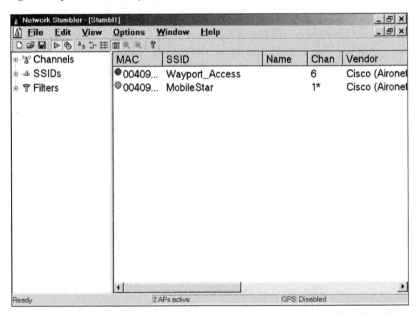

Figure 13-17: Network Stumbler and many configuration utilities display the SSIDs of every nearby wireless network.

Normally, most Wi-Fi access points send out beacon signals that broadcast the network's SSID. When a network adapter performs a radio scan, it detects those beacon signals and displays a list of nearby SSIDs in its control program. However, you can disable the SSID broadcast so the network doesn't show up on most control program scans. To connect a computer to a network whose name is not visible, you must instruct your control program to search for the SSID.

A nonbroadcast SSID is not completely invisible. A sniffer program (such as Network Stumbler) can still detect it and display the SSID, and every time a user connects to the network, the network adapter sends the SSID in a packet that can be easily sniffed. Disabling the SSID broadcast might, in some cases, make it easier for an attacker to later attack the laptop of one of your users (this is a more serious issue for businesses or corporate network administrators than for people running home networks). Because the laptop cannot know if the hidden network is available, it must constantly probe for the network, announcing its presence and giving an attacker much of the information needed to spoof the hidden network. Because a hidden network must be in a laptop's Preferred Networks list, the laptop will automatically connect to the spoofed network.

WEP Encryption

WEP encryption is an option in every Wi-Fi system, so it's important to know how it works, even if you choose not to use it. As the name suggests, the original intent of the wired equivalent privacy (WEP) protocol was to provide a level of security on wireless networks that was comparable to the security of a wired network. That was the goal, but a network that depends on WEP encryption is almost as vulnerable to intrusion as a network with no protection at all. WEP will keep out the casual snoops (and your free-loading neighbors, if they're not particularly adept at cracking encryption), but WEP is not particularly effective against a dedicated intruder. The more recent WPA encryption is always the better choice.

WEP encryption is intended to serve three functions: It prevents unauthorized access to the network; it performs an integrity check on each packet; and it protects the data from eavesdroppers. WEP uses a secret encryption key to encode data packets before a network client or an access point transmits them, and it uses the same key to decode packets after it receives them. The original standard used shared authentication, in which the access point sends a challenge packet that a client must encrypt with the proper WEP key and send back. However, this opens a significant vulnerability by allowing a snooper to watch both parts of the exchange and derive the key.

The "open" authentication method, which should be used by any network using WEP (not that any network should use WEP), simply discards packets that cannot be decrypted by the network's WEP key. Therefore, the WEP settings must be exactly the same on every access point and client adapter in the network. This sounds simple enough, but it can get confusing because manufacturers use different methods to identify the size and format of a WEP key. The functions don't change from one brand to another, but identical settings don't always have identical descriptions.

How Many Bits in Your Encryption Key?

A WEP key can have either 64 bits or 128 bits. Although 128-bit keys are more difficult to crack (but they are still pretty insecure), they also increase the amount of time needed to transmit each packet. However, confusion arises because a 40-bit WEP key is the same as a 64-bit WEP key, and a 104-bit key is the same as a 128-bit key. The standard 64-bit WEP key is a string that includes an internally generated 24-bit initialization vector and a 40-bit secret key assigned by the network manager. Some manufacturers' specifications and configuration programs call this *64-bit encryption*, but others describe it as *40-bit encryption*. Either way, the encryption scheme is the same, so an adapter that uses 40-bit encryption is fully compatible with an access point or another adapter that uses 64-bit encryption.

Many network adapters and access points also include a *strong encryption* option that uses a 128-bit key. Devices that support strong encryption are downward compatible with 64-bit encryption, but compatibility is not automatic, so all of the devices on a mixed network of 128-bit and 64-bit devices will operate at 64 bits. If your access point and all of your adapters accept 128-bit encryption, use a 128-bit key. But if you want your network to be compatible with adapters and access points that only recognize 64-bit encryption, set the entire network to use 64-bit keys.

In practice, the choice of 64- or 128-bit WEP encryption doesn't make much difference. Tools are easily available that can crack both types, although cracking a 128-bit key might take a bit longer.

Is Your Key ASCII or Hex?

The length of the key is not the only confusing thing about setting WEP encryption. Some programs request the key as a string of ASCII characters, but many others want the key in hexadecimal (hex) numbers. Still others can generate the key from an optional passphrase.

Each ASCII character has 8 bits, so a 40-bit (or 64-bit) WEP key contains 5 characters, and a 104-bit (or 128-bit) key has 13 characters. In hex, each character uses 4 bits, so a 40-bit key has 10 hex characters, and a 128-bit key has 26 characters. In Figure 13-18, the Wireless Setting screen for a D-Link access point, the 40-bit Shared Key Security field uses hex characters, so it has space for 10 characters. The D-Link program runs all 10 characters together in a single string, but some others split them into 5 sets of 2 digits or 2 sets of 5. The key looks the same to the computer either way, but copying the string when it's broken apart is easier.

A passphrase is a string of text that the adapters and access points automatically convert to a string of hex characters. Because humans can generally remember actual words or phrases more easily than hex gibberish, a passphrase can be easier to distribute than a hex string. However, a passphrase is only useful when all the adapters and access points in a network come from the same manufacturer.

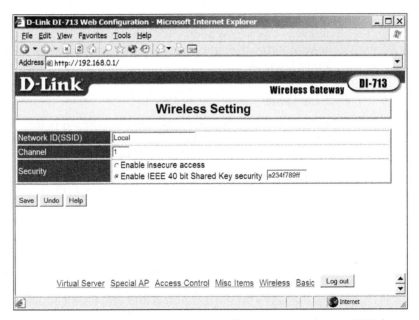

Figure 13-18: The configuration utility for a D-Link access point accepts WEP keys in hex format.

What Are the Options?

Like just about everything else in a Wi-Fi configuration utility, the names of the encryption options are not consistent from one program to the next. Some programs use a straightforward set of options such as "enable WEP (or WPA) encryption," but others use technical language taken from the formal 802.11 specification.

Some access points also offer a shared key authentication option that uses encryption when a network client has the key but uses unencrypted data with other network nodes.

Mixing Hex and ASCII Keys

Setting up a mixed network becomes more complicated when some network nodes use hex only and others require ASCII keys. If that's the situation on your network, you will want to follow these rules for setting the encryption keys:

- Convert all your ASCII keys to hex. If a configuration program demands an ASCII key, enter the characters *0x* (zero followed by lowercase letter *x*), followed by the hex string. If you're using Apple's AirPort software, you'll have to enter a dollar sign (*$*) at the beginning of a hex key.

- Make sure all your encryption keys have exactly the right number of characters.

- If all else fails, read the security sections of the manuals for your network adapters and access points. It's possible that one or more of the devices in your network might have some obscure proprietary feature that you don't know about.

WPA Encryption

WPA encryption was developed as a partial solution to the security problems that make WEP encryption less than totally secure. WPA is much safer than WEP, but cracking WPA is still possible.

WPA is more secure because it uses a method called *Temporal Key Integrity Protocol (TKIP)* to automatically change the encryption key after a specified period of time or after the system exchanges a specific number of packets. Because WPA changes the key frequently, it's a lot more difficult for a cracker to gather enough information to decipher its encryption code.

In large networks, WPA uses an authentication server to verify the identity of each network user. The server uses Remote Authentication Dial-in User Service (RADIUS) and Extensible Authentication Protocol (EAP) to exchange encryption keys with the computers and other devices that are connected to the wireless network.

In home networks and smaller business networks that don't have a server, a method called *pre-shared key (PSK) mode* uses a passphrase stored in the access point in place of the authentication server. To connect to the network, users must enter the same passphrase on their computer or other network device (or set their device to automatically enter the passphrase). When you set up WPA encryption, you must specify whether the network uses a server or PSK mode.

Any access point and network adapter that supports 802.11g or 802.11n should also recognize WPA encryption. If you're using an older 802.11b or 802.11a access point, you might be able to add WPA encryption by installing the latest version of firmware and drivers. Look in the support or downloads section of the manufacturer's website for free upgrade instructions and software.

PSK Passphrases

A WPA-PSK passphrase can be a string of either 8 to 63 ASCII characters or 64 hexadecimal digits. The passphrase that you enter into a network device must be exactly the same as the one stored in the access point. Obviously, typing 64 digits correctly is not something that you want to do frequently, so the ASCII alternative is the better choice for most users. For optimal security, the ASCII passphrase you assign to your network should be a random mixture of at least 20 characters including letters (capitals and lowercase), numbers, and punctuation marks.

A PSK network uses the passphrase to set up the initial connection between a client (such as a computer or PDA) and the access point. After the connection is in place, the TKIP assigns new encryption keys to every packet or group of packets. The PSK combines with your network SSID to calculate the final key value. Choosing a unique SSID and a strong passphrase is important.

Attackers can build large tables of SSID and PSK pairs for common network names and dictionary words, performing weeks of calculation once with the payoff of nearly instantly determining the key of any network that matches that pair of values. Choosing strong passphrases and unique SSIDs can mitigate this attack.

Using WPA Encryption

When you set up a new network, the security section of the access point's configuration software will ask if you want to use encryption, and if so, whether you want WEP or WPA encryption. Unless you're planning to run an open access network, you should choose WPA.

In many cases, the access point will offer two or more types of WPA encryption. If your network includes a RADIUS server, choose EAP. If the network has no encryption server, use the WPA-TKIP option.

For a network user, providing a WPA key is just as easy as providing a WEP key. Most network adapters made in the last couple of years automatically recognize the type of encryption embedded in each Wi-Fi signal that they detect, so the control program might ask for an encryption key without specifying whether it's a WEP key or a WPA key.

Attacking WPA Security

It was probably inevitable that somebody would take the added security features in WPA encryption as a challenge and develop a WPA cracking tool.

Several such tools are out there, so WPA does not provide the impenetrable protection that some of its proponents might want you to believe. In particular, programs called coWPAtty and Aircrack-ng both use *dictionary attacks* on WPA-TKIP networks to try thousands or millions of possible keys until they find the correct one. Fortunately, neither of these programs nor any of the others aimed at cracking WPA encryption are easy to use, and cracking a network can take a lot of time, so successful attacks on WPA are not particularly common. This technique takes time because the programs can only try about 50 different encryption keys per second, but eventually they will find the right passphrase and connect to the target network. Because each additional letter, number, or other character in a key increases the key's complexity, a long key takes much longer to crack than a short one. However, a commercial product called Elcomsoft Distributed Password Recovery uses graphics processors on video cards to "break Wi-Fi encryption up to 100 times faster than by using CPU only," so even a relatively long key is not that secure.

Completely protecting yourself against attacks might not be possible or practical, but a long passphrase that includes random numbers and punctuation marks is still a better choice than a string of words or numbers alone.

In other words, something like *hdt%mzx33wolf$fgilxxq&#smedbxor* is a better passphrase than *nostarchpressbooks*. But the only truly secure way to use Wi-Fi is to combine it with VPN encryption.

Access Control (MAC Authentication)

Most access points include an option that permits the network manager to restrict access to a specific list of client adapters. If a network device with a MAC address that does not appear on the list of authorized users tries to connect, the access point will not accept the request to associate with the network. This option can keep intruders from connecting to a wireless LAN, but it forces the network administrator to keep a complete list of users' adapters and their MAC address. Every time a new user wants to join the network, and every time an established user swaps adapters or gets a new laptop, PDA, or other device with a built-in adapter, the network manager must add one more MAC address to the list. This task is probably manageable in a home or small office network, but it could be a major undertaking for a larger corporate or campus-wide system, if it's practical at all.

MAC authentication does not provide unbreakable protection against unauthorized users because a determined cracker could monitor radio signals from approved users, intercept their adapters' MAC addresses, and load an approved address onto a different adapter. But combined with encryption and other security tools, authentication adds one more impediment in the path of a network cracker.

Every access point configuration utility uses a different format for its access lists. The manual and online documentation supplied with your access point should provide detailed instructions for creating and maintaining an access control list.

The Wi-Fi standards do not specify a maximum size for an access point's access control list, so the numbers are all over the map. Some access points limit the list to a few dozen entries, but others, such as the Proxim Harmony AP Controller, will support as many as 10,000 separate addresses. Still others accept an effectively unlimited number. If you plan to use a list of addresses to control access to your network, make sure your access point will work with a large enough list to support all of your users, with enough expansion space for future growth. As a rule of thumb, the access point should accept at least twice as many MAC addresses as the number of users on your network today.

Some access points also include a MAC address exclusion feature that allows the network manager to block one or more MAC addresses from access to the network.

Physical Security

Intruders don't always use technology to crack into a network. Sometimes they use brute-force methods. For example, if a thief steals your laptop computer, he can often use the "convenience" features of the computer's software to connect to the Internet through your network, read your email and other confidential files, and gain access to other computers connected to the same network. Other low-tech methods include *shoulder surfing*, where the bad guy watches your screen or your keyboard as you type a login name and password, and *social engineering*, in which the intruder convinces you to reveal your password or other information because she has convinced you that she has a legitimate use for it.

There are some things you can do to protect your computer and the data stored in it:

- Think like a thief and do whatever might be necessary to make the computer difficult to steal. Don't leave your laptop in plain sight in an unattended car, or walk away from it in a public location such as a coffee shop, airport, or library. In an office with cubicles or "open plan" workspaces, use a chain and lock to secure the computer to a desk, file cabinet, or other large object if you can't store it in a locked drawer or cabinet.

- Don't place your computer near a window where passers-by can see exactly what you have.

- When you're away from home or work, keep track of your laptop computer at all times.

- Log off your office computer whenever you are about to leave your desk. Don't allow other people to wander in and use your account when you're not there.

- Keep the login and password active on your laptop, and use encryption for files that contain confidential data. If somebody does steal the computer, you want it to be as difficult as possible for the thief to open and read your files.

- Install an antitheft alarm device on a PC card in your laptop or an internal card in a desktop system. If somebody tries to move the computer, disconnect cables, or open the case without entering a security code first, the alarm device will sound a very loud alarm.

- Use a tracking program such as LostPC (*http://www.lostpc.com/*) on your laptop computer. The tracking software will automatically send a "here I am" signal to a security center every time it connects to the Internet from a new location. Police and Internet service providers can sometimes use this information to locate and recover a stolen computer.

- Consider using full-disk encryption tools such as TrueCrypt for Windows or dm-crypt for Linux, so the data on it is useless if your laptop is stolen.

Windows Update and Patches

Microsoft distributes security updates and patches through the Internet at least once every month that include fixes for newly discovered security problems. You can manually check for updates and select the ones that you want to install, but it's a lot easier to let Windows automatically check for newly released update packages and install them for you. As network manager, you will want to set all the Windows computers on your network to run Automatic Updates.

To run Automatic Updates, follow these steps:

1. Right-click **My Computer** and select **Properties** from the pop-up menu. The System Properties window will appear.

2. Choose the **Automatic Updates** tab from the System Properties window. The dialog shown in Figure 13-19 will appear.

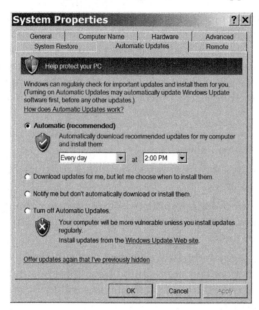

Figure 13-19: Use the Automatic Updates tab in System Properties to turn on Windows Update.

3. Choose an option to set the way your computer will handle new updates. In most cases, the Automatic option is the best choice, but if you're using this computer for programs that require most of the system's processing power, such as sound or video recording, select the Notify me but don't automatically download or install them option instead.

4. Click **OK** to save your settings and close the System Properties window.

Automatic Updates loads changes that somebody at Microsoft has flagged as essential to the computer's performance or security, but it ignores many others, including new versions of device drivers and updates that add or improve other features for Windows and some related programs. To find and select these programs, follow these steps:

1. If you aren't already connected to the Internet, connect your computer now.

2. From the Start menu, choose **Windows Update**. You can also find a link to this command in Internet Explorer's Tools menu.

3. After the Update website confirms that it has installed the software it uses to scan your computer, the site displays the Welcome screen shown in Figure 13-20. Click the **Custom** button.

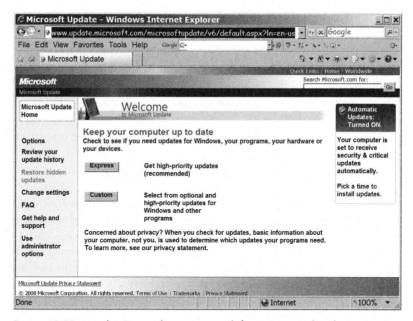

Figure 13-20: Use the Custom button to search for nonessential updates.

4. After the program completes its search for new programs, it will display a list like the one shown in Figure 13-21. Use the list of update types in the left column to display a list of available updates in each category. Don't forget to scroll down the list to see all the categories.

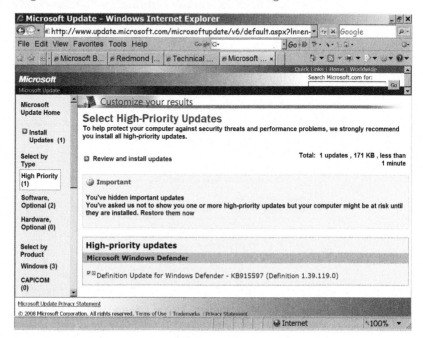

Figure 13-21: The list of update types (left) shows the number of updates available for each category.

5. Choose the updates you want to install in each category from the right panel. The number in parentheses next to *Install Updates* in the left panel shows the number of updates you have selected.

6. Click **Install Updates**. The Review and Install Updates panel will appear on the right side of the window.

7. Click the **Install Updates** button. The update program will load the updates you have selected, one at a time. If necessary, the Update routine will restart the computer to complete one or more updates.

Microsoft Baseline Security Analyzer

Microsoft's Baseline Security Analyzer is a free tool that scans computers running Windows XP and Windows Vista to identify security threats and vulnerable features and functions. You can download it from *http://technet .microsoft.com/en-us/security/cc184924.aspx*. You can use the Baseline Security Analyzer to scan your own computer, or as network manager, you can test other computers connected to yours through your LAN. Baseline Security Analyzer provides a quick and easy way to find and fix many common security issues.

Figure 13-22 shows the result of a Baseline Security Analyzer scan. For each item it identifies, you can click a link to an explanation (What was scanned) and instructions for correcting the problem.

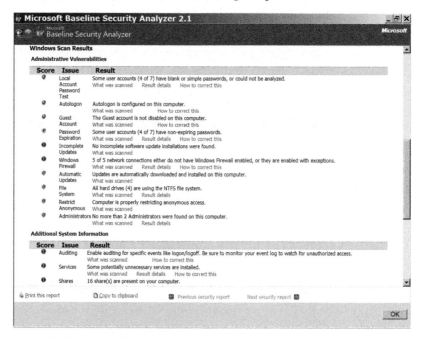

Figure 13-22: Microsoft Baseline Security Analyzer finds potential security problems and offers instructions for fixing them.

Controlling Your Own Users

As manager of your home or business network, remember that you're responsible for the security of the whole network and all the computers connected to it. Whenever it's practical, do whatever you can to encourage all your users to pay attention to security. Even if it seems easier to run their computers "wide open" without proper security measures, you are responsible for convincing them to keep their computers safe.

Denial of Service Attacks

A *denial of service (DoS)* attack occurs when your network receives a very large number of incoming connection attempts that overloads the network's capacity to respond. The volume of traffic forces the computers and routers in the network to operate at or beyond their capacity, which causes them to either flood the network with useless traffic, disrupt connections among machines, or completely disrupt network service. For example, a *mail bomb* attack might generate tens of thousands of useless email messages.

A DoS attack can make it impossible to do anything else on the network, or it can block legitimate incoming traffic, such as requests for access to a web server or exchange of email. Most DoS attacks are aimed at large businesses, government agencies, and educational institutions, so they're not a common problem for home or small business networks. Even so, it's important to know how to recognize DoS attacks and how to deal with them.

US-CERT, the United States Computer Emergency Readiness Team, has identified three basic types of DoS attack: consumption of limited resources, destruction or alteration of configuration information, and physical destruction or alteration of network components. If your small network suffers a DoS attack, you're likely to see a significant deterioration of network performance—or even a complete breakdown.

If somebody decides to target your network with a DoS attack, you can't do much to discourage them. Therefore, your best protection is to turn on the built-in filters in your firewall and modem, install all the latest security patches to your software and network hardware, and work closely with your Internet service provider at the first sign that your network is under attack. Most ISPs have more sophisticated monitoring and filtering resources that can help them identify and interrupt an attack.

In the United States, DoS attacks are a violation of federal law, so it's appropriate to ask your local FBI field office for assistance in finding and prosecuting the source of an attack.

Conclusion

As manager of a home or small business network, maintaining its safety and security is one of your primary responsibilities. The methods outlined in this chapter, combined with some commonsense attention, will allow you and your users to concentrate on the business (and recreational) use of your computer, your network, and the Internet.

14

PRINTERS AND OTHER DEVICES ON YOUR NETWORK

One of the benefits that a network brings to a small business or a household full of computer users is the convenience of sharing one or more printers among all the network's users. Rather than carrying a copy of each file to the computer connected to the printer on a disk or a flash drive, you can simply click the Print command on your own computer and let the network send it to the printer automatically.

Even a very small network might include more than one printer. For example, you might use a black-and-white laser printer for routine documents and reports, a color inkjet or laser printer for fancy presentations and school projects, and a special-purpose color printer for digital photos. If you have more than one printer, you can select the best printer for each job. Each of these printers might be located in a different room, close to the person who uses it most often, or in a central room where they're equally accessible to all of your network's users.

How to Connect a Printer to Your Network

You can connect a printer to a network in several ways: You can use an external printer server, a server built in to your printer, or an automatic switch connected directly to each printer, or you can connect through a computer. All of these methods accomplish the same thing: They send a formatted document or image to a printer that produces a paper copy. The best method for connecting a printer to your network depends on your budget, what's convenient for you, and the layout of your network.

External Printer Servers

An *external network printer server* is a device that connects to the network as a separate network node with an Ethernet port and provides either a parallel port connection or a USB connection to a stand-alone printer. Figure 14-1 shows a printer connected to a network through an external printer server.

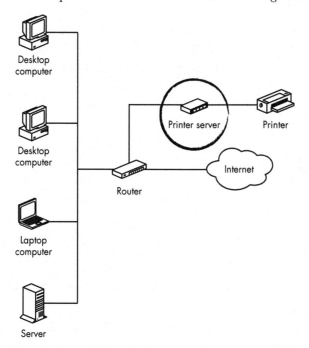

Figure 14-1: An external printer server connects a printer to a network using a parallel port or a USB port.

NOTE *When you shop for a printer server, look for one that uses the same type of printer port as your printer. Most modern printers have USB ports, but older units with parallel ports are still common. If your printer has both USB and parallel ports, use the USB port.*

External printer servers are a good choice when your network includes computers in more than one room and you have at least one spare port on the network hub or router. You can run an Ethernet cable to the server unit directly from the hub in the same room or from an unused wall outlet in another room. If you don't have enough Ethernet ports in the room where you want to place the printer server, connect the computer and the printer server to the network through an inexpensive Ethernet data switch, as shown in Figure 14-2.

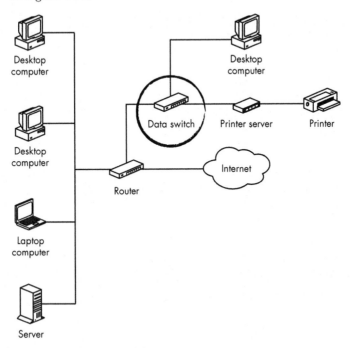

Figure 14-2: If you don't have a spare network outlet for a printer server, use a small Ethernet data switch.

NOTE *When you install Ethernet cables for your home or small business network, consider the locations where you might want to install a printer. Run an extra Ethernet cable between that room and your network hub, and use a wall outlet plate (or surface mount box) with two or more RJ-45 jacks. Use a different color jack for each outlet to make it easier to identify them at a glance.*

Adding a printer server to your network is similar to adding a computer, except that you'll have to configure the printer server remotely from a computer. The usual routine is to connect the server to the network and the printer to the server and then use a web-based configuration utility to set the server's network address and other options. Follow the instructions supplied with the server to load the printer driver.

Another advantage of using a printer connected directly to the network is that it operates independently of the other computers on the network. When a printer connects through a computer, that computer must be on all the time or you have to create a "public" account that the rest of the family or office can use to print. This setup is a lot less secure than printing through a server.

Wi-Fi Printer Servers

If your network already includes a Wi-Fi access point, you can use a Wi-Fi printer server to connect your printer to the network. The printer server should automatically detect the Wi-Fi signal from your access point and establish a two-way connection (data in and printer status out) between the printer and the computer that originated the print request. The Wi-Fi link should use all the same security tools (such as WPA encryption) as your other Wi-Fi connections.

A Wi-Fi printer shares the same wireless channel with other Wi-Fi links on your network, so a large document might slow down the network's performance, but slow performance is not likely to be an issue unless your network carries a *lot* of traffic. You can solve this problem by adding a second access point that uses a different channel and dedicating that access point to one or more printers.

WARNING *When you set up the Wi-Fi link, make sure you connect the printer server to your own access point and not to a network owned by one of your neighbors.*

A Wi-Fi printer server offers the following benefits:

- The printer may be located anywhere within range of your Wi-Fi network signal.
- You don't need a dedicated Ethernet port for the printer server.
- If you need to move the printer, you don't have to rewire the network.

Built-In Printer Servers

When you buy a new printer for your network, consider one that has a built-in network printer server along with the usual USB and/or parallel ports. The built-in printer server will perform like a printer connected through an external printer server, but it's easier to install because you don't have to connect additional cables.

Printers with built-in network interfaces are designed for small businesses and other workgroups that often produce a greater number of printed pages than a typical home network or a single user. They're often a bit more expensive than the combination of a low-end, stand-alone printer and a separate printer server device, because they're generally more durable printers with more and better features. But if your network's users print enough pages to justify a workgroup printer, the added cost will often pay for better performance.

Automatic Printer Switches

When two or more of your computers are located in the same room or adjacent rooms, an automatic printer switch might be a less expensive alternative to a network printer server. As the name suggests, an automatic switch detects print requests from two or more input connectors and automatically forwards them to the printer, and the switch returns status information from the printer back to the computer that originated the request. When it receives more than one print request at the same time, the printer switch sends the first one to the printer and holds the other requests in a buffer until the first one has completed printing. As far as each computer attached to the switch is concerned, the printer is connected directly to that computer.

A printer switch is less practical when the computers on your network are in rooms that are far apart, because a cable must run from each computer to the switch.

Using a Computer as a Printer Server

The alternative to a printer server for a network that extends beyond more than one or two rooms is to connect the printer directly to one of the network computers and send print requests from all the other computers through that one.

This approach has several advantages:

- You can use any printer connected to your computer.
- You don't need a separate printer server device or a printer with a built-in network server.
- You can locate a printer anywhere, not just where you have a free network port or outlet.
- On a network where different users have different types of printers (such as laser and inkjet, color and black-and-white, or special formats for photos or large documents), using a computer as a printer server allows everyone to take advantage of each printer's features.
- You don't need an additional port on the network hub or router.

On the other hand, this approach also has a few possible drawbacks:

- The computer acting as a printer server must be turned on whenever anybody wants to print; this could be a security issue.
- When the printer begins to print without warning, it could distract the person using the computer connected to the printer.
- As other users come into the office or workspace where the printer is located to collect their print jobs, this can be yet another distraction for the operator of the computer acting as a printer server.

If your network also uses a dedicated file server, you can eliminate the security and distraction issues by using the same computer as your network's printer server. Or if you have an older computer collecting dust in a closet, you can use it as a stand-alone printer server (although you might have to add a network interface and maybe a USB port on plug-in expansion cards). However, the most common way to use a computer as a printer server is to connect the printer to an existing computer and direct print commands from all the other computers in the network to print through the server.

In Windows, setting up a printer server is a three-step process, described in the following sections.

Turning on Printer Sharing on the Network Card

Follow these steps to turn on printer sharing on your network interface:

1. From the Control Panel, select **Network Connections**. The Network Connections window will open.

2. Right-click **Local Area Connection** and select **Properties** from the pop-up menu. To share through your wireless connection, right-click **Wireless Network Connection**.

3. Confirm that the File and Printer Sharing for Microsoft Networks option is active, as shown in Figure 14-3. If you don't see a checkmark next to this option, check the box to turn it on.

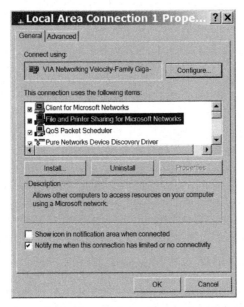

Figure 14-3: File and Printer Sharing for Microsoft
Networks must be active for you to share access to
a printer.

4. Click **OK** to save your settings and close the Properties window.

Instructing the Computer Acting as a Printer Server to Share the Printer

Follow these steps to share a printer:

1. From the Control Panel, select **Printers and Faxes** (in Windows XP) or **Printers** (in Windows Vista). A window that contains links to all of the printers and virtual printers connected to this computer will open.

2. Right-click the printer you want to share with the network. A pop-up menu will appear.

3. Select **Sharing** from the pop-up menu. The Properties dialog for that printer will open with the Sharing tab visible, as shown in Figure 14-4.

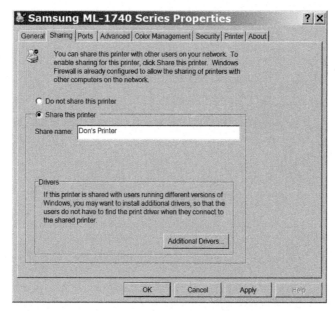

Figure 14-4: Use the Sharing tab of the printer's Properties dialog to turn on sharing.

4. In Windows XP, select the **Share this printer** option. In Vista, click the **Change sharing options** button, click **Continue** in the User Account Control window, and then select **Share this printer**.

5. In the Share name field, type a name that identifies this printer, such as **Don's Printer**.

In Windows Vista, the Sharing tab includes an option to render print jobs on client computers. If the other computers on the network use Windows XP or some other operating system, leave this option turned off. But if other Vista computers will be sending print jobs to this printer, you can speed up the printer's performance by checking this option.

Installing the Printer on Each Computer

After you set up the computer acting as a printer server to accept print jobs through your network, you must also add the server to each computer's list of printers. Follow these steps to add a network printer in Windows XP:

1. From the Control Panel, select **Printers and Faxes**. The Printers window will open.

2. Double-click **Add a Printer** to open the Add Printer Wizard. The Welcome screen will appear.

3. Click **Next**. The Local or Network Printer screen will appear.

4. Select the network printer option and click **Next**. The Browse for Printer screen shown in Figure 14-5 will appear, along with a list of shared printers connected to this network.

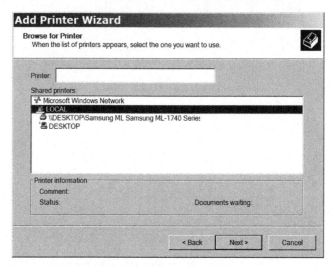

Figure 14-5: The Browse for Printer screen shows a list of all the shared printers connected to this network.

5. Select the name of the printer you want to use and click **Next**. The wizard will ask if you want to use this printer as the default.

6. If you want this computer to send print jobs to this printer as the default, click Yes. If you want it to appear in a menu as a secondary choice, click No.

7. Click **Next**. The wizard will confirm that you have added the printer to this computer's list.

8. Click **Finish** to complete the wizard and close the window. The name of the newly added printer should be visible in the Printers (or Printers and Faxes) window.

The process is similar in Windows Vista, but the Add a printer command is in the toolbar directly above the window, as shown in Figure 14-6.

1. Click **Add a printer**.

2. Click the **Add a network, wireless or Bluetooth printer** option. The wizard will display a list of all shared printers and printer servers connected to this network.

3. Select the printer you want to use from this computer and click **Next**.

4. The wizard will add this printer to your list.

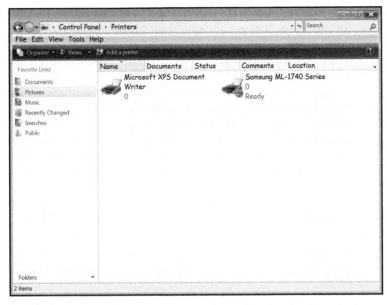

Figure 14-6: The Add a printer icon is on the toolbar directly above the Printers window.

CUPS: The Common Unix Printing System

CUPS is a printer control program for Unix and Linux systems that converts page descriptions from application programs (such as a word processor or a web browser) to the specific instructions used by individual printers. If printing from your Unix or Linux distribution requires complicated command-line instructions, CUPS can provide an easier solution; look for a free download from *http://www.cups.org/*. A CUPS driver for Windows is also available as an extension to the PostScript driver supplied with Windows. It's available at *http://www.cups.org/windows*. CUPS can print to a printer connected directly to your own computer, or through a network to a printer server.

All-in-One Devices

Most offices perform several different paper-handling activities: copying, printing, scanning, and faxing. All of these activities use some combination of the same core functions, so it often makes sense to combine several activities in a single machine that can send a digital file or scanned image to either paper or another digital file. The category of device that combines these functions is called, rather grandly, an *all-in-one device*, or simply an *all-in-one*. An all-in-one device almost always costs less and occupies less space than a separate printer, scanner, copier, and fax machine; however, the large number of features and functions often means that it's more difficult to operate than a simple single-function device.

Figure 14-7 is a functional flow chart that shows the types of sources and destinations that an all-in-one device can handle. The device can receive an image from a computer or through a telephone line, or it can create a digital copy of a physical image (such as a printed page, a transparency, or a small object placed on the surface of a scanner). The device can send the digital image to any of several different destinations: a printer, a computer file, or a distant fax machine. If your all-in-one device also includes a network interface, you can use it to accept print jobs or outgoing faxes through an Ethernet network, and you can send scanned images and incoming faxes to any of the computers connected to the same network. Some all-in-ones can also send images through the Internet as email attachments.

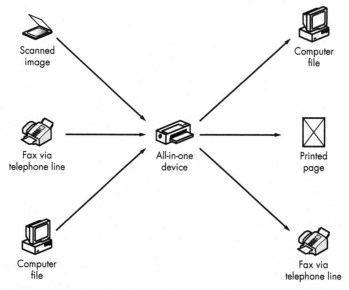

Scanned image

Computer file

Fax via telephone line

All-in-one device

Printed page

Computer file

Fax via telephone line

Figure 14-7: An all-in-one device can obtain images from different sources and send them to any of several destinations.

Each of the all-in-one's activities is a specific combination of input and output:

Scanning	Goes from a scanned image to a computer file
Copying	Goes from a scanned image to a printed page
Printing	Goes from a computer file to a printed page
Incoming fax	Goes from a telephone line to a printed page or computer file
Outgoing fax	Goes from a scanned image or a computer file to a telephone line

Computers connected to the network treat an all-in-one device like each of the separate devices. The printer shows up in the menu that Windows, Mac OS, or Linux/Unix displays when you want to print a document; like any other printer, you must add it to each computer's printer list and load a printer driver on that computer. The scanner uses either a TWAIN or WIA interface to import images directly into application programs, and fax programs detect the all-in-one as a fax machine. The copier function sends the scanned image directly to the printer, so it doesn't show up on the network.

An all-in-one that is not intended for full network operation can still operate as a networked printer. However, it's possible that the scanner and fax functions will only work from the computer connected directly to the all-in-one unit. As a rule of thumb, you can assume that an all-in-one that connects directly to the network through an Ethernet port will support all of its functions from any computer on the network. But if the unit connects to a printer through a USB port, it might not accept commands from remote computers.

Installing an all-in-one is like installing a printer: Connect the USB connector to the computer you want to use as a printer server, or connect the Ethernet port directly to the network hub or router. If the server doesn't automatically detect the all-in-one device, load the software supplied with the device. If all else fails, follow the installation instructions supplied with the all-in-one device.

15

OTHER THINGS YOU CAN CONNECT TO YOUR NETWORK
AUDIO, VIDEO, HOME ENTERTAINMENT, AND BEYOND

If you can convert information to digital data, you can transmit that data through a network and either convert it back to its original form or use it as input data for a computer. With the right kind of input and output devices, you can use the same network that shares computer resources to monitor and control industrial processes, listen to sound from a microphone or watch images from a camera, distribute audio and video through your home or business, and operate equipment by remote control. And if the network is connected to the Internet, you can do all those things to or from anywhere with an Internet connection.

Many of these network applications are extremely specialized (such as monitoring the temperature of the water in a stream), but others are often practical for a home or small business network. For example, you can use your network to watch or listen to activity in another room or to distribute audio and video files from an entertainment server to speakers and video displays in several locations around your home. This chapter explains how to connect and use additional devices with your network.

Using a Microphone and Camera with Your Network

A microphone connected to a computer or audio server can capture sounds and convert them into digital audio files. A camera (known as a *webcam*) can capture images that a computer or server can convert to still or moving image files. An audio or video server can be either a computer with an internal or external microphone or a camera (or both) or a stand-alone device that connects directly to the network. When another computer receives the same audio and/or video files through a network, it can display the images on a display monitor and play the sounds through one or more speakers or through a pair of headphones.

One widely used remote webcam service is the familiar online traffic monitor, like the one shown in Figure 15-1.

Figure 15-1: A traffic webcam uses a networked camera. This one shows cars and pedestrians on the Brooklyn Bridge.

Internal and External Controllers

A video camera can connect to a network through a controller mounted inside a computer on a plug-in PCI expansion card or as an external USB device. The controller scans the light-sensitive portion of the camera from side to side and from top to bottom at a constant rate; when it reaches the end of one row, the controller automatically moves on to the next row; when it reaches the end of the bottom row, the controller returns to the top.

At some point in the signal chain, the analog image from the camera's lens converts to a continuous digital data stream; in most cases, this occurs inside the camera itself, but some equipment might perform the analog-to-digital conversion in the controller card. As an alternative, a camera captures still images one at a time and stores them or transmits them through the network as a series of image files.

NOTE *Many camera controller cards include two or more camera inputs. In general, a multiple-input card costs more than a single-input card with similar image quality and performance.*

The computer can use a sound card or a USB or FireWire port to handle audio in a similar manner. The sound card accepts analog audio directly from a microphone or through an external amplifier, mixing desk, or other source; the USB port receives digital audio from an external analog-to-digital converter.

After the computer receives one or more video streams, audio streams, or still pictures, it can do the following:

- Store them on a hard drive or other mass storage device
- Display the pictures on the computer's video monitor as "live" images
- Play the sound stream through the computer's speakers or through headphones plugged into the computer
- Incorporate them into another program or document, such as a web page or a word-processing document
- Transmit them through the computer's network connection

The alternative to a camera connected to a networked computer is a *network webcam*—a camera and control unit that connects directly to the network as a separate node. A typical network webcam includes a remote control program on a web page that a user can operate through the network, or, with the correct set of passwords and authorization, through the Internet. Depending on each camera unit's specific features, the remote control might allow an operator to zoom the image in and out, rotate or tilt the camera, or choose a different image through the same control unit. Some network webcams also include a wireless network interface that can connect to the network through a Wi-Fi base station.

Networked Cameras and Microphones

Attaching a camera to your network—with or without a microphone at the same location—can add many useful features and functions. Anyplace where you want or need a distant set of eyes and ears, you can install a camera, a microphone, or both. Here are some examples:

Surveillance monitors   One or more cameras aimed at unattended entryways, corridors, and other locations can transmit pictures to a distant computer's video display monitor.

Baby monitors   A networked computer with a camera and microphone in a nursery or child's room can replace a conventional baby monitor transmitter unit. You can keep an eye on the baby while you work— through a small window on your desktop that contains the image from the camera in the other room.

Live conversations   When both parties have a webcam and microphone connected to their computer, it's easy to conduct a "face to face" conversation through the network.

Remote conferencing   One or more participants in a meeting or conference can participate from a remote location.

Home Entertainment Networks

A home entertainment system can distribute music, TV, movies, and other audio and video through the same network that connects your household computers to one another and to the Internet. Over-the-air, cable, or satellite TV and radio, music from a CD player or stored on a hard drive, and videos from DVDs can all provide source material for a system that can play music or display video in any room with a network connection.

There's a whole industry out there that supports very expensive home entertainment systems, complete with video-screening rooms (the high-tech popcorn maker is optional at extra cost), TV screens built into walls or rising out of hidden cabinets in the kitchen or bedroom, multiple speakers in every room, and preprogrammed mood lighting. But unless you have a spare $10,000 or $20,000 (or more—a *lot* more) to spend on fancy equipment and custom installation, those systems are not particularly practical. Most of us will have to settle (!) for something considerably less extravagant. If you've already wired your house or apartment for a data network, you can add an entertainment server and connect stereos or TVs in several rooms without spending a small fortune. You can also connect entertainment devices to your network in stages, rather than spend a lot of money at one time.

A tremendous variety of equipment and services is available that can fit within the home entertainment systems category, but for this book's purposes, I'll consider the processes of distributing music, video, and games through a home network and playing them on TVs, stereo systems, surround sound systems, and table "radios."

Music Through a Home Network

Any technology that reproduces sound has at least two elements: a *source* and a *destination*. Often one or more additional intermediate elements are between the source and destination, such as a preamplifier that boosts volume level or an analog-to-digital or digital-to-analog converter, but you'll always have a program source and a destination device that converts the signal back to sound.

For example, consider an antique gramophone like the one shown in Figure 15-2. The source of the sound is a needle that follows the vibrations in a grooved disk, and the destination is a membrane that reproduces those vibrations through a horn.

In a modern music system, the program source can include the following:

- Analog media such as vinyl disks or magnetic tape
- Digital media such as compact discs
- Broadcast radio stations
- Cable and satellite radio stations or music services
- The Internet
- Digital music files stored on a computer's hard drive or a portable device such as an iPod

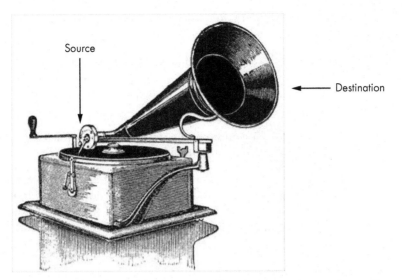

Source

Destination

Figure 15-2: The source of the music played on this gramophone is the needle on a grooved shellac disc; the destination is the horn.

The destination can be any of the following:

- Speakers connected to a home stereo system, TV receiver, or surround sound system
- Speakers connected to a computer or built into a laptop
- Headphones or a docking unit's speakers connected to a portable device such as an iPod
- A storage device such as a hard drive or a flash drive
- A tabletop or portable boom box or Internet radio

A home network can connect any of these sources to any destination. It might be necessary to convert the source from analog to digital format before it moves through the network, and you might have to convert the digital data back to analog before you play the sound through a speaker or headphones, but these are relatively minor technical details; the important point is the same network that handles other data can also distribute digital audio files. In networking terms, you can think of the devices that handle program sources as *servers* and the destinations as *clients*.

Audio Servers

An *audio server* in a home network stores music, radio programs, and other sound files that are accessible to other devices on the same network. The server can be a computer that you also use as a workstation, a server for other data files, a dedicated server for audio files, or a component in a stereo or home theater system. Regardless of their physical form, most audio servers perform these functions:

- They convert (or *rip*) audio tracks from CDs and other sources to one or more standard file formats.
- They store sound files on a hard drive.
- They distribute sound files on demand to one or more players.
- They distribute audio to the network directly from a CD, DVD, the Internet, or some other digital source.

Like any other server, a music server should have a relatively large hard drive with enough space to hold all the individual music files you want to store on it. General-purpose computers and stereo-component music servers can both perform similar services; each type has a different combination of cost, ease of use, and sound quality.

General-Purpose Computers

When you use a standard desktop or tower computer as your music server, you can use the same computer to serve other types of data. You can use free or inexpensive software such as Windows Media Player, RealPlayer, Sound Forge Audio Studio, Exact Audio Copy, or Audacity to create or convert files to your standard storage format, and you can increase the server's storage capacity by installing one or more additional hard drives.

The sound quality of the most common sound cards (and built-in sound processing on many motherboards) is adequate for casual listening. However, the quality is not as good as an "audiophile" or "studio quality" sound card or external interface unit that adds less background noise and distortion to your files. If you're creating your own files from CDs or uncompressed digital program sources, you will probably want to upgrade your sound card from the "Sound Blaster" interface supplied with your computer. On the other hand, if you get all your music by downloading MP3 files from iTunes or one of the other online services, or if you convert your music from CDs, LPs, or other sources to highly compressed MP3 files, you won't notice the difference.

The choice of operating system—Windows, Macintosh, or Linux—is a matter of personal preference; all three can work as music servers. If you're already using Windows Home Server to control your home network and share other files, the same server can stream audio (and video) to other network computers.

Microsoft's Windows Media Center, included in some versions of Windows Vista and available as a separate add-in product, is primarily a media player, but when you connect it to a device that has the Media Center Extender technology in place, you can use the Media Center computer to serve audio and video files to other computers, game consoles, and televisions.

For mixed networks, XMBC Media Center (*http://xmbc.org/*) is an excellent choice for managing and sharing media files.

Remember to configure the folder or drive that contains the server's music files as a shared resource that is accessible to other computers and devices on the same network.

Special-Purpose Music Servers

Audiophile music servers store music and other audio files on a hard drive, and they generally perform two kinds of playback: They connect directly to a stereo or home theater system as a local program source, and they also connect to an Ethernet or Wi-Fi network to serve music files to computers and audio devices in other rooms.

Music servers sold as audiophile equipment generally contain high-quality internal parts and, often, front panel text displays that provide information about the music track currently playing. Many of them, such as the McIntosh MS750, are also very expensive. Most include their own CD drives for ripping copies to the internal hard drive and analog inputs with excellent analog-to-digital converters for making digital copies of LPs and other analog source material.

A music server is an expensive alternative to a computer with a very good internal or external audio interface card or adapter, but in a serious audiophile sound system, such a server has its place; a $3,500 music server might make sense as part of a system that includes a $3,000 amplifier and a pair of $7,500 speakers. But the rest of us can accomplish the same thing for considerably less money if we're willing to use a computer instead.

Audio File Formats

Digital music players convert sound and music files in common formats to analog sounds that you can play through headphones or speakers. Some of these formats use *compressed* audio that squeezes the data into smaller files. Others use larger *uncompressed* files that maintain all the original details. The most common format for compressed audio files is MP3. The most widely used formats for uncompressed files include WAV and AIFF. Table 15-1 lists the formats that you're most likely to see.

The choice of format is a trade-off between the size of the file and the quality of the sound. As a rule of thumb, sound quality increases with file size, as measured in bits per second. A WAV file of a music track might require eight to ten times as much storage space as an MP3 file of the same recording, but the WAV file is almost always a more accurate copy of the original. The compressed MP3 file occupies less space on a hard drive and can travel across the network more quickly, but the added bits in the WAV file will mean that the music has less distortion and better frequency response (the range between the lowest bass notes and the highest treble tones). In other words, an MP3 file might sound like the recording played through an AM radio, whereas the same music played from a WAV file could sound at least as good as a very good CD player.

Table 15-1: Common Audio File Formats

File Extension	Format Name	Description
.wav	WAV or Wave (Waveform Audio)	This is Microsoft's format for uncompressed audio, which has since been adopted by others. It is widely used in audio archives.
.mp3	MP3 or MPEG Layer-3	This is a compressed format for consumer audio. It's not a high-fidelity format, but it is good enough for casual listening.
.ogg	Ogg Vorbis	This is an open source compressed format. It is widely used for free content.
.flac	Free Lossless Audio Codec (FLAC)	This is a compressed format that does not remove content from the compressed file, unlike MP3 or Ogg Vorbis. Because this format is lossless, a FLAC file is a more accurate copy of the original than other compressed file formats.
.aiff	Audio Interchange File Format	This is an uncompressed format introduced and mainly used on Apple computers.
.wma	Windows Media Audio	This is a compressed format developed by Microsoft and mainly used with Windows Media Player (but it's also supported by other players).
.ra or *.ram*	Real Audio	Th is is Real Audio's family of formats for streaming Internet audio. It is widely used by radio stations, including the BBC.
.bwv	Broadcast Wave	This is an uncompressed format established by the European Broadcasting Union for digital storage of audio files. It is similar to WAV with additional space for *metadata* (information about each file's content).

MP3 files are entirely adequate for casual listening, especially for speech, but uncompressed files can sound a lot better. The compromise between file size and sound quality is particularly important when you are loading files on an iPod or other portable device with a limited amount of storage space. For a home system, where you have little or no practical limit to the amount of storage space (you can almost always add another hard drive to the server), storing your music files in an uncompressed format, especially if you plan to listen through a good quality stereo or surround sound system, is best.

NOTE   *It's important to store archival copies of original recordings as uncompressed files, so future users will have the best possible recordings to work with. Many libraries and archives keep a high-quality WAV file as a master copy and a separate MP3 listening copy for distribution. Archiving uncompressed files is less important when you're dealing with commercially available CDs because hundreds or thousands (if not millions) of other copies are probably in circulation, but when you have the only copy, archiving an uncompressed version can make a difference.*

Many audio player programs can automatically recognize and load most common file formats. However, you might want to install more than one program, just in case your default player can't handle a file. For example,

Windows Media Player won't accept very high bit rate (24-bit/96 kHz per second) WAV files, so you'll have to play them in another program, such as Audacity or Sound Forge.

Converting from Analog Sources

If you want to distribute music and other recordings from LPs and other analog media (such as cassettes, old 78 rpm discs, and reel-to-reel tape) through your network, you must convert them to digital audio files first. This conversion is more time-consuming than ripping CDs, but it can be rewarding if you have some great old records that are not available in any other format.

If you plan to transfer a lot of analog media to digital files, it's worth the extra cost to use a better analog-to-digital converter than the one built into your computer. Professional studio-quality converters can cost hundreds or thousands of dollars, but less expensive devices such as the ones made by E-Mu, M-Audio, and Edirol, among others, will give you considerably better performance than consumer-grade sound interfaces.

Remember that the sound of your digital copy won't be any better than the sound coming from the analog original. Before you make a copy, be sure to clean the dust and grit from your LP, and make sure the needle on your record player is in good condition. Use alcohol or some other head cleaner to remove the gunk from the face of the heads before you try to play cassettes or reel-to-reel tapes.

Audio Clients

In a home network, the other half of a music distribution system is a *music client* or *audio client.* The client can be a program running on one or more of the household computers, a stereo component, a surround sound or home theater system, or a tabletop "boom box" or Internet radio. The client receives music files from a server or streaming audio program through the Internet and plays them through a set of headphones or speakers.

The quality of sound played through a network depends on several factors: the quality of the original recording, the amount of network traffic, and the quality of the client's digital-to-analog converter and speakers. For example, if you're playing a music track that originated on a noisy cassette tape through the tiny and tinny speakers in your laptop computer, the music will sound much worse than a track ripped from a CD and played through a good stereo amplifier and high-fidelity speakers. And if the network that connects the server to the client is already running close to its capacity, or if it's using a noisy Wi-Fi link, you might hear repeated drop-outs in the music when the client can't convert data packets to a continuous audio stream.

Playing Music Through a Computer

A computer used as a music client must have an internal or external audio interface, such as a sound card, an interface on the computer's motherboard, or an interface connected to the computer through a USB or FireWire port. To play a music file, open the file in an audio player program that supports the file's format, just as you would open any other kind of file. The audio output for the computer's audio interface should connect through an audio cable to a set of powered computer speakers or a full-scale stereo or home theater system.

If you're using the computer exclusively as a music client, you don't need the latest and most powerful processor or a large-screen monitor. Anything that can connect to the network and support a decent audio interface unit should be entirely adequate. If you have an older laptop that you're no longer using for other purposes, try using it as a music client; the laptop is probably more compact than a desktop unit and it might work just as well if you plug a decent audio interface into the USB port.

Most computers look like, well . . . like computers. If your stereo system is located on a bookshelf or behind glass cabinet doors in your living room, you might prefer to use a music server that matches your other stereo components. If you don't mind assembling a computer out of parts, look for computer cases (such as the Antec case shown in Figure 15-3) that look like stereo equipment. But remember that you'll still need some kind of keyboard, mouse, and monitor. On the other hand, it's often easy enough to place the computer case out of sight on the floor or in some other out-of-the-way location or to run the server through the network from another room.

Photo courtesy of Antec

Figure 15-3: Some computer cases are designed to look like stereo components.

Connecting Your Network to Your Stereo

If you don't have a spare computer, you can also run audio cables between your stereo and a nearby computer that you're using for other purposes. For example, if you have both a desktop computer and a stereo system in your home office or study, you can use that computer to feed the existing speakers through the stereo's amplifier. Even if the stereo is in another room, running audio cables through the wall or under the floor might be more practical. Figure 15-4 shows a typical system connection.

To play music from your music server, set the input selector on the stereo to the Auxiliary input (or whichever input you have connected to the computer), and use the computer's mouse and monitor to select the song or other music file you want to hear. If your computer or sound card has digital outputs (either optical or copper) and the stereo has digital inputs, use a digital cable to transfer the audio. The computer should automatically open the music file in a compatible player and feed it to the stereo.

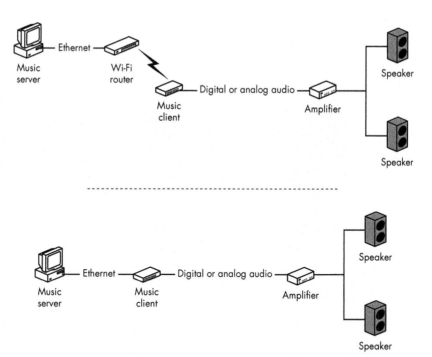

Figure 15-4: A music server can connect to a client through either a Wi-Fi link or an Ethernet cable. The client sends audio to an amplifier's analog or digital auxiliary input.

Dedicated Music Client Devices

As an alternative to using a computer, consider using a separate device specifically designed as a music client or network music player. The client device sends an instruction to find and play a specific music file (or other audio track) to the music server, which streams the requested file back to the player. The player can either send the digital stream to a converter in the audio system or convert the file to an analog signal and send the music signal to the audio system.

For example, Slim Devices makes a family of Squeezebox music clients, including the Squeezebox Classic, Squeezebox Receiver, and Squeezebox Transporter. Figure 15-5 shows the connections on a Squeezebox for a network and a stereo system. Similar products are available from Roku, Netgear, Philips, and other companies. Most of these devices are marketed as audio components, so the best place to look for a demonstration is probably a home audio retailer rather than a computer store.

Each music client manufacturer supports a different set of audio file formats; they all work with the most widely used formats, but if your library includes more obscure formats, you should confirm that a client can recognize them.

Network music players offer several benefits: They occupy less space than a computer; they're often easier to use; and they can provide sound quality as good as or better than a computer for less money. If you're buying new equipment to play music through your network, a dedicated music player can be an excellent choice; but if you already have a spare computer, you can probably accomplish the same thing without buying any new equipment (although replacing the computer's audio interface might improve the system's performance).

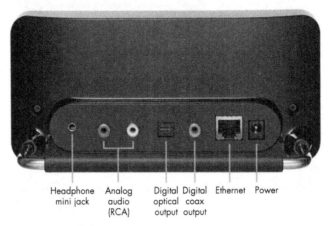

Headphone mini jack   Analog audio (RCA)   Digital optical output   Digital coax output   Ethernet   Power

Photo courtesy of Slim Devices

Figure 15-5: Slim Devices' Squeezebox connects a music server to a home audio system through an Ethernet or Wi-Fi network.

Networked Receivers and Internet Radios

It's not necessary to use a computer or a full-scale stereo or surround sound system just to listen to music from a music server or streaming radio stations and music channels through the Internet. You can find a whole category of tabletop "Internet radios" that combine the music client and speaker in a single box (sometimes with satellite speakers for stereo). In spite of the name, most Internet radios can also play music files stored on your own music server. Some also include AM and FM radios, so you can use the same device to listen to local broadcast stations.

An Internet radio works like any other network music client: It connects to your home network through an Internet port or a built-in Wi-Fi port and allows you to select files from your own server or streaming programs through the Internet. Ultimately, these devices will be as easy to use as the tabletop radio in your bedroom or kitchen; simply turn the device on, select the station, and listen. The important difference is that you're not limited to the programs on local radio stations; you can choose from thousands of radio stations and streaming music services that offer a huge variety of music, news, and other programming—many of them without commercials.

Today, Internet radios are still expensive novelties—most cost $200 or more—but if and when the price comes down, they will probably become a hugely popular alternative to radios that only receive local stations.

Video Through a Home Network

Video—in the form of movies, television shows, home videos, or files downloaded through the Internet—is yet another type of program material that you can distribute through your network. You can view videos on your computer's monitor or through an adapter on a television screen.

Video distribution through a network follows a similar structure to audio: Video files are stored on a server and transmitted to a client on demand. However, video files contain many more bits per minute of content than audio files, so the network must have a high enough capacity to handle that additional demand. In practice, this means that many Wi-Fi links (except the newest 802.11n equipment) may not be able to keep up with a video stream, and even a wired 100-BaseT network might overload if you try to push through more than one video stream at the same time.

When you want to download a movie or some other large video file through the Internet, it's often better to save the file to your computer's hard drive, rather than trying to view it as the computer receives it because the download speed is often too slow for the video player program to assemble the digital packets and display them as a continuous stream. On the other hand, when all the bits are already on a DVD or hard drive, the video player can play the stream without the need to wait for more bits to arrive.

You can think of the stream of incoming bits as a garden hose that fills a watering pail with a slow trickle of water; if you pour out water more quickly than the hose fills the pail, you must refill the pail before you can pour more water. The same thing applies to video files through a network: If the data packets that contain the video stream enter your network more slowly than the video player assembles and displays them, the player's buffer will run out of bits and stop displaying anything until it receives more.

Video Servers

A *video server* is a network server that stores movies and other video files and sends them through the network to video player programs on client computers or video players. Most video servers can also store and distribute music files. Some computer operating systems, such as Windows Home Server and its associated client programs, include software that has been optimized for video distribution, but you can also use a general-purpose Linux, Unix, Macintosh, or Windows server, as long as the server computer contains one or more relatively large hard drives with enough available space to hold very large video files.

Other media servers combine the function of a network server and a local media player into a single package. You can play music and videos through a screen and speakers connected directly to the media server or send requests to the server from other players through your network.

TiVo and Other Digital Video Recorders

The primary function of a *digital video recorder (DVR)* is to record incoming broadcast or cable television programs for delayed viewing. However, some DVRs, including TiVo, the most popular DVR in North America and Australia, can also distribute programs to another DVR through a network. By connecting a TiVo to a network, you can also download program schedules through the Internet rather than a slower dial-up telephone connection.

Most recent TiVo models, including the Series2 Dual Tuner and Series3 HD DVRs, have an Ethernet port as standard equipment. The older Series2 Single Tuner DVR requires an optional Ethernet network adapter that connects to the DVR's USB port. For a wireless connection, you must use a TiVo Wireless adapter, which is an optional accessory that connects to the DVR's USB port, or a compatible adapter made by Belkin, D-Link, Linksys, or Netgear.

Connecting to a Wired Network

To connect a TiVo to your existing wired network, follow these steps:

1. Run an Ethernet cable from the DVR to a network hub or router.
2. Press the TiVo button on the DVR and select **Messages and Settings** ▸ **Settings** ▸ **Phone & Network**.
3. From the Network Connection screen shown in Figure 15-6, select the **Change network settings** option.

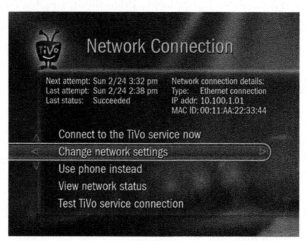

Figure 15-6: Use TiVo's Network Connection screen to configure a wired connection to your home network.

4. Follow the instructions that appear on your screen. If your network has an active DHCP server, the TiVo client will detect it automatically and display a Network Setup Complete screen. If your network doesn't have a DHCP server, select No, let me specify a static IP address, and type an IP address for this network node, the subnet mask, and numeric addresses for the node's gateway router and DNS server.

5. The DVR will test the connection. If the settings are correct, it will display a Network Setup Complete screen.

Connecting to a Wireless Network

To connect a TiVo DVR to your network through a Wi-Fi link, follow these steps:

1. Press the TiVo button on your DVR. The TiVo Central screen will appear.
2. Select **Messages and Settings** ▸ **Settings** ▸ **Phone & Network**.
3. If your TiVo is already connected to a telephone line, select Use network instead. If it's connected to a wired network, select Change network settings. Press **Select**.
4. If the wireless adapter is not already connected, connect it now. When the TiVo identifies the wireless adapter, it will display the Network Adapter Detected screen.
5. Press **Select**. The Wireless Network Name screen will appear.
6. Either select the name of your Wi-Fi network and press **Select** or, if the network does not broadcast the network's name, select **Enter network name** and follow the instructions on your screen.
7. TiVo will ask for your network password. Use the keypad on your screen to type your WEP or WPA password and then click **Done Entering Network Password**.
8. If the password is correct and your network uses a DHCP server, the Network Setup Complete screen will appear. If the network doesn't use DHCP, you will see a series of configuration screens. Type the IP address, subnet mask, and the addresses for your network's gateway router and DNS server.

Importing Programs

To watch a program that has been stored on a TiVo from a second DVR in another room, follow these steps:

1. Turn on both TVs and go to the destination player's **Now Playing List**. The other DVR will appear at the bottom of the list of available programs.
2. Highlight the name of the distant DVR and press **Select**. That DVR's Now Playing List will appear.
3. Choose the name of the show you want to transfer to this DVR and press **Select**. The Getting Program screen will appear.
4. To watch the show while you're transferring it, select **Start playing** on the Getting Program screen. When the transfer is complete, the name of the show will appear in this DVR's Now Playing List.

Playing Video on a Computer

Several of the same programs that play music on a computer can also handle video files. Windows Media Player, RealPlayer, and QuickTime include both audio and video decoders. Others such as VideoLAN (*http://www.videolan.org/*) and MPlayer are optimized for video. Like other networked files, you can use a player program on a client computer to view a video file from a server. In most cases, one or more video player programs automatically take control of specific file types, so almost all video files will automatically load into an appropriate player when you select a file from an onscreen directory or file folder.

Connecting a TV to Your Network

In rooms where you have a television set but no computer, it's often possible to use a game console or other adapter to view movies and other digital video files on the TV screen. In rooms with both a computer and a large-screen TV, it's often worth the trouble to connect the TV directly to the computer as a complement to the smaller computer monitor. The quality of pictures and text on a TV screen is not always as sharp as the same images on a computer monitor, an image from a broadcast or cable TV signal, or a DVD player, but with a bit of tweaking, it can be good enough to watch.

Connecting Directly to a Computer

To connect a TV directly to a computer, you need two things:

- An output signal from the computer that's compatible with an input to the television
- Driver software for the computer's video controller

    Your television has one or more of these input types:

- Two or more screw terminals that connect to a flat antenna cable
- A threaded socket that mates with a coaxial cable from an antenna, cable TV service, or other program source—the socket and mating plug at the end of the cable are called *F connectors*
- A circular connector with either four or seven sockets that mates with a matching multipin plug called an *S Video* (for *Super Video* or *Separated Video*) plug
- Three color-coded sockets (yellow for video, white for stereo audio left or mono, and red for stereo audio right) for analog audio-video cables— these are similar to the RCA phono plugs and sockets used in most home stereo systems
- A 15-pin analog VGA connector like the one used by older computer display monitors
- A rectangular multipin digital input known as a *digital visual interface (DVI)* connector

- A 19-pin or 29-pin digital socket known as a *High Definition Multimedia Interface (HDMI)* connector

The easiest way to feed a signal to your TV from the computer is to find a video controller for your computer that has outputs that match your TV's inputs, but that's not always possible. For example, you won't find a video controller that can directly feed an old analog TV with nothing but an F connector as signal input (or an even older set with screw terminals). The alternative is to use some kind of *adapter*—a special cable with different cables on each end—or a *converter* that changes the output signal from the computer to a signal compatible with the TV's input. For best quality with an HDTV screen, use either a DVI-to-DVI cable or a DVI-to-HDMI cable or adapter, depending on the TV's inputs. Look for an adapter or converter at an electronics retailer.

Video Output Drivers

Driver software for video controllers can come from several possible sources: bundled with your computer's operating system or supplied by the maker of the video controller or the controller's chipset or with a video converter. The control program for each driver package is different, so you'll have to follow the printed or onscreen instructions when you install the software.

Video Scaling

Putting aside the issues related to converting between analog and digital video, it would seem that there isn't a lot of difference between a TV screen and a computer monitor. But they use different methods to accomplish the same objective, and these methods create problems when you try to move from one to the other. The difficulty arises because of the way computer monitors and TV screens break an image into scan lines and pixels. For the purpose of this explanation, we can think about a still picture, but the same problems can also occur in a moving image.

In North America, an analog TV shows images as a sequence of 535 scan lines from left to right across the face of the screen; when the TV reaches the end of one scan line, it moves down to the next one. In digital TV, the screen is divided into a large number of dots called *picture elements*, or *pixels*. The method used by the TV to light up segments of scan lines or pixels is different on picture tubes and flat panels, but the number of scan lines or pixels is specified by industry standards. The size of the screen doesn't matter; the number of scan lines or pixels on a screen is always the same (there are several different standards for flat panels, depending on size and cost, but the number of pixels is constant for each standard).

Computer monitors also use pixels, but the number of pixels in an image is different, depending on screen resolution. When you change your monitor's resolution from, say, 800 × 600 pixels to 1280 × 1024 pixels, the computer adjusts the number of pixels within a 1-inch (2.5 cm) square space on the screen or any other image area.

To show a computer image on a TV screen, the controller must adjust the number of scan lines or pixels to fit the area available on the monitor. If the TV screen expects more scan lines or pixels than the incoming signal, the controller will duplicate occasional lines or pixels or it will create a new line that is a blend of the one above and the one below. If the computer sends too many scan lines or pixels, the screen will skip some of them. This process is called *video scaling*.

Video scaling has two effects: It forces the video controller to work hard to change the size (and sometimes the shape) of the image, which can slow down performance, and it sends an image to the TV screen that can suffer from smeared colors, looser focus, jagged edges, and distorted pictures. A good controller can make adjustments that minimize these problems, but don't be surprised if the image your computer displays on a TV screen (even a very good high-definition TV screen) is not as sharp as the same image on a computer monitor; a good DVI-to-HDMI image on an HDTV can be sharper than a VGA display when everything works together correctly, but a mismatched system can be considerably less impressive.

Game Consoles

The most widely used game consoles—Sony PlayStation2 or PlayStation3, Nintendo Wii, and Xbox 360—can all connect to your home network through either a wired Ethernet port or a wireless link to support multiplayer games with one or more additional consoles on the same LAN or through the Internet (they could also connect to a business network, but your employer probably would not approve).

Connecting a PlayStation

To connect through a wireless link, use the PlayStation's built-in Wi-Fi interface. To connect a Sony PlayStation to your network through an Ethernet cable, run an Ethernet cable from the game console either directly to an Ethernet hub or to a router.

To configure the network connection, follow these steps:

1. Turn off or disconnect power from your network hub, modem, Wi-Fi base station, and other network equipment, wait two minutes, and then turn everything back on again.

2. If the PlayStation console and attached display are not already turned on, turn them on now.

3. Confirm the PlayStation's connection to the Internet is active: From the XMB home menu, select **Settings ▸ Network Settings ▸ Internet Connection ▸ Enabled**.

4. Select **Internet Connection Settings** and press the ⊗ button. The PlayStation will ask "Do you want to continue?"

5. Select **Yes**. The PlayStation will ask you to select a connection method.

6. Select **Wired Connection** and press the ⊗ button. The Internet Connection Settings screen will appear.

7. Select **Easy** and press the ⊗ button. The PlayStation will scan your connection and display the current settings.

8. Press the ⊗ button again to save the configuration values. The Test Connection screen will appear.

9. Press the ⊗ button to test the connection. After approximately a minute or less, the PlayStation will display either a "Succeeded" or "Failed" message.

10. If the test was successful, the PlayStation is ready to run multiplayer games; if it fails, the PlayStation will provide instructions for fixing the problem.

Connecting a Wii

Nintendo's Wii console requires an optional Wii LAN Adapter (Model number RVL 015) to connect to a network. Follow these steps to connect a Nintendo Wii to your LAN:

1. Turn off the Wii console and plug the LAN Adapter into the console's USB port.

2. Run an Ethernet cable from the LAN Adapter to your network router or hub.

3. Turn on the Wii console.

4. From the main menu, click the **Wii** button at the bottom left. A screen showing a Data Management box and a Wii Settings box will appear.

5. Click the **Wii Settings** box. The System Settings screen will appear.

6. Click the blue arrow at the right side of the list of options to move to the second of three System Settings menus.

7. Click the **Internet** button. The Internet screen will appear.

8. Click **Connection Settings**. A list of Connection Settings options will appear.

9. Select an "empty" connection slot, with **None** shown as the connection type.

10. Select either Wireless or Wired Connection, as appropriate for your system. The console will tell you that it's initiating a test.

11. Click **OK**. The Wii console will test your connection. If it's successful, you're ready to use your game console on the network. If it fails, try one of these fixes:

   • Check your firewall settings.

   • If the console displays an error code, go to *http://www.nintendo.com/consumer/systems/wii/en/en_na/errors/iindex.jsp* to find an explanation for the code.

Connecting an Xbox 360

If you use your Microsoft Xbox 360 game console and a computer in the same room, but you have only one network jack or outlet in that room, you can run the network connection to the computer through the game console. Follow these steps to connect a Microsoft Xbox 360 console to your network:

1. Turn off or disconnect power to your computer, your network's router, hub, modem, and the Xbox 360 console.

2. If you don't have a second network outlet in the room, disconnect the Ethernet cable from the computer and plug it into the Xbox 360 console. The cable should now run from the game console to the network hub or router.

3. If you have access to a spare outlet, you don't have to disconnect the computer. Just run a new cable from the game console to the free network outlet or directly to an open port on the hub or router.

4. If necessary, plug one end of a second Ethernet cable into the Xbox 360 console and the other end into your computer.

5. Turn on your equipment in this order: modem first, router next, and then the computer. Leave the game console turned off for the moment.

6. Confirm that the computer can detect the LAN and the Internet, just as it did before you added the game console.

7. Turn on the Xbox 360 console and make sure there is not a disc in the disc tray. The Xbox Dashboard will display the Xbox Live area.

8. Assuming you have already configured things like time and language, the Gamer Profile screen will appear. If you already have an Xbox Live membership in another location, select Migrate your Xbox LIVE account. If you're setting up a new account, select Join Xbox LIVE.

9. Follow the onscreen instructions to supply your contact information and gamer profile and to create or transfer an account.

Connecting Home Appliances to Your Network

They're not widely used today (nor in many people's opinions, useful enough to justify the added cost), but home appliances with Internet connections are available, and more will probably come along in the next few years. Networked connections can allow you to control your household TV, refrigerator, microwave oven, and other appliances through the Internet or from a mobile telephone—even when you're away from home. Combined with built-in diagnostic modules, a network connection will also make it possible to identify problems and notify a service bureau that can either send back a software fix or dispatch a repair person before the problem turns into a catastrophic failure.

Remember the classic science-fiction nightmare in which all your household appliances communicate with one another and conspire to take over your life? When you connect everything to your home network, that fantasy is one step closer to reality.

Several specifications for networked home appliances have been established in order to assure that appliances made by different manufacturers will communicate with one another through a home network, including the Living Network Control Protocol (LnCP), developed by LG Electronics and adopted by several other (mostly Korean) manufacturers, and the Association for Home Appliance Manufacturers' (AHAM) standard for Connected Home Appliances (CHA-1). It's too early to know whether LnCP, CHA-1, or some other specification will ultimately emerge as an industry-wide standard, but it's likely that some method for exchanging data among appliances and other devices through a home network will become common within the next few years.

If you buy a network-compatible "smart" home appliance today, it will probably use an Ethernet port to connect to your home network. Depending on the specific applications built into each appliance, it might use a control panel or remote control unit, dedicated client software, or a web-based interface to run the appliance's communications functions.

Home Automation

Other home network applications can control your house's heating and air conditioning systems, open and close draperies, adjust the lighting, communicate with a burglar alarm or home security service, operate lawn sprinklers, and control the filters and temperature of your swimming pool, among other activities. The interface between the network and the control device can be either a direct Ethernet link or a controller that follows the low-voltage X.10 standard.

Remote Sensors and Controls

When you connect a remote interface device to your LAN, you can monitor environmental conditions or the performance of unattended equipment and operate equipment by remote control through your network. Many possible applications for this kind of networked remote activity are available, including the following:

- Monitoring the temperature in an equipment room, a freezer, or "cold box"
- Measuring and monitoring air or water temperature, wind speed, water flow in a stream or other body of water, and other environmental conditions
- Monitoring power levels
- Monitoring and responding to alarms
- Turning AC or DC power off and back on again in order to restart "hung" equipment
- Monitoring normally open or normally closed intrusion alarms (such as open doors or windows)

- Remotely controlling and adjusting isolated equipment
- Tracking any other condition that can be measured or monitored with a digital sensor or operated with a relay

Most of these applications are more practical for relatively large businesses and government agencies that operate in several locations (such as a county- or statewide system of radio transmitters or a scientific study that allows researchers in multiple locations to track environmental conditions through the Web), but some can be adapted for a home or small business network. For example, a water detector in the cellar might trigger an alarm or send an email message, or an intrusion alarm, a fire alarm, and a remote temperature sensor in a barn could all connect to a network on a farm through a Wi-Fi link to a computer or other monitoring device in the house. Or with the right kind of equipment connected to your home network, you could send an instruction through the Internet from your workplace in case of a sudden snowstorm that would turn on heating coils embedded in your driveway and melt the ice before you arrive home. For that matter, you could even operate a model railroad through your network, but you'll need somebody near the tracks to take care of derailments and other scale-model disasters!

Remote controls, thermostats, sensors, and monitors are specialized devices, but they're widely available through industrial sources and from retailers and mail/web-order suppliers of home automation equipment.

WARNING   *Every remote sensor and control that connects to your network through a wire or cable increases the network's sensitivity to lightning strikes. Remember to use appropriate lightning suppression wherever practical.*

Bar Code Readers and Remote Data Entry

One more possible use of a small business network could be remote entry of information to a central computer. This might include a portable bar code reader used for inventory control or property management, security devices for controlled access, and networked cash registers and other point-of-sale devices.

If You Can Convert It to Digits, You Can Put It on the Network

The most familiar uses of a data network are the ones that involve a computer or a game console, but the same network can also handle other forms of digital data. Today's technology makes it possible to convert almost any kind of information to digital form; if you can't find off-the-shelf equipment and software that can do the job you have in mind, you can probably assemble a system from standard parts and software.

As you install your home network, think about it as a household utility— just like electricity, telephone service, and water. Even if you only use your network to connect computers to the Internet today, it's entirely possible that new and unexpected uses will appear in the future.

16

OTHER NETWORK
APPLICATIONS

Most people use a network for a limited number of purposes; they share files and messages, connect to the Internet, and maybe play multiplayer games or listen to music and watch videos from a server. But once you have your home or small business network up and running, you can use the network to accomplish some things you might not have expected.

This chapter describes a handful of other useful network applications. None of these is reason enough to install a network, but if you have come this far, you're already using the network for other purposes. Consider the network programs and services in this chapter as *lagniappe*, a little extra that might enhance your networking experience.

Remote Desktop

Remote Desktop programs allow another user, with your permission, to take control of your computer through a network. When a remote control program is active, a network manager or service technician can distribute and install new or updated software, provide help and remote assistance, and view information on other computers. Remote Desktop programs are a standard feature in Windows XP, Windows Vista, and Macintosh.

Several open source remote desktop programs for Linux and Unix are also available, including Virtual Network Computing (VNC), FreeNX, 2X Terminal Server, and X Display Manager Control Protocol. You can find links to downloads for all of these programs at *http://blog.lxpages.com/2007/03/13/remote-desktop-for-linux/*. For Mac-to-Windows remote access, try Microsoft's Remote Desktop Connection Client for Mac (*http://www.microsoft.com/mac/products/remote-desktop/*). For Windows-to-Mac, use a Windows-based VNC client such as RealVNC or TightVNC. You will find more information about VNC later in this section.

Windows Remote Desktop

Windows Remote Desktop transfers control of a client computer to a host. The host mirrors the screen display from the client, and the host's mouse and keyboard control the programs running on the client. When Remote Desktop is active, the client computer displays a blank screen and doesn't respond to keyboard or mouse input until the host releases control.

Remote Desktop makes the person running the host computer a sort of *superuser* who can take control of a client computer, so several controls are built into the system that limit this kind of access: First, the user of the client must set the computer to accept Remote Desktop access, and second, the person running Remote Desktop on the host computer must have an account (usually with a password) on the client computer. In other words, if you turn off Remote Desktop on your computer, other people can't use it without your permission.

In Windows XP, the remote access tool is called *Remote Access*; in Windows Vista, it's known as *Remote Desktop*. Computers running Windows Vista Starter, Windows Vista Home Basic, Windows Vista Home Basic N, or Windows Vista Home Premium won't accept incoming access, but you can use Remote Desktop to take control of another computer running some other version of Vista. Windows XP Home Edition won't accept access from any Windows Vista machine.

Configuring Windows for Remote Desktop Access

To configure a Windows XP computer to accept Remote Desktop access, follow these steps:

1. Right-click **My Computer**. A pop-up menu will appear.
2. Select **Properties** from the menu. The System Properties window will open.

3. Click the **Remote** tab. The dialog shown in Figure 16-1 will appear.

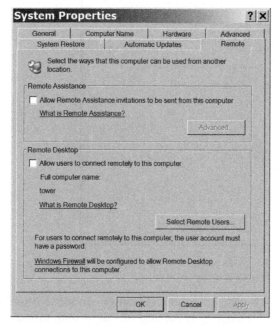

Figure 16-1: The Remote tab in System Properties controls inbound and outbound access to the Windows Remote Desktop utility.

4. To use this computer to control other computers remotely on your network, check the **Allow Remote Assistance invitations . . .** option in the Remote Assistance area.

5. To permit another computer on your network to take control of this computer, check the **Allow users to connect remotely . . .** option.

6. When Allow users to connect remotely to this computer is turned on, anybody who is logged on to another machine on the same network with the same username as an Administrator account on this computer—and who uses a password to log into this computer—can request remote access. To allow a non-Administrator to use Remote Access, click the **Select Remote Users** button, click the **Add** button in the Remote Desktop Users window, and then type the account name for the person who you want to allow to use Remote Access.

7. Click the **OK** buttons in each of the open windows to save your data and close the windows.

To configure Windows Vista for Remote Assistance, follow these steps:

1. Right-click **My Computer**. The System window will appear.

2. Click **Remote settings** in the Tasks list on the right side of the window. The System Properties window will appear with the Remote tab visible, as shown in Figure 16-2.

Figure 16-2: Use the Remote tab in System Properties
to turn Remote Assistance on or off.

3. Check the **Allow Remote Assistance connections to this computer**
   option. Activating this option will allow both inbound and outbound
   remote access.

4. Click **OK** to save your settings and close the Properties window.

Using Remote Desktop

To take control of another computer using Remote Desktop in Windows XP
or Remote Assistance in Windows Vista, follow these steps:

1. Select **Start ▶ All Programs ▶ Accessories ▶ Remote Desktop Connection**.
   A dialog similar to the one shown in Figure 16-3 will appear.

Figure 16-3: Use the Remote Desktop Connection
dialog to specify the computer you want to control.

2. Type the name of the computer you want to control, and click **Connect**.
   Your screen will go black, except for a control tab near the top of the
   screen and a Log On box.

3. Type a valid account name and password for the target computer in the Log On box and click **OK**. The screen on the distant computer will go dark, and you will see an image of the distant computer's desktop on your screen.

You can now control the distant system with your own computer's keyboard and mouse. You can open files, run tests, and load programs though the network. However, a user looking at the distant computer's screen will see nothing but a dark screen.

When a new Remote Desktop connection opens, it fills the client computer's screen, but you can reduce the size of the Remote Desktop window and see your own computer's desktop and Start menu by clicking the sizing icon on the Remote Desktop tab at the top of the screen. This will allow you to copy text, data, or files between the two computers.

To return control to the local user, click the **X** on the control tab near the top of the screen.

NOTE   *If you try to use an account without a password to take over a Remote Desktop connection, you will get this error message:* Unable to log you on because of an account restriction. *If you see this message, go to Control Panel ▶ User Accounts on the target computer, select Change an account to assign a password to your account, and then try connecting again.*

Virtual Network Computing (VNC)

Virtual Network Computing (VNC) is a system that allows one computer (the *client*) to gain remote access to a second computer (the *server*) and to use the first computer's mouse and keyboard to control the second computer. In general, VNC is not as fast as the Windows and Macintosh remote desktop programs, but it's more flexible. Unlike the Microsoft tools described in the previous section, VNC is not limited to any operating system; you can use any VNC client (or viewer) to control any VNC server—even if the two computers use different operating systems.

Several VNC-based programs are available that offer clients and servers for more than one operating system, including RealVNC (*http://www.realvnc.com/*), UltraVNC (*http://www.uvnc.com/*), and TightVNC (*http://www.tightvnc.com/*). Several others are limited to Linux and Unix operating systems. For descriptions and links to additional versions, go to *http://www.linux.com/feature/43165.*

MaxiVista: Adding a Screen

MaxiVista is a slick set of network tools for Windows that allows you to extend your computer's display to one or more additional computers connected to the first computer through your network or to operate two or more computers with the same mouse and keyboard. It can also allow you to use the Windows clipboard across two or more computers through the network. These tools aren't for everybody, but under certain conditions, an extended keyboard or shared controls can be hugely convenient. MaxiVista is available in a free demo version from *http://www.maxivista.com/*.

MaxiVista comes as two programs: a server program that runs on the main computer and a client program that runs on each of the secondary machines. Except for the network connections that are already in place, MaxiVista doesn't require any special hardware.

All of MaxiVista's controls are on the server; the only setting on each client turns the program on or off. The server automatically detects each active client and includes controls that you can use to select either an extended desktop or remote control of client computers.

Multiple Monitors

Extending the size of your screen display by adding an additional monitor is one of those things that sounds extravagant, but just about everybody who tries it is convinced that the second screen makes them much more productive. Because you can keep two or more windows open at the same time without the need to bring one of them to the top, you can work more efficiently; just for starters, you can drag text, figures, or data from one document or program to another, view large documents and graphics without scrolling from one end of a document to the other, and keep a web browser or video surveillance window open on one screen while you work on the other. If you're writing code or working on a web page, you can save your work and immediately see what your latest changes look like in an application window or a browser. And in many Windows programs, you can drag one or more toolbars away from the main program window to the second screen in order to make more of your work visible.

Two (or three or more) monitor screens on your desk will change the way you work with your computer. Figure 16-4 shows a desktop extended across two laptop computer screens.

Figure 16-4: Windows can show a single large window extended onto two or more screens.

If you have an old monitor in the back of a closet, try adding it to a computer. Even if the monitor isn't the same size as your main monitor, it will still work and be an improvement over a single screen.

The easiest way to add another monitor to your system doesn't require MaxiVista or any other special software—simply plug the monitor into a spare VGA or DVI connector on your computer. If your video controller doesn't have an extra video output, install another video controller card in an empty expansion slot. Don't worry about high performance and memory unless you're playing bleeding-edge games; you can use an old PCI video card with as little as 8 or 16 MB of memory from your junk box or a second-hand computer store.

None of this requires MaxiVista. You can use the Display Properties controls in Windows to extend your desktop to additional monitor screens. But if you want to use a laptop computer as your second screen, or if you already have two or more networked computers on the same table or countertop, MaxiVista allows you to use the monitors on those additional computers as extended screens and switch back to normal use when that's more convenient.

If you already have both a laptop and a desktop computer, MaxiVista allows you to try an extended screen without the need to haul out any extra hardware; just plug your laptop into the network, install the free trial version of MaxiVista, and reconfigure your Display Properties settings (as shown in Figure 16-5).

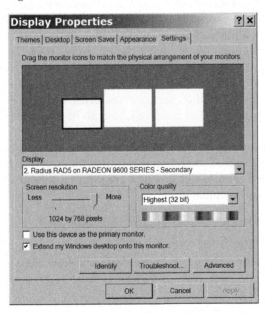

Figure 16-5: The Display Properties dialog includes an option that can extend the Windows desktop to two or more monitor screens.

Remote Control

When you're already using two or more computers in the same room, it's often a nuisance to move among the keyboards and mice that control them. MaxiVista includes a Remote Control feature that allows a single keyboard and mouse to transmit signals through a network to multiple computers.

To use MaxiVista's Remote Control, turn on **Remote Control** mode in the main computer and drag the mouse cursor to the desktop of the computer you want to use. When you select or open a program with the mouse connected to the main computer, the main keyboard will work with that program.

The shared clipboard is part of MaxiVista's Remote Control function. Simply use the mouse from the main computer to select and copy a file, folder, block of text, or other object to the clipboard just as you normally copy objects on a local computer. Then move the mouse cursor to the target computer, open a program (or select an already open window), and paste the contents of the clipboard.

Synchronizing Files

Any time you collaborate with somebody else on a project, you run the risk that each copy of the document (or drawing or spreadsheet or any other record of your work) will accumulate a different set of changes. It's essential to maintain some kind control that synchronizes everything.

File synchronization software compares computer files across a network and incorporates all the additions, moves, changes, and deletions from each copy into all the others. When the file synchronizer finds a conflict between two versions, it can flag the differences and allow a human editor or project manager to decide which version to accept. Most file synchronizers compare and update the contents of folders or directories, but they don't open and change individual files—you must make an all-or-none decision about each file.

Some synchronizers are limited to Windows or Macintosh computers, but others can compare files stored on computers that use different operating systems. Here are some programs that are either available at no cost or as try-before-you-buy downloads:

- Synchronize It! (*http://www.grigsoft.com/winsin.htm*)
- GoodSync (*http://www.goodsync.com/*)
- Microsoft SyncToy (*http://www.microsoft.com/downloads/*—search for *SyncToy*)
- DirSync Pro (*http://directorysync.sourceforge.net/index.html*)
- FreeFileSync (*http://sourceforge.net/projects/freefilesync/*)

Instant Messaging and Live Communication

As the name suggests, *instant messaging (IM)* is the process of sending text or other data that arrives at its destination almost immediately. The most common forms are *text messaging*, in which the participants use their keyboards to conduct a conversation on a display screen, and *audio* or *video messaging*, where a microphone and/or a camera replace or supplement the keyboard.

Live messaging is more immediate than email because it arrives on the recipient's screen as soon as the originator hits the Send button, rather than waiting for a mail server to forward each message. Assuming the distant computer is turned on and the messaging program is running, the text appears on the screen or the sender's voice comes through the computer's speakers immediately. Live messaging makes it possible to conduct a text-based conversation through the network, without the time delay that comes with sending and receiving email.

The most common uses for instant messages involve brief questions and answers such as requests for specific items of information ("Hey Sarah, I'm on the telephone with a customer. How many Size 4 gizmo brackets do we have in stock?"), invitations to face-to-face meetings ("Can you meet me in ten minutes in my office?" or "Do you have plans for lunch?"), and purely social exchanges among friends and family. IM has also become the medium of choice for online gossip among teens and preteens.

IM has a specific place in the hierarchy of communication methods. It's less formal and more immediate than email or facsimile (fax), less intrusive than telephone calls, and more civilized than shouting from one room to another. In some businesses and families, IM is an essential part of the culture; others hardly use it at all. For an extensive study of instant messaging and the way people in business use it, take a look at "Interaction and Outeraction: Instant Messaging in Action" (Proceedings of Conference on Computer Supported Cooperative Work, 79-88 New York: ACM Press, *http://dis.shef.ac.uk/stevewhittaker/outeraction_cscw2000.pdf*). The authors of this study offer some interesting insights, but they have buried them under some seriously dense academic language, using highfalutin words like *dyadic* and *ethnomethodology*.

Just about every messaging program has a similar structure: It displays a list of other users, with an indicator that shows whether each user is currently available to receive a message. Users might not be available because their messaging program is not active or because they have set the program to not accept incoming messages. To start a conversation, click the intended recipient's name. When a message arrives, it appears in a pop-up window on the recipient's screen (some programs also sound an audible signal when they receive a new message).

NOTE   *Instant messaging is not the same as online chat, but the experience is similar. The difference is that chat takes place among two or more participants who connect to a common channel (a* chatroom). *When you join a chat, you instruct the program to connect to a specific chatroom. Instant messaging appears to connect two participants' computers directly to each other, so you specify the name of the other participant rather then the channel. After you make the initial connection, there's not much difference between chat and IM.*

Servers vs. Peer-to-Peer Messaging

Instant messaging services can use two different structures: through *message servers* that receive all messages and forward them to their ultimate destinations and *peer-to-peer* systems that forward each message directly from its source to its destination. Figure 16-6 shows both types. Just about every Internet-based IM service uses a server; messaging services within a LAN are usually peer-to-peer.

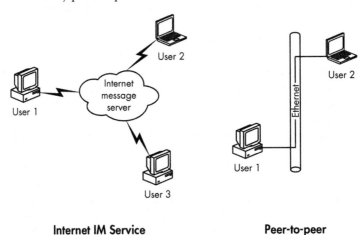

Internet IM Service   **Peer-to-peer**

Figure 16-6: Internet instant messaging servers and peer-to-peer chat use different structures to accomplish similar objectives.

Internet-Based IM Services

Most IM uses one of the services that send and receive messages through the Internet, such as AOL Instant Messaging (AIM), Windows Live Messenger, Google Talk, or Yahoo! Messenger, or a service that exchanges messages with a mobile telephone. Other messaging programs are available that operate within a LAN.

Unfortunately, many IM services are self-contained networks; for example, you can't use Google Talk software to send a message to an AIM account. However, several third-party programs—such as Pidgin (*http:// www.pidgin.im/*); Trillian (*http://www.ceruleanstudios.com/*); and meebo (*http://www.meebo.com/*)—are available that can exchange messages with people on different services from a single contact list and message window.

To set up a new IM account with one or more of the major services, go to their respective websites:

- Google Talk (*http://www.google.com/talk/*)
- Jabber (*http://www.jabber.org/*)
- AIM or AOL Instant Messenger (*http://www.aim.com/*)
- Yahoo! Messenger (*http://messenger.yahoo.com*)
- Windows Live Messenger (*http://get.live.com/messenger*)
- Gadu-Gadu, based in Poland, with Polish-language screens (*http://www.gadu-gadu.pl*)

In-house LAN messaging offers several advantages over Internet messaging services for exchanging messages within a business or a household. It's more secure and more private because the messages never leave the LAN. And they aren't exposed to spam and other unwanted messages from strangers through the Internet. In addition, they don't use bandwidth between the LAN and the Internet, so they don't interfere with other activities, and they don't require a separate account for each user with an IM service (although the major IM services all offer free accounts). More importantly, a local messaging system controls all of your messages within the LAN, rather than sending everything to an outside service.

Messaging Through a LAN

Many LAN messaging programs are available, all with similar feature sets. Some are limited to a single operating system, whereas others offer compatible versions for exchanging messages between different computer types. In most cases, the same program must be running on each computer connected to the LAN; you can't assume that two different LAN messenger programs will automatically recognize each other.

SoftRos Lan Messenger (*http://messenger.softros.com/*) is typical of this category. As Figure 16-7 shows, the program displays a list of people who are currently logged into their computers, with an icon that shows each person's status (Available, Busy, or Away). To send a message to another user, simply click that person's name and type your message in the pop-up Conversation window.

Figure 16-7: LAN messenger programs list the names of available users.

When a message arrives, the recipient's computer sounds a signal and displays the message in a pop-up window like the one in Figure 16-8. The same window appears on both the sender's and the recipient's computers. To continue the conversation, type the text in the Message text box and click **Send**.

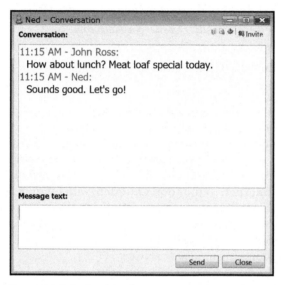

Figure 16-8: Both sides of a message exchange appear in the conversation window.

The same program also allows users to transfer files through the LAN.

If you don't like the SoftRos package, there are plenty of others, each with a slightly different screen layout and features. A web search for "LAN messenger" will produce dozens of links to descriptions and download sources.

Messaging Through a Virtual Private Network

When you connect to a LAN through a virtual private network (VPN), the LAN treats your computer just like every other network node, even through you might be hundreds or thousands of miles away from the rest of the network. Chapter 13 explains how to set up and use a VPN.

VPN connections are commonly used for IM, although you can also use a public IM service to accomplish the same thing. To set up an IM through a VPN, follow these general steps:

1. Establish your VPN connection to the LAN.
2. Run your LAN messaging program.
3. Choose a connection through the VPN and select the person with whom you want to exchange messages.

Audio and Video Messaging

In some situations, there's value to adding sound and pictures in text messages. The world's telephone companies spent many years and huge amounts of money trying to develop a successful commercial "picturephone" service as a supplement to traditional voice telephone calls, but it never happened until they repackaged it as "videoconferencing." Adding pictures to telephone service seemed like a good idea but it turned out to be too expensive and too intrusive to be practical for individual users. As a business proposition, call-based picturephones were a complete flop.

But less expensive video devices and higher bandwidth have made it possible to send and receive both still pictures and full-motion video through computer networks. As a result, many people have added online cameras (*webcams*) and microphones to their systems.

Both Microsoft's Windows Live Messenger (shown in Figure 16-9) and Apple's iChat support video conversations in parallel with their text messaging services. They're both designed to operate through the Internet, but there's nothing to stop you from using them to conduct conversations with other people on your LAN.

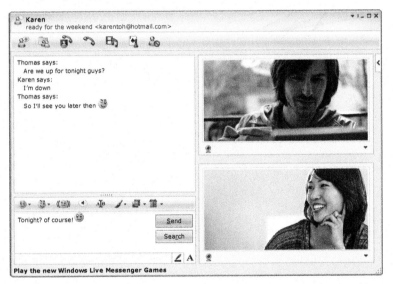

Image courtesy of Microsoft

Figure 16-9: Windows Live Messenger can add video images to simple text.

17

TROUBLESHOOTING

When your network is working properly, it's all but invisible; you can send and receive files through the network between any pair of computers or other connected devices. But when a connection fails, or one of your users can't find a network node, or any of a truly amazing number of other possible problems occurs, as the local network expert, it's your job is to fix it. Network problems always have a specific cause (or combination of causes), even if that cause is not obvious.

Too often, a network error message will say something like "ask your network manager for assistance." But when the network manager is *you*, that message doesn't tell you how to solve the problem. This chapter offers some tools and methods that will help you identify and solve most network problems.

General Troubleshooting Techniques

The key to successful troubleshooting is to follow a logical problem-solving process, rather than simply trying things at random until you stumble upon the correct solution to your problem. Most people who spend a lot of their time fixing things use a system like this without a formal plan, but if you're new to repairing computers and networks, consider using the techniques in this chapter as a guide.

Many of these suggestions are common-sense answers, rather than complex technical procedures. Don't overlook them; otherwise you can spend hours tracing a circuit or trying to find a bad connection just because somebody has unplugged a cable.

Remember that a problem that appears in your network might really be located on one of the computers or other devices *connected* to the network. In many cases, you will want to look for problems in the Windows, Macintosh, or Linux/Unix operating system as well as on the network itself.

Define the Problem

The first step in solving a problem should be to identify the symptoms. Remember that computers and networks don't break down completely at random. Every piece of information you can find about a problem can help you isolate and solve it. Is the problem a failure to connect to a particular computer through the network, or an error message, or a file transfer that takes longer than usual? Is it limited to a single computer, or does it appear all over the network? Have any of the lights on your network router, switch, or modem changed color or gone dark? Does the problem occur when you are using a particular program or only when a certain desk lamp (or vacuum cleaner or any other electrical device) is turned on? As you identify symptoms, make a list—either on paper or in your mind.

If you see an error message, copy the exact text onto a piece of paper. You might have to restart the computer or go to another computer to search for information, and you will need the specific wording of the message. Don't ignore the cryptic code numbers or other apparently unintelligible information. Even if the message means nothing to you, it could be the key to finding the help you need.

Sometimes you can identify a pattern in the symptoms. When more than one user reports the same problem, ask yourself what those users have in common: Are they all trying to use the printer or connect to the Internet at the same time? Are they connected to the network by Ethernet cables or Wi-Fi? Does the problem happen at the same time every day?

If you're lucky, defining the problem can tell you enough to fix it. For example, if the Power LED indicator light on your modem is off, that's a good indication that the power cable is unplugged, either at the wall outlet or on the modem itself. If everybody has trouble connecting to the Internet during a rainstorm, maybe water is leaking into the telephone cable that carries your Internet connection from the utility pole to your house (that happened to me—the repair guy told me that the cable had been there since about 1927).

More often, your list of symptoms will be a starting point that you can use to search for more information. As you analyze the problem, ask yourself these questions:

What caused the problem?   Did it occur when you or another user ran a specific program or tried to connect? Does the problem seem to be related to some other action? If you try the same action again, does the same problem occur? Did it first appear when you turned on a computer?

What has changed?   Have you installed new hardware on the network or loaded new software on the server or another computer? Did you recently update the router's firmware? Have you made any other change to the network or another connected computer, even if the change seems unrelated to the problem?

What else happened?   Have you noticed any other problems or unexpected events? Has another network user experienced a similar problem at about the same time?

Is this a new problem?   Have you ever experienced this problem or something similar before?

Look for Simple Solutions First

Look for easy solutions before you start to tear apart hardware or run complex software diagnostic routines. Nothing is more aggravating than spending several hours running detailed troubleshooting procedures, only to discover that restarting a computer or flipping a switch is all that was needed to fix the problem.

Restart Everything

The first thing to try when an otherwise unexplainable problem occurs is to turn off each network component—one at a time—wait a few seconds, and then turn it back on again. Sometimes that's all you need to do to clear a program or a chunk of memory that is stuck on the wrong setting and return it to the correct value. If possible, use the operating system's shut-down process to turn off the computer in an orderly manner; don't use the power switch or reset button unless the computer won't respond to a mouse or keyboard command.

NOTE   *Don't turn off your computer until you have copied the text of any error messages on the screen. Sometimes the same problem will produce a different message after you restart (or none at all), and the text of the original message might be a useful troubleshooting tool.*

When you restart a computer, don't use the Restart option; that can leave some settings at the same values rather than resetting them to the default startup configuration. You should turn off the computer completely, count to ten, and then turn it back on.

If the problem continues after you restart the computer, try restarting the modem, Wi-Fi access point, or network router. If a device doesn't have an on/off switch, disconnect the power cable, wait a few seconds, and plug it back in. After you restart each device, check to find out if the problem still exists. If the problem still occurs, move on to the next device.

Check the Plugs and Cables

If a single computer can't connect to the network, confirm that the physical cables providing those connections are not unplugged. Be sure to check both ends of each cable. If the whole network can't find the Internet, check the cables connected to the modem. If possible, examine the cable itself to make sure it hasn't been cut someplace in the middle.

Almost all routers, switches, modems, and network adapters have LED indicators that light when they detect a live connection. If one or more of these LEDs has gone dark, check the connection.

Most data plugs and sockets maintain solid connections, but it's possible that a plug might have come loose without separating itself from the socket, or a wire inside the plug might have a bad contact. If you suspect a loose connection, try wiggling the cable while you watch the LED indicator that corresponds to that socket. If the LED lights and goes dark as you shake the cable, try a different cable.

If you can't connect through a newly installed wall outlet, make sure the wires inside the outlet are connected to the correct terminals at both ends of the cable inside the wall (at the outlet and at the data center).

To quickly confirm that data is passing through the network to and from each computer, use the tools supplied with the computer's operating system to display network activity. In Windows, use the Networking tab in the Task Manager; in Linux, use the ethtool command (ethtool *interfacename* | grep Link). If the computer reports that no link is available, a cable is disconnected or the network adapter or hub has a problem.

Check the AC Power

Every device connected to the network probably has an LED indicator that lights when the device is connected to AC power. When a connection fails, look at the front of each device to confirm the power light is on. If it's not, check the device's power switch (if it has one) and both the plug at the back of the device and the plug or power supply that plugs into the AC outlet.

If you use a power strip or an uninterruptible power supply, make sure that the master power switch is turned on and the power unit is plugged into an AC outlet.

If the network fails but your computer still works, a fuse or circuit breaker might have blown in the room containing the network switch, router, or other control device.

Check the Settings and Options

Look for other switches and settings that might interfere with a device's operation. For example, make sure that the network printer is online and that no Error LED indicators or messages are visible in the control panel. Or if you're having trouble with a Wi-Fi connection, make sure your computer hasn't associated itself with the "wrong" base station and connected to one of your neighbors' networks instead of your own.

Isolate the Problem

If your search for simple solutions to a network problem or failure doesn't produce an answer, the next step is to identify the physical location where the problem is occurring. Although it's easy (and often appropriate) to think about a network as an amorphous cloud that exists everywhere at the same time, when you're looking for a specific point of failure, you must replace that cloud with a detailed map that shows every component and connection. If you don't already have a network diagram in your files, consider drawing one now.

Most problems offer some kind of hint about their location: If just one computer's connection to the network has failed, but all the others work properly, the problem is probably in that computer or its network link. But if nobody on the network can connect to any other computer or to the Internet, the problem is probably in a server, router, or other central device. Start searching for the source of a problem in the most logical device.

If you have a hardware problem, it's often effective to isolate the problem by replacing individual components and cables one at a time until the problem goes away. If the problem disappears when you install a replacement, that's a good indication that the original part was the source of the problem. If the replacement is a relatively expensive item like a router or a printer, you might want to send it back to the manufacturer for replacement or repair, especially if it's under warranty. But if you replace a cheap part like a cable or a network interface card, it's often easier to just throw it away and buy a new one.

Similar techniques can work with software. If a computer connection fails, try shutting down each program running on that computer, one at a time, and then try to reestablish the connection. If you recently installed a new program, driver, or update, try uninstalling the new software and test the connection again. If the connection works, the conflict is between the new software and your network connection or device driver. In Windows, try restarting the computer in Safe Mode and re-establishing the connection; if it works in Safe Mode, you know that the Windows operating system is not the source of the problem.

Retrace Your Steps

Even if a network problem appears without warning, the problem was probably caused by something that has changed within the hardware or software. Therefore repeating your steps can often help identify and solve it.

Keep Notes

As you try to identify and solve a problem, keep a record of what you have done. Describe each problem you encounter and what you did to fix it in a simple log or notebook. Note configuration settings, websites that provide useful information, and the exact location of any options or control programs that caused the problem or helped solve it. Keep this on paper, rather than in a text file stored on the computer, so you will be able to access it if the computer breaks down again.

If the same problem appears again, your log will tell you exactly what you did to fix it the first time; rather than stepping through all the same unproductive troubleshooting techniques again, you can go directly to the correct solution.

One excellent approach is to keep a network notebook in a loose-leaf binder. Among other things, your notebook should include the following:

- The configuration settings and passwords for each modem, router, Wi-Fi access point, and other device connected to the network
- The numeric IP addresses for your Internet connection, DNS servers, default gateway, and subnet mask
- The numeric addresses used by your LAN
- The make, model, serial number, and MAC address (if you can find them) of each hub, switch, router, modem, Wi-Fi access point, network adapter, and other network device
- A list of channel numbers, SSIDs, and passwords for your Wi-Fi network
- The telephone numbers and other contact information for your ISP and the telephone company or cable service that supplies your physical Internet connection
- Instruction manuals for each modem, router, access point, or other network device
- A list of your network's users, including names, telephone numbers, and logins
- A diagram that shows how each computer and other device connects to the network
- Passwords for each network server
- Account names and passwords for your email service
- A list of rooms that have wall-mounted network outlets and the label on the other end of each cable
- A log of adds, moves, changes, and deletions to your network
- A log of repairs, including:
  - The date and time each problem appeared
  - A description of each problem
  - What you did to fix the problem

- The time and date of each call to a technical support center
- The name and telephone number of each technical support person you talk to
- The *trouble ticket* number or case number assigned to the problem by each support center

WARNING   *Your network notebook might contain confidential information such as passwords and information about user accounts. Therefore, you should to keep it in a secure location such as a locked cabinet or drawer.*

Viruses and Other Nasties

If you can't find an obvious solution to a network problem, it never hurts to run a complete scan for viruses, worms, Trojan horses, and spyware on each computer connected to your LAN. Even if you have firewalls, up-to-date antivirus programs, and other network security software running on all your computers, it's possible that something might have slipped through your defenses.

Several antivirus program vendors offer free online scans that might identify a virus that your resident program might not catch. As part of your troubleshooting routine, run a full scan with your usual network security programs and also use one or more of these online scans:

Trend Micro HouseCall   *http://housecall.trendmicro.com*

Symantec Security Check   *http://security.symantec.com/sscv6/default.asp*

BitDefender Online Scanner   *http://www.bitdefender.com/scan8/ie.html*

Kaspersky Online Scanner   *http://www.kaspersky.com/virusscanner*

ESET Online Scanner   *http://www.eset.com/onlinescan/*

Panda ActiveScan   *http://www.pandasecurity.com/homeusers/solutions/activescan/*

Use an online scanner made by a different supplier from the one that came with the antivirus program resident in your computers. Each company employs a slightly different set of rules for finding and isolating viruses, so you will want to take advantage of more than one approach.

Other Common Problems

It's not practical to describe every possible network problem, but there are a few that occur more frequently than others. If the problem in your network is not described in this chapter, try the Windows Network Problem Solver described in "The Collective Wisdom of the Internet" on page 247 (for computers using Windows), or search for information about the problem in the web pages devoted to your own operating system.

Configuration Settings

When you can't connect your computer to the Internet, but other computers on the same network can connect, check the computer's network configuration settings to confirm that the default gateway and the DNS server are present and correct. If none of the network's computers can find the Internet, check the settings on the network's router or modem.

To confirm that the gateway and the DNS server are alive and operating properly, try sending ping requests to their numeric addresses. If you don't receive a reply, look for a problem in the gateway or the server, or in the equipment and cables between your computer and the target.

DHCP Settings: DNS and Default Gateway

When a DHCP server is active on your network, and your own computer (or the one you're troubleshooting) is set to accept DHCP settings, the computer should automatically connect itself to the network. But if there's no DHCP server, or if the computer is not configured to accept DHCP data from a server and the settings on the computer itself are missing or incorrect, the computer won't connect.

To confirm that the DHCP settings are correct, follow these steps:

1. Check the modem, router, Wi-Fi access point, or other device that normally acts as DHCP server for your network. If the server is active (and other computers on the network are connecting normally), the problem is in your computer; if it's not active, either turn it on or confirm that this network doesn't use DHCP.

2. Open the network configuration settings utility in your computer. If the DHCP server is active, confirm that the computer is set to accept data from the server; if the network does not use DHCP, make sure the addresses for the DNS server and the default gateway (or gateway router) are correct.

If the DNS server settings in your computer or DHCP server appear to be correct, it's possible (but unlikely) that the DNS server itself is not working. Try adding the address of one of the OpenDNS servers (208.67.222.222 or 208.67.220.220) as an alternative to your usual DNS server's address.

Failed Connection to a Specific Site

When you try to connect to a specific website or other Internet service, you will sometimes see an *Unable to connect* message instead of the web page or other screen you were expecting. When this happens, immediately try some other address that takes you to a site in a different geographical location; for example, if you can't connect to *The New York Times* website, try a site based in Germany or Australia. If you can connect to the second address, you can safely assume that the problem is at the first address, and not in your own computer or network. If you can't connect to any site, look for a local problem such as your computer, the LAN, or your Internet service provider.

An Alternate Connection to the Internet

When your Internet connection breaks down, it's not possible to use that connection to consult technical support websites or send email to your network provider. Therefore, it's often helpful to have a backup method for connecting at least one of your computers to the Internet. It might be a neighbor's Wi-Fi network (with their permission, of course), a nearby library or coffee shop that offers Internet access, or a link through a dial-up telephone line and modem.

Before you have a problem, ask your Internet service provider if they offer dial-up access along with their high-speed services. If they do, ask them for a dial-up account as an emergency backup, and make a note of the access telephone numbers, login name, and password in your network notebook.

The Collective Wisdom of the Internet

Any problem that occurs on your network has happened before to somebody else. You have an excellent chance of finding a description of the problem and instructions for fixing it someplace on the Internet.

This is where defining the problem carefully becomes important. If you're working with a Windows-based network, the Microsoft Knowledge Base at *http://support.microsoft.com/* can be particularly useful; if Microsoft's technical support people have ever had to deal with a particular problem, they have probably included instructions for fixing it in the Knowledge Base. Similar resources exist for Macintosh networks and servers at *http://www.apple.com/ support*, and for Unix and Linux systems in the Support sections of each distribution's website.

Other online sources for useful troubleshooting information include manufacturers' technical support centers, independent newsgroups and web forums, and sites such as Wikipedia and HowStuffWorks.com that offer descriptions and explanations of various types of technology. If those sites don't answer your question, try a more general web search. Type a few keywords that describe the problem (such as "XP can't find network printer") or the exact text of an error message into a web search tool and follow each of the links to read about other people's experiences under similar circumstances. Remember that quotation marks around phrases instruct the search sites to search for the entire phrase rather than individual words.

One particularly helpful tool for troubleshooting networks is the Windows Network Problem Solver at *http://winhlp.com/wxnet.htm*, shown in Figure 17-1. The Problem Solver is an interactive list of symptoms that links to instructions for solving the most likely cause of the problem. If you take the time to carefully answer each of the questions in the problem definition form, the Problem Solver can be a remarkably effective tool.

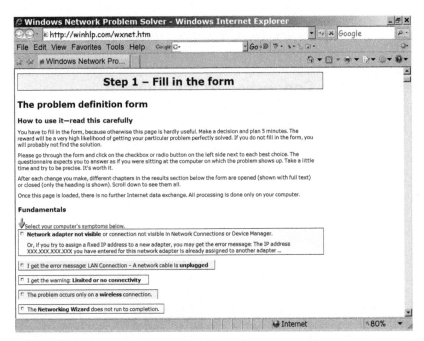

Figure 17-1: The Windows Network Problem Solver is an excellent interactive trouble-shooting tool. This screen image shows only a small portion of the page; scroll down for additional information and instructions.

Software for Troubleshooting

Several software programs can gather and display useful information when you're trying to understand what's happening inside your network. These programs are available as free or trial downloads, so you don't incur a cost when testing them.

Network Magic

Network Magic (*http://www.networkmagic.com/*) provides a graphic display of the devices connected to a LAN, as shown in Figure 17-2, and a central control point for adding new network devices or changing the existing network configuration. It can also perform some basic troubleshooting tests and automatic repairs.

Protocol Analyzers

Microsoft Network Monitor (go to *http://www.microsoft.com/downloads/* and search for *Network Monitor*) and Wireshark (*http://www.wireshark.org/*) are free protocol analyzers that capture and display data as it moves through your network. In other words, they grab each block of data (a *frame*) as it passes in or out of your computer, and they display the contents of the frame along with detailed information about the form and structure of each frame. Figure 17-3 shows a data capture in Network Monitor, and Figure 17-4 shows a Wireshark screen. The two programs capture the same data stream, but they handle and display it differently. The programs are available at no cost, so you might want to install both of them. Protocol analyzers are also known as *network sniffers.*

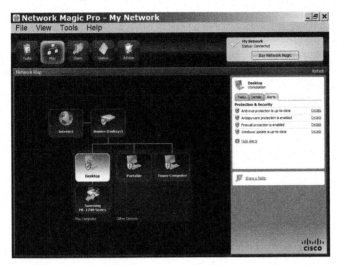

Figure 17-2: Network Magic scans your LAN and displays all the devices connected to it.

Most of this data display looks like hexadecimal gibberish, but it contains the actual text of messages, conversations, and other transactions, along with all the commands and status messages that move through the network. Most of the time, you can allow your computer and the network plumbing to handle the data in background. But when something goes wrong, the data captured by a protocol analyzer can help you identify what's causing the problem.

For example, if the amount of incoming or outgoing traffic moving through your network increases, the network may be sending or receiving many requests every second. This could be a hacker's denial of service attack, or a computer that has innocently latched itself into an endless program loop. Either way, you will want to identify the source and take action to make it stop. When this happened to me, I used Wireshark to find the numeric IP address of the computer that was originating the bogus messages and a whois program to identify that computer's owner; then I sent an email explaining the problem and asking them to fix it. The data stream stopped within an hour.

A network sniffer can also identify a device within your own network that becomes infected or has some other problem that interferes with proper operation. By running the sniffer program on more than one computer, or even inserting a sniffer at a router, a modem connection, or other interface point, you can often isolate the source of a problem.

You won't use a protocol analyzer very often, which is probably okay, because it's a complex and tedious process. But when you need to know what's moving through your network, an analyzer can give you information that you won't find anywhere else.

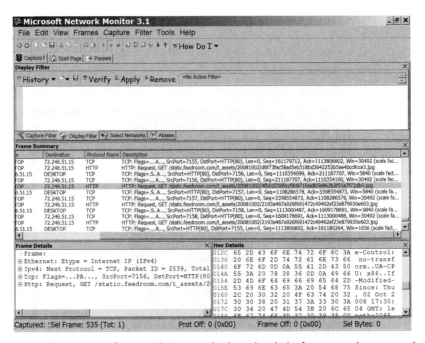

Figure 17-3: Microsoft Network Monitor displays detailed information about network data.

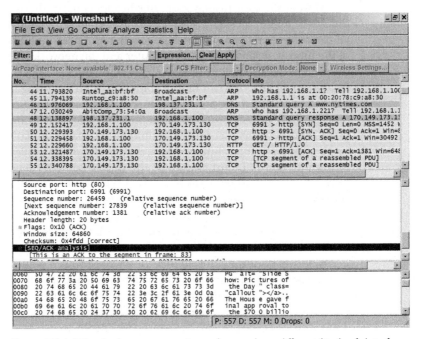

Figure 17-4: Wireshark uses contrasting colors to show different kinds of data frames.

ISP Problems

As a formal or informal network manager, you're often on your own when you're trying to find and fix a problem on your LAN, but if you or one of your users discovers a problem using the Internet, you might need help from your Internet service provider's (ISP's) support center and the people who run the computer or network at the other end of your connection.

Therefore, you should find and keep the telephone numbers and email addresses of the ISP's help desk and the network tech center at the telephone company, cable TV service, or other company that provides the physical connection between your own LAN and your ISP. The people who answer calls in those support centers are there to help you, and they will often have tools that can test and monitor your network connection. When you talk to a support representative, ask for the case number or trouble ticket number that they have assigned to your problem; if you have to call back later, the case number will lead the person who takes your call to the notes about earlier calls.

Don't Panic

Finally, keep calm. Your network does not have a mind of its own. If you take a logical and organized approach to finding the cause of a network problem, you will probably solve the problem without developing (or enlarging) an ulcer. Over time, you will recognize particular symptoms and know how to home in on the most effective diagnostic tools and techniques.

If you can't find the problem after searching for an hour, walk away for a few minutes. Make yourself a sandwich, have a cup of coffee or a glass of lemonade, or go for a short walk. The network will still be there when you get back, and you'll feel better about it. Approaching the problem with a fresh mind can often be the most effective possible way to solve it.

INDEX

headers, 11–13, *12*
Hewlett-Packard (HP), 95
hex encryption keys, 180–181, *181*
hidden networks, 179
High Definition Multimedia Interface
      (HDMI), 217
    cables, 219, 220
high-gain directional antennas, 85
high-speed modems, 109
home appliances, 8, 222–223
home automation, 8, 49, 51, 223
home entertainment systems, 7–8, 48, 49,
      203, 206
Home Phoneline Networking Alliance, 17
HomePlug, 17, *17*
HomePNA, 17
home run wiring, 51–52, *52*, 53
home security devices, 8, 205
hosting services, 105
host names, 43
Hotmail, 105
hotspots, 77–78, 89
HOWTO, 159, 164
HP (Hewlett-Packard), 95
HTTP. *See* HyperText Transfer Protocol
      (HTTP)
hubs
    data, 30, 55
    designing, 47
    Ethernet, 29, *29*, 80, 220
    network, 120
    overview of, 28–30, *29*, 111
    for printers, 193, 201
hybrid wireless networks, 89
HyperTerminal programs, 22
HyperText Transfer Protocol (HTTP),
      24, 39
    web servers, *158*

I

IANA (Internet Assigned Name
      Authority), 37, 38, 157
IBM, 82, 94
iChat, 237
IDE hard drives, 97
IEEE (Institute of Electrical and Elec-
      tronics Engineers), 21, 78
ifconfig, 43
IM (instant messaging), 7, 233–237
incremental backups, 100
indicator lights, 75
individual bits, 10, *10*
industrial electronics suppliers, 57

.*info*, *40*
Infrared Data Association (IrDA), 20
    ports, 20–21, *21*
infrared networks, 20–21, *21*
input/output (I/O) ports, 4, *18*,
      18–19, *19*
instant messaging (IM), 7, 233–237
Institute of Electrical and Electronics
      Engineers (IEEE), 21, 78
Intel, *88*, 164
internal controllers, 204–205
internal expansion cards, *72*, 72–73
Internet Assigned Name Authority
      (IANA), 37, 38, 157
Internet-based IM services, 234–235
Internet connections, network, 110–115,
      111, *112*
Internet Explorer, 24, 174
Internet Protocol (IP), 35–36, 54, 123,
      123, 126
    addresses, 36–41, *38*, 42, 45, 86
      computer-to-network connections
        and, 118, 124, 126–128, *127*
      domain names and, 38–41, *40*
      dynamic, 37–38, 86, 109
      firewalls and, 157
      fixed, 37–38, 109, 118
      network-to-Internet connections
        and, 110–115, *111*, *112*
    filters, 159
    networks, 162
Internet Protocol Properties window, *123*
Internet radio, 209, 214
Internet Relay Chat (IRC) servers, 39
Internet service providers (ISPs), 22, 31,
      41, 110, 113, 114
    problems, 251
Internet-to-network connections, 6,
      107–115, *108*, *111*, *112*
I/O (input/output) ports, 4, *18*,
      18–19, *19*
IP. *See* Internet Protocol (IP)
IPConfig, 41–43, *42*
iPhone, 77
IP Masquerade, 164
iPod, 8, 206, 207, 210
IPsec network links, 162, 163, 164,
      169, 173
IPX networks, 162
IRC (Internet Relay Chat) servers, 39
IrDA. *See* Infrared Data Association
      (IrDA)
ISA Ethernet adapters, 72

ISM bands, 80
ISPs. *See* Internet service providers (ISPs)
iTunes, 24

J

Jabber, 235
jacks. *See* ports
Jameco, 57
jumper cables, 56

K

Kaspersky Online Scanner, 245
KDE, 104, *128*, 128–129, *129*, 148, *148*, 149
Kerberos, *158*
keyhole slots, 63–64, *64*
Konquerer file manager, 148, *148*, 149–150, *150*

L

L2TP (Layer Two Tunneling Protocol), 162, 163–164, 169
LANguard, 158
LANs. *See* local area networks (LANs)
Lantronix UBox 4100, *99*
laptops
   interface adapters, 81–82, *82*
   network adapters, 73–74, *74*
Laughing Squid web hosting, 45
Layer Two Tunneling Protocol (L2TP), 162, 163–164, 169
LED indicator lights, 240, 242–243
Level 1–5 access, 133–136
Leviton, 67
LG Electronics, 223
limited backups, 100
line of sight, 85
LINK indicator lights, 75
Linksys, 216
Linux
   backup files, 100, 104
   computer-to-network connections, 117, *127*, 127–129, *128*, *129*
   CUPS printer control program, 199
   file servers, 94–95, 96, 215
   file sharing, 131, 147–150, *148–150*
   firewalls, 154–159, *155*, *158*, 164
   network adapters, 73–74
   network-to-Internet connections, 115
   OpenVPN for, 173
   remote desktop programs, 229

text commands for, 43
troubleshooting info, 247
VPN clients for, 172-173
VPN servers for, 164
wireless control programs, 87
LinuxCD, 95
Linux Online!, 104
live conversations, 205, 233–237
Living Network Control Protocol (LnCP), 223
local area connections, 42, *42*, 122–123, 196
local area networks (LANs)
   addresses, 37–38
   computer-to-network connections, 117–123
   connections to, *20*, 21, 32, 41, 49, 55
   data transfer speeds, 14–15
   Ethernet, 14–16, 71
   file sharing, 137
   firewalls, 154–159, *155*, *158*
   game consoles, 220–222
   instant messaging, 234–236, *235*
   network-to-Internet connections, 107–115, *108*, *111*, *112*
   overview of, 31–32, *32*
   remote terminals, 23, *23*
   security methods for, 91–92
   troubleshooting for, 248–251
   VideoLAN, 218
   VPNs and, 159–161, *160*, *161*, 163
   Wi-Fi and, 54, 77–78
   wireless security, 54, 89–92, 174–184, *175*, *178*, *181*
LostPC, 185
LPs (music), 208, 209, 211

M

MAC
   addresses, 43, 91, 184
   authentication, 184–185
Macintosh OS X, 35, 43, 44
   backup files, 100, 103–104, *104*
   computer-to-network connections, 117, *124*, 124–127, *125*, *126*, 127
   file servers, 94–95, 96, 99, *99*, 215
   file sharing, 131, *134*, *135*, 143–147, *144–146*
   IP addresses, 112, *112*, 118
   network adapters, 73–74
   network security, 184–185
   network-to-Internet connections, 115
   OpenVPN for, 173

remote desktop programs, 226–229, *227, 228*

troubleshooting info, 247

wireless control programs, 87

Mac-to-Windows remote access, 226

mail servers, 24

M-Audio, 211

MaxiVista, 229–232

Mbps (megabits per second), 3

McIntosh MS750, 209

Media Center Extender, 208

media sharing, 143

meebo, 234

megabits per second (Mbps), 3

mesh topologies, 28

messages, sending, 11, 13–14

message servers, 234

messaging, 233–237

microphones, 8, 204, 205

Microsoft

    Baseline Security Analyzer, 188, *188*

    Knowledge Base, 247

    MSN Messenger, *158*

    Protocol Analyzers, 248, *250*

    Resource Kit, 163

    SQL, 95

    SyncToy, 232

    TechNet articles, 163

    Windows. *See* Windows

    Xbox 360, 220, 222

microsoft.com, 44

microwave radio links, 3

mini-PCI cards, 81–82, *82*, 84, 87

MoCA (Multimedia over Coax Alliance), 17

modems, 6

    cable, 110

    combination boxes, 33

    configuring, 86

    dial-up, 109

    DSL, *62*, 110

    high-speed, 109

    installing, 59, 61, 62–64, *63*

    location of, 50

    network-to-Internet connections, 108–115

    null, 19, *19*

    PTSN, 21–22

    telephone line connections and, 21–23

modular structured wiring center, 59, 63

modulation, 6, 108

monitors, multiple, 229–232, *230, 231*

motherboards, 70

mounting brackets, 56, *56*

mounting frames, 59

MPEG Layer-3 (MP3) files, 208, 209–210, *210*

MPlayer, 218

MSN Messenger, *158*

Multimedia over Coax Alliance (MoCA), 17

music clients, 211, 212, 213

    devices, 213–214, *214*

music servers, 7–8, 24, 207–209, 212–213, *213*

Muuss, Mike, 43

N

.name, 40

names and addresses, 36–41

NAS (network-attached storage) devices, 93, 95, 97–98, *98*, 100, 108

NAT (Network Address Translation), 37, 67, 157–158, 159

National Electric Code, 51

Nautilus file browser, 147–148, *148*

.net, 39, *40*

NetBEUI networks, 162

NetBSD, 159, 164, 173

Netgear, 161, 213, 216

Netscape Navigator, 174

network adapters

    for laptops, 73–74, *74*

    USB, 73

Network Address Translation (NAT), 37, 67, 157–158, 159

Network and Sharing Center, 136–138, *137, 138*

network applications

    MaxiVista, 229–232, *230*

    messaging, 233–237

    multiple monitors, 229–232, *230, 231*

    overview of, 225

    remote controls, 232

    remote desktop programs, 226–229, *227, 228*

network-attached storage (NAS) devices, 93, 95, 97–98, *98*, 100, 108

network commands

    ifconfig, 43

    IPConfig, 41–43, *42*

    ping, 36, *43*, 43–44

    TraceRoute, 36, *44*, 44–46, *45*

network-compatible home appliances, 223

The Electronic Frontier Foundation (EFF) is the leading organization defending civil liberties in the digital world. We defend free speech on the Internet, fight illegal surveillance, promote the rights of innovators to develop new digital technologies, and work to ensure that the rights and freedoms we enjoy are enhanced — rather than eroded — as our use of technology grows.

PRIVACY EFF has sued telecom giant AT&T for giving the NSA unfettered access to the private communications of millions of their customers. eff.org/nsa

FREE SPEECH EFF's Coders' Rights Project is defending the rights of programmers and security researchers to publish their findings without fear of legal challenges. eff.org/freespeech

INNOVATION EFF's Patent Busting Project challenges overbroad patents that threaten technological innovation. eff.org/patent

FAIR USE EFF is fighting prohibitive standards that would take away your right to receive and use over-the-air television broadcasts any way you choose. eff.org/IP/fairuse

TRANSPARENCY EFF has developed the Switzerland Network Testing Tool to give individuals the tools to test for covert traffic filtering. eff.org/transparency

INTERNATIONAL EFF is working to ensure that international treaties do not restrict our free speech, privacy or digital consumer rights. eff.org/global

EFF.ORG

ELECTRONIC FRONTIER FOUNDATION

Protecting Rights and Promoting Freedom on the Electronic Frontier

EFF is a member-supported organization. Join Now! www.eff.org/support

STEAL THIS COMPUTER BOOK 4.0
What They Won't Tell You About the Internet

by WALLACE WANG

This offbeat, non-technical book examines what hackers do, how they do it, and how readers can protect themselves. Informative, irreverent, and entertaining, the completely revised fourth edition of *Steal This Computer Book* contains new chapters that discuss the hacker mentality, lock picking, exploiting P2P file-sharing networks, and how people manipulate search engines and pop-up ads. Includes a CD with hundreds of megabytes of hacking and security-related programs that tie in to each chapter of the book.

MAY 2006, 384 PP. W/CD, $29.95
ISBN 978-1-59327-105-3

UBUNTU FOR NON-GEEKS, 3RD EDITION
A Pain-Free, Project-Based, Get-Things-Done Guidebook

by RICKFORD GRANT

This newbie's guide to Ubuntu lets readers learn by doing. Using immersion-learning techniques favored by language courses, step-by-step projects build upon earlier tutorial concepts, stimulating the brain and increasing the reader's understanding. This book covers all of the topics likely to be of interest to an average desktop user, such as installing new software via Synaptic; Internet connectivity; working with removable storage devices, printers, and scanners; and handling DVDs, audio files, and even iPods. It also eases readers into the world of commands, thus allowing them to work with Java, Python, or other script-based applications; convert RPMs to DEB files; and compile software from source.

JUNE 2008, 360 PP. W/CD, $34.95
ISBN 978-1-59327-180-0

HACKING, 2ND EDITION
The Art of Exploitation

by JON ERICKSON

While many security books merely show how to run existing exploits, *Hacking: The Art of Exploitation* was the first book to explain how exploits actually work—and how readers can develop and implement their own. In this all new second edition, author Jon Erickson uses practical examples to illustrate the fundamentals of serious hacking. You'll learn about key concepts underlying common exploits, such as programming errors, assembly language, networking, shellcode, cryptography, and more. And the bundled Linux LiveCD provides an easy-to-use, hands-on learning environment. This edition has been extensively updated and expanded, including a new introduction to the complex, low-level workings of computer.

FEBRUARY 2008, 480 PP. W/CD, $49.95
ISBN 978-1-59327-144-2

THE BOOK OF WIRELESS, 2ND EDITION

A Painless Guide to Wi-Fi and Broadband Wireless

by JOHN ROSS

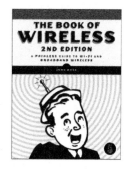

This plain-English guide to popular wireless networking standards shows readers how to connect to wireless networks anywhere they go. After an introduction to networking in general and wireless networking in particular, the book explains all available standards, including all flavors of wireless Ethernet (Wi-Fi), along with new standards like WiMAX and 3G networks. Readers will learn how to use wireless software to connect to the Internet wherever they are, rather than waiting until they're in range of a public Wi-Fi hot spot. *The Book of Wireless* offers information about all of the currently available wireless services for Internet access, with advice on how to understand the important differences between them such as cost, speed, and coverage areas. For readers setting up home networks, the book contains useful advice about choosing and setting up hardware and software, securing networks using WEP and WPA, and setting up a wireless connection for VoIP.

JANUARY 2008, 352 PP., $29.95
ISBN 978-1-59327-169-5

THE MANGA GUIDE TO ELECTRICITY

by KAZUHIRO FUJITAKI, MATSUDA, *and* TREND-PRO CO., LTD.

The Manga Guide to Electricity teaches readers the fundamentals of how electricity works through authentic Japanese manga. Readers follow Rereko, a denizen of Electopia, the Land of Electricity, as she is exiled to Tokyo to learn more about electricity. In no time, graduate student Hikaru is teaching her the essentials, such as static electricity and Coloumb's law; the relationship between voltage, resistance, and current; and the difference between series and parallel electrical circuits. Using real-world examples like flashlights and home appliances, *The Manga Guide to Electricity* combines a whimsical story with real educational content so that readers will quickly master the core concepts of electricity with a minimum of frustration.

MARCH 2009, 232 PP., $19.95
ISBN 978-1-59327-197-8

PHONE:
800.420.7240 OR
415.863.9900
MONDAY THROUGH FRIDAY,
9 A.M. TO 5 P.M. (PST)

EMAIL:
SALES@NOSTARCH.COM

WEB:
WWW.NOSTARCH.COM

COLOPHON

The fonts used in *Network Know-How* are New Baskerville, Futura, and Dogma.

The book was printed and bound at Malloy Incorporated in Ann Arbor, Michigan. The paper is Glatfelter Spring Forge 60# Antique Eggshell, which is certified by the Sustainable Forestry Initiative (SFI). The book uses a RepKover binding, which allows it to lay flat when open.

UPDATES

Visit *http://www.nostarch.com/networks.htm* for updates, errata, and other information.

CPSIA information can be obtained
at www.ICGtesting.com
Printed in the USA
BVOW07s1458250416

445501BV00005B/31/P

9 781593 271916